Marquis de Sade and Continental Philosophy

Marquis de Sade and Continental Philosophy

Lode Lauwaert

EDINBURGH
University Press

Edinburgh University Press is one of the leading university presses in the UK. We publish academic books and journals in our selected subject areas across the humanities and social sciences, combining cutting-edge scholarship with high editorial and production values to produce academic works of lasting importance. For more information visit our website: edinburghuniversitypress.com

Edinburgh University Press Ltd
The Tun – Holyrood Road
12(2f) Jackson's Entry
Edinburgh EH8 8PJ

First published in hardback by Edinburgh University Press 2019

Typeset in 10.5/13 Warnock Pro by
IDSUK (DataConnection) Ltd, and
printed and bound by CPI Group (UK) Ltd,
Croydon, CR0 4YY

A CIP record for this book is available from the British Library

ISBN 978 1 4744 3069 2 (hardback)
ISBN 978 1 4744 3070 8 (paperback)
ISBN 978 1 4744 3071 5 (webready PDF)
ISBN 978 1 4744 3072 2 (epub)

Contents

Acknowledgements vi

Introduction 1

1. Godlessness, Purity and Simulacra 7
2. The Terror of Writing 39
3. Apathy, Energy and Transgression 62
4. Ethics and Modernity 89
5. Sadism as Formalism 117
6. Literature and the Clinical 142

Conclusion 168

Notes 171
Bibliography 204
Index 222

Acknowledgements

First of all, I wish to express my thanks to the Institute of Philosophy in Leuven for giving me the opportunity and the space required to work on this project.

I would like to thank Paul Moyaert for the hours he has devoted to discussing the topic of the book and for his passionate comments on what I presented to him. I have learned a great deal from him over the years, and thank him for his encouragement and jocularity during this time.

I also wish to thank Anneleen Masschelein, Karin de Boer, Tomas Geyskens, Laurens ten Kate, Arthur Cools, Rudi Visker, Roland Breeur, Eli Noé, Willem Styfhals, Pieter Adriaens, Stéphane Symons and Dominiek Hoens for offering feedback on my texts.

Will Britt and Reham Elnory helped me to understand Deleuze's interpretation of Sade and Masoch during our weekly meetings at Boston College. Without their insights, suggestions and recommendations I wouldn't have been able to write the chapter that I wanted to write.

In the continental tradition, Lacan's writing on Sade is one of the most difficult texts to read. During our meetings and animated discussions in Ghent, Jens De Vleminck, Gertrudis Van de Vijver, Boris Demarest, Filip Geerardyn and again Paul Moyaert made the text more understandable and less obscure to me (although it would be misplaced to say that Lacan's interpretation of Kant and Sade is totally clear to me).

Introduction[1]

The statement that Foucault made in 1970, that one day, the twentieth century may be Deleuzian, is well known. Less well known perhaps is the fact that over 100 years ago the avant-garde writer and poet Apollinaire made a similar claim about 'the divine Marquis de Sade'.[2] He stated: 'this man [Sade] who seemed to represent nothing throughout the nineteenth century may well dominate the twentieth'.[3] In the first part of the quotation, the author of *L'œuvre du marquis de Sade* refers to the fact that, during the first decades after his death in 1814, Sade was only mentioned indirectly and sporadically.[4] Sade was read during the nineteenth century by various well-known writers, but extensive studies about his life or work were not yet written at that time. We will see that this changed at the turn of the twentieth century. It was then that there was an increasing interest in Sade's life and work, which continued well into the twentieth century.

To conclude, however, that the curiosity cabinet of the illustrious Marquis de Sade has dominated the intellectual climate for the past hundred years would be to grossly exaggerate. However, Apollinaire's words did not turn out to be entirely untrue. From the first years shortly after the Second World War until well into the 1960s, the work of the Marquis was read intensively and commented upon in French philosophical circles. For two decades, the following leading philosophers wrote a great deal about the literature of Marquis de Sade: Pierre Klossowski, Maurice Blanchot, Georges Bataille, Jacques Lacan, Roland Barthes and Gilles Deleuze.[5] On this basis, we can say that Apollinaire has, in a sense, been proven right. Sade has not dominated the past century, but his literature was prominently present for more than twenty years after the Second World War, and is explored in the works of a number of prominent French post-war philosophers.[6]

From a historical point of view, it is not surprising that these French philosophers were looking at literature. Indeed, throughout history many philosophers have written about literature. We can think of Plato's discussion of Homer; Hegel dedicates a few pages to Diderot's *Le neveu de Rameau*, for example; and Heidegger discusses Hölderlin, among others. The fact that philosophers engage with literature was very much the case in France after the Second World War. All of the above-mentioned thinkers devoted numerous pages to literature in the broadest sense of the word: Klossowski writes about Gide, Blanchot about Mallarmé, Bataille about Baudelaire, Lacan about Joyce, Barthes about Brecht, and Deleuze about Proust. But despite this, two things stand out with regard to the philosophical reception of Sade in France after the Second World War.

First of all, it is remarkable that a large number of philosophers wrote about the same author during the same short period of time between 1947 and 1967. It may be that each of them was individually interested in several authors at the same time and that, for example, Kafka's literary oeuvre enjoyed the attention of, among others, Bataille and Deleuze. The fact remains that no fewer than six philosophers wrote about Marquis de Sade in a short space of time.

Secondly, and more importantly, it is remarkable that, in addition to the work of, among others, Kafka and Proust, philosophers also read the literature of D. A. F. de Sade. It is hardly surprising that a psychiatrist such as Richard von Krafft-Ebing, a writer like Honoré de Balzac or a surrealist like André Breton was interested in Sade, but it is curious that philosophers also discussed the oeuvre of the Marquis.[7] Isn't the world that Sade unfolds in his literature populated by brutal torturers, murderers and hotheads who, in a delirium of destruction, subject others to muggings, scalping, flagellation or massacre? Is the Sadean universe not known for the many erotic and scatological passages in which the libertines smear each other with their excrements and are, moreover, sexually aroused by them?[8] Isn't it also true that hardly anything happens in Sade's writings and that what happens is nothing more than an endless repetition of the same thing? In other words, doesn't a reading of Sade's work quickly degenerate into boredom?

And aren't the philosophical passages that follow the erotic images merely gratuitous and superficial chatter that is of zero importance in the history of philosophical thinking?

Therefore, at first glance, it is rather strange and surprising that six renowned philosophers paid quite close attention to these cruel, peculiar and monotonous texts. Consequently, the question arises of what these French philosophers read in this oeuvre, which they apparently could not ignore. Why did the work of the libertine Marquis de Sade enjoy the interest of French philosophers after 1945? Where – and this is the central question around which the various essays turn – did French post-war philosophers' interest in Sade's literature come from?

Some will probably suggest that those thinkers dealt with Sade because they wanted to go against the academic elite who preferred to write more soberly about someone like Kant, and for whom the aphrodisiac of the Marquis was only food for psychologists. The French interest in Sade, one might think, was nothing more than an adolescent provocative gesture. The problem with this hypothesis is that it does not explain why it was precisely the Marquis's oeuvre that was intended to provoke the elite. There were many other forms of literature with which one could achieve the same effect. Moreover, this explanation does not hold up because various thinkers have been writing about Sade's work on multiple occasions over the years. This would not be the case if they were simply to write in order to provoke a reaction.

Therefore, there is probably a stronger link between Sade, on the one hand, and French post-war philosophy, on the other. However, I do not want to suggest that this connection is the result of philosophical questions or problems that are almost spontaneously highlighted by the oeuvre itself. The reason why Sade was being written about may not be the same as the reason why philosophers usually deal with the work of Proust or Kafka, for example. The fact that philosophers write about both authors is usually due to the fact that their oeuvre, of its own accord, gives rise to reflection on time or the law, respectively. I suspect that the Sade studies are not rooted in Sade's own oeuvre but have their origins elsewhere. This presumption is based on the observation that the French philosophers who are at the centre of this debate have something maniacal about them, in a sense. By this I mean that, for a certain period of time – and some until the end of their lives – this group of philosophers returned regularly to the same subject matter or often formulated the same idea. The thinking of the above-mentioned French philosophers centred on a number of themes or ideas. The related concepts that characterise this thinking also constantly return. Bataille's thinking about religion and eroticism, for example, must be understood against the background of the theme of transgression, while the experience of writing is a recurring theme in Blanchot's work. Another example is Klossowski, who was intrigued by the idea of gnostic purity and who often used the notion of simulacrum to map out another theme, namely the theme of what he calls 'the pathological artist'. On this basis, I put forward the hypothesis that French philosophers after 1945 were interested in Sade because his literature illustrated and reflected the themes and ideas that constantly recur elsewhere.

The expectation is, therefore, that in the studies of the philosophers, Sade is always examined from a different perspective. More concretely, it is expected that, for example, Bataille approaches the Sadean world from the notion of transgression, Blanchot focuses on the experience of writing in Sade and Barthes' reading is formalistic. Despite these differences in content, it is nevertheless expected that a similarity will arise, namely that the French post-war philosophers wrote about Sade because this enabled them to further explore and elaborate the ideas and the themes that fascinated them. In order to investigate whether this is the case, I will take sufficient time to explain the Sade studies of Klossowski, Blanchot, Bataille, Lacan, Barthes and Deleuze as clearly as possible.

When I write 'as clearly as possible', I am referring to the fact that these French philosophers do not always present their thinking in the most accessible way. Anyone who has ever read something of, say, Lacan – and this is happening today, rightly or wrongly, less and less – will undoubtedly agree. His texts are often written in a sloppy and incoherent way, in a language that can usually only be understood by those already familiar with his ideas. For some Lacanians, this is precisely a reason to engage with his thinking and admire it; for those who dislike the writing of Lacan, however, it is a reason to dismiss *le maître absolu* as an obscure non-philosopher. In view of the structure of the present book, both attitudes make little – if no – sense. My task is therefore, after Descartes, to produce clear and distinct ideas, in order to gain insight into the Sade reception in French post-war philosophy. This objective also implies that I am going to write about these studies not from an external but from an internal perspective. In other words, I will not evaluate the perspectives or compare, at the end of the journey, the studies with one another. Both would undoubtedly provide interesting literature, but do not serve the purpose of this study. In short, I will stand not outside but inside the Sade studies, and trace the track on which they move. Or, to say it with an expression that fits seamlessly with the subject of this book: *I'll cook the shit and serve it*, without, however, giving points.[9]

Before I start, I would also like to draw the reader's attention to the following. All the philosophers who will be addressed in the following chapters, ranging from Klossowski through Lacan to Deleuze, experienced their intellectual climax after the Second World War. Moreover, they all belonged to a movement that made a name for itself not only in philosophy, but also far beyond it: literature, sculpture, film, etc. We usually define this movement as 'postmodernism', a concept which, because of the different contexts in which it has been used, has different meanings. Of course we will only use the philosophical interpretation, in which the central idea is that man is not the subject of reality, but is the expression of something that transcends or traverses humanity: language, nature, drives, energy, etc. From a postmodern perspective, man is not the centre of the world, but is taken out of that centre by something non-human, which is why that type of thinking can be summed up by terms such as 'desubjectification' and 'decentralisation'. The reason why I mention that is that we can expect that thought to be reflected in the Sade interpretations that will be discussed in the next six chapters. Precisely because these French thinkers all belong to the same philosophical movement, we will not be surprised if it soon becomes clear that the idea of decentralisation or desubjectivation is also in the background of the Sade interpretations. If that is true, it means that the present study can in a sense be read as an introduction to (philosophical) postmodernism via the oeuvre of the libertine writer Marquis de Sade.

The latter offers us at least one good reason to thoroughly study the sometimes recalcitrant Sade interpretations of Deleuze and his contemporaries (as we will do in this book). After all, isn't philosophical postmodernism one of the most exciting currents in the long history of Western philosophy? And can we understand contemporary thinkers like Badiou and Meillassoux without looking at their predecessors?

1[1]

Godlessness, Purity and Simulacra

I Introduction

In a contribution to an issue that the literary magazine *L'Arc* dedicated to his oeuvre in 1970, philosopher and artist Klossowski focused on his predilection for certain authors. He stated that he had long since become 'captivated by the mental or plastic constructions that directly emerge from pathology'.[2] Klossowski's interest was extended to those works originating from a 'pathological' nature.[3] One of these 'pathological' authors was Sade, to whose life and work Klossowski devoted a number of studies. In fact, among the post-war French commentators on Sade, Klossowski was the writer that devoted the greatest number of pages to the fate and oeuvre of Sade.

Klossowski's interest in Sade can first be felt in 'Éléments d'une étude psychanalytique sur le marquis de Sade' from 1933. This text was the first written on Sade by one of the French philosophers whose interpretations of Sade I examine. One year later, he published 'Le mal et le négation d'autrui dans la philosophie de D. A. F. de Sade' in *Recherches philosophiques* and in 1936 he wrote 'Le monstre', a short text that appeared in the journal *Acéphale.* A few years afterwards he gave two lectures on Sade, the first of which was in 1939 when he presented the text 'Le marquis de Sade et la révolution' to the Collège de Sociologie, to which intellectuals such as Bataille belonged. The second was in 1941 when he gave the lecture entitled 'Le corps du néant' to the Dominicans of Saint-Maximin. In 1947, he compiled these lectures with the first essays and several earlier unpublished texts to form *Sade mon prochain.*[4] The collection was published exactly twenty years later bearing the title *Sade mon prochain, précédé de:*

Le philosophe scélérat, in amended form, with several texts either removed or reworked.[5] He also added 'Le philosophe scélérat' to the collection in 1967. This text is a revised lecture from a conference organised by the avant-garde group Tel Quel on 12 May 1966.[6]

In 'Le philosophe scélérat', Klossowski sheds light on three aspects of Sade's literary work. Firstly, he notes that libertine actions do not follow any explicit plans but are more reflective of gratuitous gestures. He then relates that quite a few libertines enjoyed a certain fondness for sodomy. Lastly, Klossowski points out that it was not only male libertines and virgins drifting through Sade's world, but also androgynous figures, of whom Juliette is the most salient example. Although gestures, sodomy and androgyny initially appear to have little in common, Klossowski reveals one similarity. He contends that all of these facets signify the radically modern reality of the Sadean universe. The gratuitous acts, anal sexuality and androgyny all indicate that Sade is a far-reaching form of modernity. How are we to understand this rather curious assertion? What is particularly modern about a gesture or sodomy? And in what sense does androgyny suggest a break with pre-modernity? I shall answer these questions in the second part of this chapter.

In the third part, rather than focusing on 'Le philosophe scélérat', I will focus on the texts that were included in the first edition in 1947, which Klossowski wrote during the 1930s and 1940s. During this period, it was not philosophy that was his predominant interest, but theology. This led him to translate the meditations of Johann Georg Hamann and read the works of Aurelius Augustinus. Klossowski's theological interests also left their mark on his interpretation of Marquis de Sade. He finds a correlation between Sade and Gnosticism and suggests that sadistic pleasure is an example of what scholastics call *delectatio morosa*. He also claims that concealed within Sade's brand of natural philosophy is a doctrine of salvation. That interpretation is surprising in two ways. Is Sade not a well-known atheist who rejected all forms of religiousness? In addition, the interpretation appears to be directly contradicted by Klossowski's readings of twenty years later.[7] Nevertheless, it is noteworthy that secondary literature pays little heed to Klossowski's first interpretation.[8] In the third part, I examine Klossowski's theologically inspired interpretation of Sade.

Finally, Klossowski addresses not only the universe that Sade reveals in his literature but also the fate of Marquis de Sade as a person. In the 1930s and 1940s as well as in the 1960s, he also relates Sade's literature to his own life. More specifically, Klossowski states that literature and writing played a particular function in the life of the Marquis. Literature represented a kind of healing process for certain issues with which he struggled. Marquis de Sade, according to Klossowski, was characterised by a disturbance to his well-being caused by a certain constantly recurring thought, for which he turned to literature as a remedy. In the last part of this chapter, I discuss this psycho-biographical interpretation of Sade. In the process, it will become clear why Klossowski regarded Sade in particular as his neighbour.[9]

II Enduring the Death of God

In 'Le philosophe scélérat' from 1967, Klossowski asserts that the Sadean universe is an exponent of modernity. This claim is based on a number of striking observations. For example, Klossowski draws attention to several aspects such as the erratic, unpredictable nature of the sadistic act, the androgynous figure and the sadist's preference for sodomy. In the following, I will first illustrate these aspects. Then I will explore the way in which they indicate that Sade's literature is an expression of modernity.

Gesture, Androgyny and Sodomy

In *Les 120 journées de Sodome*, Sade describes the libertine lifestyle that transpired for four months in the Black Forest's Château de Silling. The male libertines – the Bishop, the Président de Curval, the Duc de Blangis and Durcet – have four narrators at their disposal. At the beginning of each month, one of the four is chosen to entertain the libertines every night with erotic and scandalous stories. Duclos is the first. She tells of her time working in a brothel at a young age where the women were not so much there to gratify the visitors sexually, but rather to satisfy their peculiar preferences. She recounts the story of a banker who demanded that a red-haired girl jump around until beads of sweat dripped down her body. Others had a preference for rotten teeth, sweaty feet or vomiting girls. Suddenly, however, the President of the libertine gathering interrupts Duclos' story. He complains that Duclos is providing too few details about the bodies, the people, the actions and the clothing, etc. Duclos continues, thereby meeting the expectations of the President. But once again she is interrupted, this time by the Bishop: '"One moment, Duclos", said the Bishop upon seeing that she was about to proceed. "I have on my own account a need rather more pressing than to piss. It's had me in its grip for an age and I have the feeling it's got to go."'[10] Then the Bishop calls his niece and a young boy and goes with them into the next room. Just a few minutes later, Duclos continues her story again where she had left off.

This scene is a good example of what, according to Klossowski, was one of the central aspects of the Sadean universe: the gesture.[11] By this, he certainly does not wish to suggest that we are to view the world of Sade as one stemming from generosity. Nor is Klossowski referring to the voluntary or involuntary movements of the hands, arms and head that accompany an explanation or are used to communicate a specific meaning, for example. The Sadean gesture is most certainly a movement of the body, but that movement is solely focused on sexual satisfaction and is also completely meaningless. There are three additional aspects of the gesture that stand out. Firstly, the gesture is as abrupt as it is fleeting. For example, the Bishop interrupts the story of Duclos without warning so that he can satisfy himself, but then returns just as quickly to continue listening to the narrator. Secondly, the libertine has no control over the gesture. The scene cited above is not based on any particular decision that the Bishop has made to first stop Duclos' narration and then withdraw briefly. The significance of the scene does not lie with the Bishop, and the gesture is not an expression of his freedom. Its entire significance is that of a sexual impulse for which the libertine is nothing more than a passive vehicle. Finally, as is evident from the President's complaint, the libertine is primarily interested not in wild stories but in meaningless details. The gesture does not evolve from the story, but rather from that which is concealed in the story and lies in the far reaches of the narrative. This reflects the pointed, sudden and brief character of the gesture. Moreover, any arbitrary detail can cause the gesture to surface: a rotten tooth, a drop of sweat, a grey hair, etc. Any minor trigger could be sufficient cause for the urges to re-emerge. This indicates that the gesture should be understood as an expression of a compulsion that cannot wait to manifest.

According to Klossowski, the world of Sade was characterised not only by the gesture but also by the androgynous.[12] The assertion that androgynous figures are a part of Sade's literature seems curious at first glance. After all, is it not the case that the Sadean scenario rests on a strict separation between the 'male master' on the one hand and the 'female slave' on the other? However, Klossowski notes that the 'women' in Sade's literature do not have primary or secondary feminine sexual characteristics and that their genitals are more like those of men. For example, Madame Champville, one of the four narrators from *Les 120 journées de Sodome*, is introduced as follows: 'Her mouth was lovely, still fresh, missing no teeth as yet, she was flat-chested but had a belly which was good [. . .], her mound was rather prominent, and her clitoris protruded three inches when well warmed.'[13] And of one of her male customers Duclos states: 'a prick whose incredible littleness, I assure you, isn't worth the bother describing.'[14] Furthermore, Klossowski recalls that philosophical speeches were generally handled by a 'woman' and that it was often the case that 'women' such as Madame de Saint-Ange in *La philosophie dans le boudoir* acted as 'teachers'. For Sade, speech-giving and associated pedagogical roles belong not to the 'man', as was traditionally the case, but to the 'woman'. Finally, Klossowski also notes that the short, abrupt and uncontrolled gesture is the exclusive territory of the 'male' libertines. That is noteworthy, as according to Klossowski, the gesture seems more fitting to the spontaneity, impulsiveness and capriciousness of women. Based on these observations, however, Klossowski asserts that we cannot conclude that there is only 'a simple symmetrical reversal of the [. . .] schema of differentiation' in Sade.[15] Strictly speaking, the Sadean universe is not populated by men and women. Sade's characters are androgynous 'male women' and 'female men'. They represent what falls between the masculine and the feminine.

In addition, Klossowski, as the sole commentator on Sade among the French, pays close attention to the fact that with Sade, it is not the genitals that are paramount, but rather anal sexuality.[16] The fact that the libertines preferred sodomy is apparent from the title *Les 120 journées de Sodome*, which is a reference to the city in the Bible that belonged to the Pentapolis. In addition, Sade introduces the four libertines in the aforementioned book as follows:

> And such, dear reader, are the four villains in whose company I am going to have you pass a few months. Roughly all that we can say at the present time is that they were generally susceptible of an enthusiasm for sodomy, that the four of them had themselves buggered regularly, and that they all four worshipped behinds.[17]

The preference for sodomy is a recurring theme in most of Sade's novels. In *Le philosophie dans le boudoir*, for example, Dolmancé repeatedly declares his penchant for sodomy: 'I acknowledge my weakness [sodomy]. I admit as well that in all the world there is no mode of pleasure-taking preferable to this.'[18] However, that does not mean that Sade's 'male women' have no interest in other 'male women.' Klossowski emphasises that they do indeed make love with 'female men,' only they have a preference for their rear ends. For example, we read in *Les 120 journées de Sodome*: 'He insisted upon having his women enveloped in a sheet so that her face and breast would be entirely hidden from him, the single part of her body that he wanted to see, and which had to be of the highest degree of excellence, was her behind.'[19] The preference for sodomy is rooted in a particular view of nature, upon which I will further elaborate in the following section. Nature, according to the libertines, is undoubtedly focused primarily on allowing its powers to flourish to the fullest. However, if humankind utilises the powers that nature has bestowed upon it in order to propagate, then this in turn inhibits nature's productive capacity. This means that the 'male woman' who does not engage in vaginal intercourse is acting in accordance with the will of nature. In contrast, those who do reproduce are acting against nature and will be punished for doing so.

Radically Modern

When the four libertines in *Les 120 journées de Sodome* welcome the boys and girls to the Château de Silling, they not only show them the rigid daily regime and the clothing they are to wear, but they also give them a number of explicit restrictions and commands. One of the commands includes: 'The name of God shall never be uttered save when accompanied by invective or imprecations, and thus qualified it shall be repeated as often as possible.'[20] In the same manner, a certain Madame Delbène in *Juliette* states: 'Let's be guided by mature reflection and, deciding upon the existence of a God only after careful sifting of what has just been advanced, let's be persuaded, as I said, that the whole notion of God is nothing but illusions and phantoms.'[21] Such passages are repeated frequently in Sade's prose and are not seldom followed by blasphemous tirades. The libertine does not believe in God and fiercely berates whoever may dare to doubt God's non-existence. Their constant emphasis on atheism is, according to Klossowski, an expression of the godlessness of the Sadean universe. The world populated by Sade's libertines is deeply permeated by the death of God. This manifests itself not only in the renunciation of God's existence but also, according to Klossowski, in the aforementioned aspects of the gesture, androgyny and sodomy. How are we to understand this?[22]

In 'Sade et la révolution', Klossowski refers to the condemnation and guillotining of Louis XVI. His death symbolised the end of a stable, God-centred form of society that had dominated the European continent for several centuries, namely that of feudalism. At the head of this medieval society was the king, who derived his powers from God, of whom he was the primary representative on earth. At the bottom of the hierarchy was the serf, who was lent farmland by a lord. In that respect, feudalism was a reflection of creation. Just as God gave man life, the wealthy feudal lord gave the serf a livelihood by providing him with solid ground from which to draw his sustenance. That does not mean, however, that man would find happiness between the walls of a fortified medieval castle. He still bore the consequences of Original Sin that God pronounced upon the first man. This transgression was an expensive one for humankind. Humans were expelled from paradise and continued to suffer from a dreary earthly life, withdrawn from the light of eternal life, until deep into the Middle Ages. This suffering implies that feudal society focused not on the temporal but rather on the eternal life, where mankind would be delivered from their sins. This means that their fate was completely in the hands of God. Only He could grant mercy to mankind. This does not mean that God guaranteed salvation. Mankind could hope and pray for His redemption by aligning with the Will of the Lord and by keeping His Word as much as possible, but there was no assurance that the Lord would save mankind from their fall.

The death of Louis XVI in 1793 symbolised the dissolution of an unwavering order built upon and devoted to God. With the beheading of the king, mankind also killed God. It is from this death that modern, secular society was born. The origins of modernity, therefore, lie in the destruction of every reference to a point transcending the world, through which the world is supported and in which it also enclosed. In fact, according to Klossowski, abandoning that reference to God is a necessary but insufficient prerequisite for truly constituting a new, modern era. It is not enough, according to Klossowski, to merely exchange transcendence for absolute immanence. When something in the world is put forward on which life is based and to which life is oriented, the connection to a point that supersedes the world will disappear, but not the fact that there is something from which reality originates and to which mankind can cling. In other words, being radically modern not only involves severing the bond to an eternity that lies beyond the *saeculum*, but also means that nothing is deified in transient life in the sense that nothing may contend to support, sustain or safeguard life. For Klossowski, modern man must radically embrace and endure godlessness. The empty place that God has left may not be filled with something from which reality is derived and to which mankind can adhere or conform. In short, fully embracing modernity means assuming and affirming the instability, uncertainty and fluidity of life. It is at this very point that many fail and that the libertine characters from Sade's oeuvre succeed, according to Klossowski.

Take, firstly, the difference between man and woman. In modernity, that difference is no longer understood from a superior, religiously embedded perspective. Rather, the arbitrariness of that distinction becomes more pronounced. However, this has not resulted in the disappearance of the classical dichotomy and all the expectations and conditions associated with it. Even in modern, secular culture, a permanent distinction modelled on physical differences still exists through which everyday life is upheld, ordered and oriented. In their androgyny, Sade's characters break with the driving force of that symbolic order, and for that reason, Klossowski contends that these figures endure the death of God in a radical sense. Secondly, Klossowski states that although modernity has brought about the death of God, it has not left that empty space open. Although it may very well be that modern man is no longer guided by the Word of God, the foundation of reality is now based on the free and autonomous capacity to reason of the *cogito*. Justifications, according to Klossowski, are completely absent in the Sadean universe, such as seen in the departure from the Château de Silling where Duclos is suddenly interrupted by the Bishop. The man does not allow himself to be swayed by his powers of reason, but merely acts as a conductor for a fluctuating, spasmodic gesture which, once it begins to impose itself, pulls the ground out from under him, depriving him of any foothold. Thirdly, modern life has detached itself from a *telos* anchored in nature and is no longer focused on greater goals, but nonetheless holds on to life and wants to continue living. However, being radically modern also means that safeguarding life is no longer the ultimate aim. That is exactly the rationale that the libertines adopt in Sade's literature. They vehemently oppose the concept of pregnancy and are only interested in each other as long as their backs are turned.

III The Desire for Purity

In the introduction to this chapter, I pointed out that Klossowski emphasised the distinction between his second, modern Sade reading and his first interpretation of Sade from the 1930s and 1940s. During those years he did not recognise Sade as a radical offshoot of modernity, but associated Sade's philosophy of nature with a salvation-oriented movement in Christianity, Gnosticism. Furthermore, Klossowski compared sadists with nineteenth-century romantics. Finally, he also claims that libertine pleasure is a form of *delectatio morosa*. In the following, I highlight the earlier, theologically inspired interpretation of Sade's oeuvre. Afterwards, I will demonstrate in what sense Sade's concept of nature coincides with Gnosticism, to what degree the sadist is a romantic and how sadistic pleasure is a form of *delectatio morosa* according to Klossowski.

Sadism and Gnosticism

In the opening line of 'Esquisse du système de Sade', Klossowski indicates the purpose of the section.[23] He states that in the pages that follow, he will focus on the theoretical passages from Sade's literature. He begins with the observation that the backgrounds from which the libertines deliver their presentations and monologues are not always the same. He identifies at least three perspectives.

The first perspective is atheist, but inspired by Christianity. In order to illustrate this, Klossowski refers to *Dialogue entre un prêtre et un moribond*.[24] This dialogue begins with a question from a priest to a dying atheist libertine on whether he feels remorse about his life. The libertine confirms this and repents. The priest believes his remorse is a good reason to forgive his sins. Great, however, is his surprise when the libertine then says he is not sorry for his great many sins, but because he has sinned too little. As the dialogue continues, the libertine expresses his regret. Klossowski draws attention to the surprising turn that the conclusion of the dialogue takes. The conversation ends as follows: 'All human morality is contained in these words: make others as happy as you yourself would be, and never serve them more ill than you would yourself be served.'[25]

The second point of view that Klossowski identifies is from a theological angle. That is evident from the exposé from Saint-Fond in *Juliette*.[26] In this, he refers to a divine being, and in particular to the Supreme Being of Wickedness.[27] That being is characterised by the fact that it is steeped in malevolence. Evil is the essence of *L'Être Suprême en méchanceté*, according to Saint-Fond. The reason Saint-Fond has brought forth this being is that he wants to establish that one need not feel guilt when one causes suffering in others. Considering that the origin of the world is complete and total maliciousness, logic implies that mankind should live accordingly.

Thirdly, Klossowski examines the passages from Sade's literature pertaining to natural philosophy.[28] What emerges from those passages is that the libertine refers first and foremost to nature rather than to God in order to construct reality. Klossowski observes, however, that the concept of nature that Sade at times portrays is strikingly similar to the Supreme Being of Wickedness. Some of Sade's libertines perceive nature not as a blind force but as one ascribed with a will, more specifically, an evil will. Some libertines believe that nature, just as the divine Supreme Being, is pure evil. She causes wars, epidemics and earthquakes not in a quest to achieve natural balance, but because she takes pleasure in committing evil deeds. Nature is not an a-teleological force of perpetual creation and destruction but one characterised by a lust for evil for evil's sake.

These three perspectives initially appear to have little in common. While the first perspective describes a liberal libertine to whom the *regula aurea* is the core of morality, the second and third perspectives present a Supreme Being of Wickedness and a force of nature with an evil will respectively. However, Klossowski points out that the three perspectives also have a shared meaning. Each point of view adopts a moral vocabulary.[29] Regardless of the perspective taken, Klossowski concludes that the libertines use a moral vernacular throughout a large part of Sade's literature. Nevertheless, there are also passages in which this is not the case. According to Klossowski, this is evident in the fourth part of *Juliette*, in which Juliette and Clairwil go to Rome to meet Pope Pius VI, otherwise known as Braschi. His reasoning is also mostly philosophical in nature, but the Pope does not perceive nature in moral terms. Nature, as Braschi understands, is neither good nor evil, but morally neutral. What concept of nature do the two libertines obtain from the Pope?[30]

Klossowski emphasises that Pope Pius VI does not think of nature as a random force. Nature, according to the Pope, is largely comprised of an intangible force that it primarily wants to cultivate to its fullest through the creation of life. It generates that life by infusing its force into matter. Once it has created that life, however, tensions emerge between nature and its products, arising from the fact that this newly forged life can itself create life. After nature has imparted its force into matter, that force is used by the products of nature to propagate. The tension lies in the fact that the products of nature act as a competitor to nature. Because they produce new life themselves using these natural forces, they deprive nature of the possibility of fully utilising its own forces. For that reason, nature wishes not only to forge new life, but also to destroy the products it has created. Nature concentrates on the death of its own products, not because it gains pleasure from destroying life but because it is a means of regaining power, making it possible to bring about new life. In turn, these new products will themselves reproduce, once again inhibiting nature's productive possibilities. In short, nature is doomed perpetually to kill its own creations because its will fully to cultivate its own forces is obstructed by the very products that result from the cultivation of that force. According to Braschi, this culminates in the desire to destroy all life, meaning that nature endeavours to maintain the original purity of its forces that have not yet been infused into matter.[31] For this, it relies on the sadist. Nature calls upon the sadist to murder, allowing for the release of its powers. The sadist does not kill because he enjoys the destruction or suffering of the victim. These murders are intended to cure nature of its metaphysical suffering resulting from the fall of its forces into matter.

It is that view of nature that is central to Klossowski's literature. Of this concept, which he at times refers to as 'a pneumatology' and at others as 'a mythical cosmology', he writes the following in 'Sous le masque de l'athéisme': 'it is impossible not to recognize the whole ancient system of the Manichean gnosis, the visions of Basilides, Valentinus, and especially Marcion.'[32] Before we can understand that, we must first explain what Gnosticism entails.[33]

Gnosticism is the doctrine of the Gnostics. These mystical religious figures are grouped into a wide variety of movements. For example, there are the Gnostics who formed a pagan salvation movement in late antiquity and who have no ties to Christianity. There is also the Gnostic movement that arose at the same time as Christianity in Syria, North Africa and Asia Minor, quickly coming into contact with Christian doctrine. When Klossowski associates Sade with Gnosticism, he is referring to that brand of Christianity of which Basilides, Marcion and Valentinus are the most prominent representatives. These Christian-inspired Gnostics ventured to Rome, where they enjoyed a great deal of support as a result of the spiritual poverty they encountered in decadent Rome. They were denounced by the Church, however, as their broad base of followers posed a threat to the Church's authority, as well as for a number of other substantive reasons. One of the disputes arising between the Church and the Gnostics was over the birth of Jesus. According to the Gnostics, Jesus was not born of Mary in the conventional manner, but was poured forth from her as water from a pipe. Despite the Church's denunciation, the Gnostics did not disappear. Gnosticism lived on in North Africa, in movements such as Manichaeism. In Europe, there were also traces of Gnosticism in medieval sects such as the Cathars.

Despite the range of movements – and the related differences between the systems of teaching – virtually all Gnostics fundamentally agree on several points. All Gnostics profess belief in the existence of a deity who is neither good nor evil, and who escapes human comprehension. Yet that deity reveals itself in a succession of emanations. God is the first to emerge, followed by thirty emanations or Aeons in pairs, which become increasingly weak the further they move away from their divine origin. Together with God, who, according to the Gnostics, is akin to the God of the New Testament, the Aeons form the pleroma, or the divine world. The human world, however, is not a product of the evangelical God. That world was created by a Demiurge who, according to Gnostics such as Marcion, bears a similarity to the God of the Old Testament and who is situated between the God of the pleroma and earthly life. However, the Demiurge was not able to create the human world on its own accord. He was only able to do so after a cosmic mistake had occurred that for the Gnostics was equivalent to the Fall of Man: Sophia, the last of the emanations, sought to gain knowledge of the unknowable God. This arrogant pride, void of any respect for the cosmic order, resulted in the last Aeon falling out of God's grace, and subsequently being expelled from the pleroma. The fall of Sophia allowed the Demiurge to create the human world, which was made up of a mixture of matter and the last emanation.

As is evident from this 'mythical cosmology', it appears that, according to the Gnostics, the pleroma precedes life on earth chronologically. Earthly life only arose after Sophia's cosmic mistake. To this, the Gnostics link the idea of the primacy of the divine sphere over the human world. To them, the human world represents the impure whereas the divine is equated with purity. Nevertheless, this concept of the origin of life on earth is evidence that the human world was a product of divine procreation. Earthly life was created by the Demiurge, forged from matter and Sophia, the last emanation of the divine. According to the Gnostics, man is unaware of this procreation from the outset and is not capable of becoming aware on his own. In order for man to become aware of his divine conception, he requires the help of Jesus, a non-physical manifestation of the Aeon Logos that descended to the earth. Jesus reveals to mankind its origin and allows mankind to become aware of its divinity. In negative terms, Jesus makes mankind aware of its *natura lapsa*. Through the intervention of Jesus, man comes to realise that because of the physical materiality of his body, he is an expression not of God's love but of decay. This insight creates a desire for a non-material condition. The realisation that the divine dwells in him, and that it is defiled by the body, awakens the desire to live in accordance with the divine origin. Man achieves this convergence with the divine being that he always was by destroying what he is. More explicitly, this implies actions such as the need for man to purify his body and earthly burdens through strict asceticism.

From the foregoing, it appears that Gnosticism assumes a more limited concept of salvation, rather than one based on the Old Testament. For the Gnostics, salvation does not necessarily lie in curing diseases or in the liberation of oppression and slavery. The Gnostics understand salvation primarily as *apokatastasis*. This is a theological concept that refers to the restoration or restitution of an original condition or a condition that has been undermined by external factors. According to Klossowski, the triad 'demise–creation–restoration' also characterises Sade's view of nature. Under the mask of Sade's atheistic philosophy of nature lies the desire for the return to a primordial, uncorrupted condition, according to the title of a chapter from Klossowski's collection of essays. Furthermore, Gnosticism and Sade's view of nature not only relate on a formal level, but also show some remarkable similarities in terms of content, according to Klossowski.[34] We can identify at least three such similarities.

The first similarity is that earth's material reality, just as with Gnosticism, represents a reality of decay from the viewpoint of nature. According to the Pope, nature comes to this realisation because it observes that its will to fully cultivate its powers is diminished by its own products. It recognises that its creative capacity is inhibited because its creations utilise the forces it has infused into their matter for procreation. In short, nature, according to Klossowski, suffers from the fall of its forces into matter.[35] The second agreement lies in the fact that the desire for a pure, non-material condition also arises in nature, based on the awareness of decay. As is the case with the

Gnostics, the concept of material contamination awakens the desire for an original, prelapsarian condition that remains uncorrupted by material life, *in casu* the intangible force of nature. The third similarity is that nature also defines salvation as the detachment of matter and life in accordance with the concept of non-material purity. Nature pursues this paradisiacal condition with the assistance of the ruthless sadist, who liberates nature from its metaphysical suffering, which was also characteristic of the heretical Gnostics.

Based on these similarities, we can conclude that when Klossowski focuses on the passages related to Sade's philosophy of nature, he does not necessarily regard Sade as a radical offshoot of modernity. Sade is an extension of an age-old mystic-religious movement of salvation which held as central not the idea of progress, but rather the memory of and desire for an original past. Nevertheless, Klossowski also indicates a number of differences. We can identify at least three distinct points.

Firstly, Klossowski indicates that the Gnostics assigned Jesus an important role, although they rejected the concept of Jesus' death on the cross as a redemption from mankind's sins. Jesus, according to the Gnostics, is the mediator of salvation. It is only after the appearance of Jesus that man can become aware of the divine light that is present within him. This image corresponds to the descending motion that starts in the pleroma and arrives at humankind. Sade's concept of salvation, on the other hand, as Klossowski notes, evokes the image of an ascending movement. In Sade's philosophy of nature, nature is not the saviour of mankind. On the contrary, the cruel sadist liberates the forces of nature from their fall into matter.[36] The second difference is related to the first, and is that nature, unlike the Gnostics, does not try to bring about its own salvation, but relies on external assistance in order to redeem its powers. While the Gnostic is able to save himself after awakening the knowledge of his divine self as a result of the coming of Jesus, nature relies on the sadist as *Soter* to release its forces from material life. Thirdly, Klossowski states that salvation is entirely impossible for Sade, unlike for the Gnostics. This is not only because nature calls upon the assistance of the sadist for its own salvation, but because the murders caused by the sadist can never achieve the intended goal.[37] The sadist will never succeed in disconnecting the force of nature from matter.

The reason for this is that nature continues to produce unabated, continuously infusing its forces into matter. In spite of its desire for the return of its lost, uncorrupted origins, nature cannot rid itself of its will to permeate its forces into matter. In short, there is no remedy for the suffering of Sade's nature. Nature is doomed to linger in the break with its immediate presence.

Sadism and Romanticism

In our culture, the loss of virginity has a special meaning, particularly in reference to women. The focus is on the context and the right person during defloration. However, the significance of defloration is found not only in the act itself, but also in what it symbolises, namely a transition into adulthood. That idea resonates in *La philosophie dans le boudoir,* for example, when the following is said to Eugénie shortly after she has been deflowered: 'Yet there you are, dear heart, half deflowered, there you are, arrived at a woman's estate.'[38] The importance of defloration has to do not with breaking the hymen, but with what this symbolises, namely a break with a past symbolised by virginity. This means that virginity is a symbol for a phase in life that is not concerned with the pursuit of goals, the inclusion of responsibility, the defence of interests, or a focus on productivity.

In this case it is almost impossible not to recall the Holy Virgin Mary, who occupies an exalted position in Christian cultural history as she was chosen by God to be the mother of Jesus, the incarnation of the Word. Due to her unique role as mediator between God and humanity, the dogma of the immaculate conception was brought into being. Mary was received into the womb of her mother Anna without the stain of original sin and thus born immaculate. The reason why Mary was born as a result of an immaculate conception is that Jesus, who was to redeem mankind, would have otherwise been born to a woman stained in sin, thus also becoming a bearer of original sin.[39] From that same perspective, Mary also remains a virgin, at least up to and including the birth of Jesus, and is impregnated not through the conventional means of conception, but by the Holy Spirit.[40] Given the Neoplatonic background of Christianity, any form of conception involving the flesh of Mary's husband would have meant that Jesus would have originated from a sinful act. While virginity symbolises a phase that precedes adulthood in our culture,

Mary's virginity was an indicator of the absence of sin. Both views share the understanding of virginity as a symbol of purity.

I refer to virginity here because Klossowski points out in the section 'L'hommage à la vierge' that virginity is central in the Sadean universe. Contrary to any preconceptions one may have, the libertines have no interest in women who have already had their first sexual experiences and are looking to refine their sexual pleasures through all manner of bizarre experiments. The libertines are primarily interested in being accompanied by girls who are unspoilt sexually. For example, that requirement is heard in the beginning of *Les 120 journées de Sodome* when the four libertines are to choose eight girls out of a total of 144 who will accompany them for four months. Part of the selection process progresses as follows: 'She was to spread her legs with her buttocks wide open in order to be carefully examined for her virginity.'[41] This demand for virginity is associated with the tight, young bodies of girls not yet affected by time. For example, we can consider Aline, the daughter of the Bishop from *Les 120 journées de Sodome*, as the prototype of the Sadean victim:

> She was the most youthful of the four, she had just become eighteen; she had a fetching, exuberantly healthy, and almost pert little countenance; a little turned-up nose, brown eyes full of expression and vivacity, a delicious mouth, a most shapely though somewhat tall figure [. . .]. A pair of the most voluptuous buttocks that ever a libertine eye may behold. [. . .] and when she was presented to the assembly, she was thoroughly a maid.[42]

The virginity of the young female characters from the Sadean universe does not merely represent refreshing youthfulness. Their virginity also symbolises metaphysical purity. According to Klossowski, the girls resonate a purity that has a deeper meaning, as is the case with the Holy Virgin Mary. The Sadean virgins, Klossowski writes, are the image of a 'divine' purity not yet touched by material life.[43] The fact that they evoke this image is due to the aura of invulnerability that their bodies radiate. No matter how violently the girls are raped, the young virgins recover quickly, the blush returning to their cheeks afterwards as a sign of their impeccable health. The perpetual restoration of the virginal bodies is evoked by a presence that transcends the mortal body and is not bound by material substance. In other words, the Sadean virgins are a reflection of the intangible power of Sade's philosophy of nature, which I have outlined in the section above.

When Klossowski discusses the sadist's attitude towards 'divine' virgins, he repeatedly refers to nineteenth-century Romanticism.[44] This movement contains the central notion that in the modern world, under the influence of the rationalism of the Enlightenment, the bond between man and nature has disappeared.[45] The idea that modern man is no longer in harmony with nature resonates, for example, in the well-known words of the German romantic, Novalis: 'We have lost the world, and the world has lost us.' Romantic suffering, referred to as 'the spleen' by Baudelaire, expresses an awareness that this break with the ruins of the past is irreversible. At the heart of this romantic grief is a suffering felt as a result of what has disappeared and can no longer be restored. At the same time, the desire for restoration can also be felt in this suffering. The romantic would not mourn this irrevocable break if he did not wish for the past to return. This suffering is therefore the expression of both the realisation of the impossible resurrection of the past and the longing for its return. In other words, the romantic represents a part of modernity, but his nostalgia reflects the fact that he is not yet fully steeped in the modern concept of life.

The fact that Klossowski refers to romanticism in the middle of his discussion on the sadist's attitude towards virgins gives rise to the suspicion that he also believes the sadist is suffering. At first glance, this appears to be a rather curious statement. Anyone skimming through a few pages of Sade's oeuvre quickly discovers that it is not the sadist but the virgins who undergo pages of severe anguish. The sadist does not seem to suffer but appears to enjoy the terrible suffering he causes his virgins. How then are we to understand the suffering of the sadist? Where does Klossowski believe that suffering lies? In what sense does this correspond to the grief of the romantic?

To answer those questions, we can refer to examples such as *Juliette*, in which a libertine asserts that it is not beneficial for a woman to remain a virgin until marriage. He adds:

> The pseudo-virtue called chastity, unmistakably the most ridiculous of existing superstitions in that this mode of being does

> nothing in the slightest to make others happy and wreaks incalculable harm on the prosperity of everyone [. . .] every sane mind ought first of all to give chastity an eminent position amongst the most odious devices whereby man has seen fit to encumber and rout the inspirations of Nature.[46]

This is evidence that the libertine does not view those who choose to remain virgins in a particularly positive light. The reason he gives for this is that virginity does not contribute to happiness or well-being. This explanation is a moderate, rationalised expression of something different, namely the extreme frustration that the virgins trigger. The libertine is not someone whose sexual desire is aroused by young, unspoilt girls. Nor does he fall in love with those who evoke the image of a 'divine' purity. No, declares Klossowski, the libertine is characterised by extraordinary irritation with regard to virginity. More particularly, he is bothered by what that virginity symbolises, namely intangible purity.[47]

Central to Klossowski's interpretation, however, is not the irritation as such, but its origin. In this, Klossowski emphasises that the girls remind the sadists of their inevitable bond to their bodies.[48] The virgins are disturbing because their purity brings to mind the fact that the sadist is inextricably connected to his body. The irritation that the pure virgins provoke is a frustration with his own impurity. However, this preoccupation with the body would not disturb the sadist to such an intense level if he were not fascinated by the intangible purity he prefers over his own body. The fact that he is irritated by this connection to his body betrays an attachment to an ideal of purity that the sadist imagines he once possessed but which was irrevocably lost.[49] This is precisely where Klossowski pinpoints the suffering of the sadist. Just as with nature, the sadist grieves for the impossible return of his ideal purity. The sadist is not characterised by the jubilation or pleasure he takes in causing pain but rather, he is a *homo nostalgicus*, gloomy and melancholic man suffering from the unattainable restoration of the past. Sade's entire oeuvre, according to Klossowski, is permeated by one long, drawn-out, nostalgic scream.[50] That cry is what separates the sadist from the romantic. Both long for the merging of a divide, but at the same time are steeped in awareness of the irreversible loss of an ideal.

Despite the suffering that the sadist and the romantic share, Klossowski also points to a difference between the two. The distinction lies in the way they deal with the suffering they face as a result of this irreparable loss. One possible reaction is to inflate or exaggerate the suffering. That is the reaction of the romantic, wallowing in his suffering and plagued with guilt. This sense of guilt stems from the fact that he belongs to the new, modern era and therefore also shares in the responsibility for man's break from nature. Through intense suffering, the romantic hopes to rectify his feelings of guilt with regard to the lost past.[51]

The case of the sadist is different. He does not exaggerate his suffering and does not stubbornly cling to the past. According to Klossowski, the sadist attempts to free himself from his suffering by releasing the shackles of his past.[52] Thus, the sadist does not compensate for the loss. The force of all his efforts takes a more radical approach, attempting to make the loss disappear by severing his bond with the ideal of purity. The sadist, according to Klossowski, aims to destroy the past that lives on inside of him. What does not exist cannot be lost, reasons the sadist, and therefore cannot cause suffering. Klossowski asserts that it is from this intent that we are to understand the sadist who drags out pure, 'divine' virgins for torture. What the sadist is doing, according to Klossowski, is projecting his unattainable ideal onto the victim. When he strikes down hard on the virgins, he is battling against this unattainable ideal and attempting to destroy his past. In short, sadism is an attempt to break free from the past by projecting that past onto someone else and kicking it hard.[53] Even if the sadist is not at the service of nature, according to Klossowski, he does not commit cruelty for the sake of pleasure or because he enjoys destruction. The sadist is cruel because he wants to heal himself of his nostalgia by freeing himself from his ideal.

Despite the fact that the romantic and the sadist both long for the past and at the same time recognise that the loss is irreversible, there is also a point of distinction between the two. Unlike the romantic, whose guilt shows that he remains attached to the past, the sadist goes one step further and attempts to rid himself of his damaged ideal. Destroying the purity of the virgins is an attempt to break with the past. However, Klossowski frequently draws attention to the fact that the atrocities committed in Sade's literature never cease and are constantly repeated.[54] Every page introduces a new set of girls that the sadist vanquishes as mercilessly as the ones before. This perpetual repetition signifies that the sadist does not succeed in his objective. Considering the aim of his cruelty, he would then stop those atrocities if he had indeed achieved his goal. In other words, although the sadist attempts to kill his past, his repeated actions suggest that the past continues to exert its power and will not allow itself to be eradicated. The sadist attempts to break free of his past but fails to do so. The past casts a perpetual shadow over the sadist's here and now, and it is in that sense that the sadist is ultimately no further along than the romantic.

The Slow Enjoyment of Repetition

Klossowski also addresses the pleasure the sadist feels, which in his view is a form of *delectatio morosa*.[55] The first term in that expression means 'pleasure' or 'desire'. The epithet *morosus*, as Klossowski points out, originally has two meanings. The first meaning of *morosus* is 'strange'. In this case, *morosus* is related to *mos*, which means 'habit'. The reason for this lies in the fact that the people in antiquity considered the habits of others strange. Secondly, *morosus* also means 'sad'. Here, *morosus* is derived from the term *mora*, which means 'delay'. *Morosus* acquired the meaning of 'sad' in the sense that a delay implies that the focus of achieving a predetermined goal has been impeded. This leads to the intended result not being achieved, at least not as long as the delay lasts. Failure to achieve the goal is accompanied by sorrow.[56]

Klossowski points out that the compound expression *delectatio morosa* originated from scholasticism.[57] More specifically, the expression is used in moral theological debates pertaining to the relationship between guilt and pleasure. The scholastics draw a distinction between primary and secondary pleasures. Both represent the enjoyment of fantasising about forbidden actions over an extended period of time without the intention of turning that fantasy into reality. The difference lies in the fact that primary pleasures emerge involuntarily, whereas secondary pleasures stem from the intervention of the will. According to medieval theologians, only those who are guilty of both consciously envisioning sinful thoughts as well as taking pleasure in them are guilty. It is this form of pleasure that they refer to as *delectatio morosa*. According to Klossowski, this confirms that for the scholastics *morosus* does not mean 'sad'. In scholasticism the meaning of *morosus* refers to *mora*. *Delectatio morosa* in scholasticism means 'slow pleasure' or 'pleasure of some duration'. If one entertains a notion for an extended period of time and this results in pleasure, then this is indeed a pleasure of some duration.

Shortly after elaborating on the meaning of *delectatio morosa* in theology, Klossowski states that the sadist not only commits cruelty and discusses philosophy, but also engages in fantasies. By this Klossowski does not mean that the sadist is a dreamer.[58] While the dreamer detaches himself from his free will and fills his mind with images that spontaneously create associations, the sadist unifies his imagination with his will. Furthermore, Klossowski makes a distinction between the sadist and the ascetic, who purifies his mind from the notions to which sensual desire is normally directed.[59] The ascetic frees himself from his sensory nature and opens himself to the divine. The sadist, on the other hand, does not empty his mind but focuses on images of actions for an extended period of time, which he then also turns into reality. More specifically, he fills his mind with images of virgins whom he himself tortures, and focuses on the concept for a long time. The resulting pleasure is consistent with the secondary pleasures referred to by the expression *delectatio morosa*. The enjoyment the sadist experiences is also a pleasure taken in an idea that extends over time and, just as with secondary pleasures, there is a taboo associated with the content of that idea.

When secondary literature addresses the section '*Delectatio morosa*', it deals exclusively with that aspect of Klossowski's interpretation.[60] It does not pay heed to the fact that Klossowski explicitly states that there are several forms of *delectatio morosa* present in Sade's literature, and that the pleasure of the sadist engaged in fantasy is not the only form.[61] Another form of *delectatio morosa* that Klossowski identifies is not a pleasure derived from inner observations but a pleasure associated with the actual realisation of the content of the sadist's fantasies, in other words the mistreatment of the 'divine' virgins. In what sense is that pleasure a form of *delectatio morosa*?

We have seen earlier that the cruel deeds have the specific purpose of making the sadist forget the past, although he is not able to achieve that goal. The repetition of the torture indicates that the past continues to exert its power beyond the will of the sadist and that he therefore fails to leave the past behind. The failure of the predetermined goal initially causes disillusionment. The sadist is at odds with a limitation that heightens his disappointment. After a while, however, as Klossowski states, the disappointment fades as the sadist begins to long for the failure itself. Although the sadist is initially focused on an objective, as the number of atrocities committed increases, the sadist wants nothing more than to achieve the failure of his intent.[62] The sadist wants this failure because after a time the goal of committing the offence has disappeared and is replaced by cruelty itself. In the course of the rapid successions of crimes resulting from the goal not being achieved, the crime and the original goal become dissociated and the crime itself becomes the goal. Repetition severs the bond with the goal and leads the sadist to desire nothing more than the pointless repetition of the same actions. This repetition is where the pleasure of the sadist originates, which is no longer an expression of failure, but represents the fact that the goal now lies in the action itself. Sadistic pleasure is therefore not rooted in a disposition or an error during development but is an effect of repetition. That pleasure is a form of *delectatio morosa*: it lasts a long time and is of some duration. The reason is that it stems from an activity that continues constantly and extends over time.

IV The Relationship between Sade's Life and Work

Klossowski also interprets Sade from a psycho-biographical perspective. In this way, he understands Sade's literature as a solution to a problem with which the Marquis struggles. That is the case in both Klossowski's first and later studies of Sade. In 1967, however, he adds something more. One solution for a problem in Sade's life includes not only the written content but also a certain literary technique. It is in the sense that Sade's literature has something to solve that Klossowski sees him as his neighbour. In order to understand that, we first have to examine the relationship between Klossowski's own life and work.

Klossowski the Maniac

In an interview from 1982, Klossowski says: 'I am neither a novelist, nor a philosopher, nor even an artist before I am a maniac – a pure and simple maniac.'[63] By that he does not mean that he is primarily a pervert or that he is always out to seduce women and share a bed with them. Here, Klossowski is referring to the fact that his life gravitates around a force that never ceases to exert itself. It is this force around which his life revolves that drives him and compels him to draw, paint and write. It plagues him obsessively, forcing him to continue drawing, painting and writing maniacally. How are we to understand that? What does Klossowski's life revolve around? Why does it prompt him to become an artist? What is this issue that Klossowski is facing? And in what sense do Klossowski's activities as an artist pose a solution to that issue?

Let's start with a brief look at *Les barres parallèles*, Klossowski's most famous drawing. The female figure, Roberte, is central in that drawing. Her wrists are tied to the point where the vertical poles and the horizontal beams of the gymnastics equipment meet. Next to her, there is a large male figure standing on a chair, and on the other side a shadowy dwarf squats, holding her left ankle. This peculiar scene is also reflected in the trilogy of novels *Les lois de l'hospitalité* (1965), in which Klossowski describes how the man standing violently unfolds Roberte's clenched right fist, places her fingers between his lips, tastes her nails and licks her palm.[64] Although Roberte first resists, she can soon no longer control herself. She surrenders to the pleasure that the man awakens in her. This is evident from details we see in the drawing such as her head falling slightly to the side and her half-open eyes staring downward. It also shows how Roberte attempts to conceal the physical signs of her pleasure with her right thigh. After this bizarre scene, the standing man faints, and the dwarf releases Roberte from her restraints.

Klossowski refers to the *Les barres parallèles* drawing as he does his other creations, as a 'simulacrum'. Klossowski derives this term from Augustine, who in *Civitas Dei*, in the wake of the Roman scholar Marcus Terentius Varro, draws a distinction between natural, political and mythical religion.[65] Augustine has no interest in the first form of religion, the one with which philosophers primarily occupy themselves. His attention focuses exclusively on the political religion of urban life and the mythical religion that takes place in the theatre. More specifically, he establishes that there is a difference between the two forms of religion. In the temples, the gods are revealed as guardians of urban life and much is sacrificed to them to ensure the prosperity of the city that they protect. This is in stark contrast to the theatres outside the official temples. There, actors and actresses portray the gods as licentious, immoral beings. That depiction is chutzpah, according to Augustine. From the perspective of his Neoplatonic Christian notion of a true and benevolent God, it baffles him that one might give a theatrical depiction of the gods as obscene and immoral. More importantly, the Fathers of the Church assert that the two religions are incompatible. The portrayals of the gods in the theatres cannot be reconciled with the gods worshipped in the temples who are responsible for prosperity and well-being in the city. These portrayals, Augustine concludes, are nothing more than simulacra, or 'deceptive notions'.

Augustine is only able to view the actors as deceptive insofar as he assumes that the gods coincide with their political function.[66] According to Klossowski, that portrayal of the gods is too one-sided. It may be true that the Roman gods are responsible for prosperity in the city, and they allow themselves to be known as such insofar as they are in the public sphere. Klossowski asserts that there is also a different aspect of the gods that is not displayed in the temples that transcends these political values, namely eroticism. According to Klossowski, it is that aspect which is depicted in the theatres. The obscene and immoral actions performed by the actors and actresses are not deceitful, but representations of the erotic, non-functional, shadowy side of the gods. Despite the fact that this interpretation differs from Augustine's view, Klossowski still adopts the term 'simulacrum'. For him, the fact that the actors are simulacra means that they reveal an aspect of the gods which would normally remain concealed. He further emphasises that the actors and actresses do not merely mimic the eroticism of the gods. The relationship between the actors and the gods cuts deeper than the mere outward relationship between the depiction and the depicted. Klossowski describes that relationship in terms of 'incarnation' or 'embodiment'. By this, he means that the actors play a role in the divine and that they present the hidden side of the gods. The simulacra are an expression of the dark side of the Roman gods, and the wild eroticism of the gods is expressed in the actors.

Klossowski continues to use the term 'simulacrum' in the sense described after his reading of Augustine and his interpretation of Roman theatrical plays.[67] This is also the case when he comments on his drawing *Les barres parallèles*. The drawing is not a mimesis of some cherished scene from Klossowski's love life. It is an embodiment of the fact that there is something left unspoken in his life. That something remains unexpressed in words, not because he does not want to speak about it or because he wants to hide something from the public. The neglect stems from an inability to speak.[68] Klossowski was overwhelmed by an event, more specifically his marriage to Denise Morin-Sinclair in 1947, which escaped his words and imagination, and in that sense was foreign to him. For example, he relates, albeit in the third person, the experience of his marriage in the following: 'Such abundance is offered to him, that it would erase him if he were not to find a response to this abundance that overwhelms him.'[69] The result is that this experience has permeated deeply into his life and that something foreign is still present in his life. When relating an event, a distance emerges between the speaker and the event about which they are speaking. The person speaking does not necessarily internalise the experience, but instead keeps that experience on the outside, without absorbing what has happened. To this end, Klossowski is not capable of allowing the experience into his psyche and thus continues to ramble on as a stranger to it. He calls that experience his 'pathos'.

Klossowski's life revolves around an experience that defies description and depiction, which, because it escapes words and imagery, continues to invoke 'exorcism' or 'externalisation' as he often puts it. He tries to achieve this with his artworks. Klossowski draws, paints and writes in order to free a space between himself and the foreign experience that is close to his skin. From that perspective, he incorporates some aspects in his drawings, paintings and novels that are foreign to the scenario and that fall outside the bigger picture.

Take, for example, *Les barres parallèles*. It is clear to the viewer that the man on the chair and Roberte are sexually aroused. The licking of the palm, the presence of the dwarf and the gymnastic equipment, however, make certain that the scene no longer resembles conventional eroticism. The fact that there are aspects of this scene that do not merge with the whole reflects something different, namely the fact that there is something in Klossowski's own life that escapes his imagination. Furthermore, just as with the actors in the Roman theatre, we must also understand the significance of the drawing. For Klossowski, *Les barres parallèles* is an embodiment of the fact that an experience continues to exert itself on him but at the same time remains foreign to him. Klossowski incorporates elements into his work that are foreign to the larger context in order to take the fact that something alien remains present, and place it outside himself and into his work. Thus, the drawing is not an attempt to express and illustrate the experience itself, which is impossible in the case of Klossowski. He is expressing not an aspect that he extracts, but an aspect that escapes him. This externalisation frees him from the fact that something is escaping his imagination, at least for the moment. The fact that one work saves him from the foreign experience does not mean that the experience itself is more distant. Afterward Klossowski must continue working, which is why he is deemed a maniac.

Living and Writing

As mentioned previously, Klossowski not only discusses Sade's reflections on philosophy, the cruel scenes in which virgins are abused, the spasmodic gestures and the androgyny. In his first texts and in the text he adds to his collection in 1967, Klossowski also addresses the life of Sade. More specifically, he connects Sade's literature with an aspect of Sade as a person. To which aspect does Klossowski refer? And what, in his view, is the link between this aspect and Sade's work?

In 'Le philosophe scélérat', as discussed in the first section, Klossowski states that sodomy is central in the Sadean universe. In addition, in 1967, he points out that this is also Sade's personal preference.[70] Sade's preference is for sodomy, both with women and with men, as evidenced by a well-known affair in June 1772. After that affair, the Marquis was sentenced to death. The reason for this was not only that he intended to poison prostitutes but also that he had sodomised girls. Sade's preference for sodomy continued throughout his lifetime and did not cease, not even when he was in prison. For example, in 1781 in a letter from the prison in Vincennes, he wrote to his wife that she should send him bottles and tubes with a circumference of six inches. When she answers that she does not understand how he would be able to put it in his trouser pockets, he notes in the margin of the letter: 'I don't put it into my pocket. I put it elsewhere, where it still turns out to be too small.'[71] And two years later he writes to her in a letter in which he becomes rather upset about those who do not share his preference: 'I kiss your behind well [. . .] anyone who moves away from the vase must burn in hell.'[72] The fact that Sade prefers sodomy over vaginal intercourse is not only felt in circumstances to which it is suitable. Even when sitting in his prison cell, it is not the case that Sade only occasionally fantasises about sodomy. Sade, according to Klossowski, is haunted by his desire for sodomy, which is constantly weighing down on him. Klossowski does not mention any special event in Sade's life that could explain his obsession. He does state, however, that Sade is unable to express verbally this extraordinary interest in sodomy, which escapes his understanding, just as is the case with Klossowski's own experience with his marriage.[73] This means that Sade also clings to a preference that is at the same time alien to him. In short, according to Klossowski, sodomy is Sade's pathos. His life gravitates around the idea of sodomy which, because he has no access to it, incessantly plagues him in every pore of his body. This already shows us that, according to Klossowski, Sade's life can be interpreted in postmodern terms, namely as haunted by an obscure force that decentres the subject.

Just as with Sade himself, the characters in his literature also prefer sodomy. They have good reasons for this. Madame de Saint-Ange, just after her homosexual friend Dolmancé has prepared Eugénie for what he calls 'sodomite amusements,' states the following:

> Imagine nothing of the sort, sweet little fool [Eugénie]; there is not the least wrong in diverting a man's semen into a detour by one means or by another, because propagation is in no wise the objective of Nature [. . .], the less we propagate, the better; and when we avoid it altogether, that's best of all.[74]

Madame de Saint-Ange is referring here to the concept of nature that we mentioned in the previous section. This view is that nature consists of a powerful force that it initially intends to develop fully by creating new life. After a time, however, tensions arise between man and nature. Human reproduction, after all, prevents nature from developing its powers to the fullest. That tension disappears when human sexuality, as in the case of sodomy, is decoupled from reproduction. In short, the sodomite does not live at odds, but rather in accordance, with nature. This is the conclusion drawn not only by Madame de Saint-Ange but also by many other characters from Sade's oeuvre. The idea that sodomy is in accordance with nature is mentioned repeatedly. Klossowski not only compares those passages with the passages in which a Supreme Being of Wickedness appears or in which the libertines attribute an evil to nature. He is also exploring their origins and claims that they have non-philosophical roots. More specifically, Sade writes these philosophical passages because they give his preference for sodomy a scope that goes well beyond his personal life. This depersonalisation creates space between Sade as a person and the alien driving force within him. It is through his own preference for sodomy within the larger, natural-philosophical perspective that we understand that he is attempting to sever the ties to that preference and liberate himself from the forces that persist.[75]

Klossowski interprets the relationship between Sade's life and work as such in 'Le philosophe scélérat', the text he added to his essay collection in 1967. However, it is not the case that Klossowski only considered the life of the Marquis many years after his first texts about Sade. He also discusses the relationship between Sade's life and work in the texts included in the first version of *Sade mon prochain* from 1947. In those texts, he states that Sade's oeuvre reverts to 'his pathos', namely 'a mystery that does not cease to exert itself'.[76] The difference is that during the 1930s and 1940s, Klossowski pointed not to the idea of sodomy as Sade's pathos but to that which also characterises his characters, namely the idea of an intangible purity. Marquis de Sade, according to Klossowski, obsessively longs for those who do not seem to be bound to a physical body and who radiate pure 'divinity'. Klossowski contends that this desire does not have its roots in a particular event but that it is an original, irreducible fact expressed early in Sade's life.[77] The first person to represent the ideal of purity for him was his mother.[78] However, she was not able to fulfil that ideal for long. According to Klossowski, at some indeterminate moment in Sade's childhood, her physicality revealed itself. The young Marquis interpreted this as his mother's betrayal of her own purity. The result is that Sade began to despise his mother and mother-in-law as well as all maternal values such as care and devotion.[79] Nevertheless, Sade remained obsessed with his ideal. According to Klossowski, this obsession explains Sade's love for Anne-Prospère, a canoness and younger sister of Sade's wife. The ongoing re-emergence of this notion of purity, a concept that confounds him and that continues to exert itself, prompts Sade to speculate about a pure force that has not yet fallen in nature. That speculation, according to Klossowski, takes the idea of purity into a larger, more impersonal perspective, keeping the strangeness that continues to stir in Sade at a distance.

Based on the foregoing, it appears that the similarities between Sade and Klossowski are not to be understood on a substantive level. Neither during the 1930s and 1940s nor in 1967 does Klossowski see Sade as his neighbour because he recognises himself in Sade's peculiar sexual preferences. Klossowski's interest in Sade is due to the fact that he too is plagued by an alien force that continues to persist and that Sade also attempts to place what is close to his skin at a distance. In both his early texts and the texts of 1967, Klossowski states that Sade's attempt focuses on the content of a concept that is both imposing and elusive. Sade tries to keep this concept that escapes his understanding at a distance by placing its contents in a broader context. In 'Le philosophe scélérat', Klossowski states that this attempt fails. The reason for this is that the obsessive thoughts, just like Klossowski's experience with marriage, remain an enigma and cannot be encapsulated in a broader perspective.[80] At the end of the same text, he mentions a second attempt by Sade to express his pathos in spatial terms. This attempt deals not with the content of the alien force, but with the fact that Sade is escaping something.

The starting point of Klossowski's interpretation is the conclusion that the philosophical reflections are constantly interspersed with scenes that are at times purely orgiastic and at other times cruel. The libertines begin to speculate about a nature that aims to infuse its forces into matter, but before they finish with the thought of a nature that desires to be released from its creations, they interrupt their session to enjoy a momentary pleasure. That continuous interruption of the theory by palpable experience may be intriguing or exciting at first, but according to Klossowski, it quickly leads to boredom. Moreover, Klossowski contends that this constant interruption of the progress of thought by the *tableaux vivants* imparts a strange, peculiar character to Sade's text. The reason for this is that the erotic and cruel passages repeatedly describe the same actions. This constant repetition kills the meaning of the text. The strangeness of Sade's literature thus lies in the fact that the theoretical reflections are interrupted not by erotic scenes but by passages that, after a time, no longer say anything and which therefore fall out of line with the text and are removed from it. According to Klossowski, that strangeness in the text is the embodiment of the observation that a foreign thought continues to plague Sade. Therefore, the erotic and cruel passages are not deceitful representations but simulacra in the Klossowskian sense. Repetition is the literary technique that Sade uses to pursue the strangeness that continues to haunt him externally. This technique does not, however, imply that the idea of sodomy and purity escapes his understanding, nor can it prevent this strangeness from continuing to present itself. Nevertheless, repetition helps Sade rid himself of the experience of strangeness for a moment. It is that stylistic lesson that Klossowski draws from his reading of Sade and that served as a source of inspiration for the production of drawings such as *Les barres parallèles*.

V Conclusion

With the title *Sade mon prochain*, borrowed from St Benedict Joseph Labre in the eighteenth century, Klossowski suggests that he was interested in Sade because Sade's oeuvre reflects Klossowski's own sexual preferences and fantasies. In the third section, however, I demonstrated that Klossowski's interest lay in interpreting Sade as an illustration of what he calls a 'pathological artist'. This interest in an author who, through his work, tries to come to terms with a problem that accentuates and besieges him also led Klossowski to Friedrich Nietzsche (although it remains to be seen, since Klossowski's reading is highly speculative, whether it was really the case that Sade needed to deal with the personal problem Klossowsi had in mind). It is also because of the latter that he considers Sade to be his neighbour. In the second section, we have seen that the enjoyment of the sadist, according to Klossowski, is an example of what the scholars call *delectatio morosa*. This expression returns in those texts from Klossowski's oeuvre in which he gropes for hidden erotic traces in the history of Christianity. This quest forced Klossowski to study theology during the German occupation and to go to the seminary. During these years he not only delved into Augustine, but also became intrigued by the idea of gnostic purity. This interest is reflected in his Sade interpretation. According to Klossowski, we must understand both nature and the sadist from the point of view of the ideal of immaterial purity. This theologically inspired reading is completely absent from the text he added to *Sade mon prochain* in 1967. In it, he does not interpret Sade from a theological perspective but reads his oeuvre as the radical offshoot of what modernity means to him. This interpretation is non-scientific and reflects his interest in Nietzsche during this period, which is also expressed in a translation of Nietzsche and in his well-known study *Nietzsche et le cercle vicieux*.

2[1]

The Terror of Writing

I Introduction

Among the French post-war philosophers who have written about Sade, there is no one who has worked on literature as thoroughly and for as long as Blanchot. Literature, more particularly the literary experience of writing, is the pivotal point on which Blanchot's intellectual activities turned. This is clear from the letter he wrote to the Italian writer Elio Vittorine in 1963: 'All my life has disappeared in a research movement that is perhaps the experience of writing and for which I tried to bear the responsibility in a poor but absolute way.'[2] However, this interest in literature and the activity of writing was not immediately apparent. During the 1930s, Blanchot was first and foremost a journalist and political activist. Only after a sudden break with his political activism in 1938 did his interest in literature come to the fore. In 1941, Blanchot wrote his first novel and in the same year started a literary chronicle, which he continued until the end of the war.[3] In the decades that followed, Blanchot wrote several more novels, and established himself as a renowned literary critic. He wrote about contemporaries including Marguerite Duras, Michel Leiris and Francis Ponge, as well as about eighteenth- and nineteenth-century literature, focusing, for instance, on the work of Friedrich Hölderlin, Stéphane Mallarmé, Herman Melville and others.

Among these authors, Blanchot kept an important place for Sade, to whose work he dedicated three essays. Blanchot's first text on Sade, which appeared in *Critique* in 1946, is entitled 'Quelques remarques sur Sade'.[4] His second text, 'À la rencontre de Sade', was published in *Les Temps Modernes* the next year and builds on his first study. This second study was later retitled 'La raison de Sade', and was published three times: twice with a study on the nineteenth-century French writer Comte de Lautréamont and on a third occasion, together with a text on Restif de La Bretonne.[5] Blanchot's third study on Sade was published four times under two different titles: In 1965, 'L'inconvenance majeure' was included as a foreword in both 'Français, encore un effort si vous voulez être républicains' and in *Nouvelle Revue Française*; 'L'insurrection, la folie d'écrire' was included in the book *L'entretien infini* in 1969 and published again in 1986 alongside his second study.[6]

Although Blanchot's three essays on Sade are quite lengthy, this does not mean that he focuses on Sade's work in isolation. On the contrary, in these essays Blanchot actually refers less to Sade's literature than to the works of other authors including Kafka and Mallarmé. It becomes clear that Blanchot considers Sade to be very important; this can be seen from a passage in 'La littérature et le droit à la mort', probably Blanchot's best-known text, which I will refer to several times later in this chapter.[7] In this passage, Blanchot briefly discusses Sade and states the following: 'Sade is the writer par excellence.'[8] This points to why Blanchot is interested in the work of the Marquis. Blanchot is specifically interested in mapping out the experience of writing in general and looks to Sade because he fits the image of the ideal writer. This is striking for two reasons. Firstly, it seems odd that Blanchot, who was mainly interested in innovative, avant-garde authors, would select Sade's work, which was rejected in the eighteenth century, mainly from moral considerations. Secondly, Blanchot repeatedly underscores that Sade's literature is annoying to read. This negative qualification of Sade's work seems at first sight to contradict the fact that Blanchot celebrates Sade as an ideal writer. What is Blanchot's ideal? And in what way does Sade fit this image?[9]

I will address these questions via a detour that runs through the idea of revolution, an idea that is central to Blanchot's life in the 1930s.[10] In that period, he had joined the *Jeune Droite* movement, which opposed the socioeconomic disorder that arose after the Wall Street stock market crash in 1929. According to the Catholic intellectuals' movement, this market crisis was merely the symptom of a much more fundamental and far-reaching crisis. The roots of the disorder of the 1930s, according to *Jeune Droite*, pointed to a crisis of the anthropology and values underpinning Western culture since the Enlightenment. According to Blanchot and his supporters, an intellectual and moral revolution was required to overcome this fundamental crisis. When Blanchot, two years before the outbreak of the Second World War, suddenly turned away from his revolutionary ambitions, this did not mean that the idea of revolution disappeared from his life. Instead of participating in the sphere of organised political movements as such, Blanchot would focus on the idea of revolution in his new field of interest, namely literature.

In order to map out the activity of writing, he constantly employed terms such as 'Terror' and 'revolt'. At the end of the 1930s, Blanchot not only made the movement 'from revolution to literature', to quote the title of a text from 1937, but also thought of literature as itself revolutionary.[11] This is also the case when he comments on Sade's work. The link between Sade's work and the French Revolution – more specifically, the radical offshoot of it: the 'Terror' – contradicts the impression that a first superficial reading of Sade leaves behind. After all, isn't Sade the heir of an aristocratic family? And is the Sadean universe not populated by popes and graves? What then is the connection between Sade and Terror? And what does that clarify that about Sade's literature and authorship?

In the third part of this chapter I will discuss two essays that Blanchot included in *L'entretien infini*, in which he presents several philosophical and historical cultural considerations. In these essays, Blanchot writes more specifically about our book and knowledge culture, and also about humanism. It is remarkable that he connects these larger reflections to his views on literature. Although he does not mention Sade in that context, on the basis of my explanation in the second section, I will show that Blanchot has Sade in mind in both essays. This will lead to the initially surprising thesis that, according to Blanchot, Sade's activity of writing – and not the cruel content of his literature – calls into question two pillars that underpin our culture.

II The Ideal Writer

It is known that Sade actively participated in the French Revolution and the Terror during his lifetime and, in his reading of Sade, Blanchot gives a great deal of weight to this. According to him, however, we should resist the temptation to understand Sade's participation in the Terror regime from the perspective that he was simply looking after his own interests. Sade did not participate in the Terror regime because he wanted to prevent his aristocratic past from haunting him under that new regime, which would have led him to the guillotine. Blanchot maintains that the ties between Sade and the Revolution lie deeper.[12] According to Blanchot, the reason why Sade moves into the political arena is because what is happening there is in line with, and responds to, his own views as set out in his letters and speeches. In what follows, I will show that, according to Blanchot, there is a close connection not only between the Terror and Sade's political views, but also between the Terror and Sade's literature. Therefore, I rely on the passage from 'La littérature et le droit à la mort' that has been cited above. In this passage, Blanchot states not only that Sade is the author par excellence, but also that every writer feels close to the Revolution and Terror.[13] Although Blanchot does not explicitly refer to Sade in this context, I will show on the basis of a number of passages from Blanchot's Sade studies that therein he further elaborates his thesis from 'La littérature et le droit à la mort' via Sade's literature. More specifically, I will argue that, according to Blanchot, Sade's oeuvre is closely linked to the work carried out during the reign of Terror, both in terms of content and in terms of Sade's style. This explanation will then bring to light the sense in which Sade corresponds to the image of the ideal writer.

Terror, Protest and Negation

Regarding the content of Sade's oeuvre, Blanchot refers to, among other texts, Sade's political-philosophical diatribe 'Français, encore un effort si vous voulez être républicains' from *La philosophie dans le boudoir*.[14] The topics tackled by Sade in this text can be grouped into two categories: religion and morality. He explains that, in the new France, Christian idols should be destroyed, and that murder, incest and theft should not be punished; indeed, one of Sade's characters argues that the latter transgressions must be required. Blanchot, however, is interested not so much in what is or is not prohibited in Sade's ideal republic. Rather, he is interested in the fundamental structure of Sade's new republican state.

In order to describe that structure, Blanchot relies on a passage in Sade's political diatribe in which it is stated that, in the future, the republic will face attacks from surrounding countries.[15] Sade claims that the republic's response to such attacks will need to consist of resistance. To cope with threats from the outside, the country should focus on the external enemy. This view, Blanchot holds, makes clear that Sade does not understand the republic as a constitution, meaning that, for Sade, the republic is not based on a principle which provides society's steadfastness from within. The republic that Sade has in mind, then, should be understood not as a solid autonomous ground, but rather in terms of its relation to an outside, to which the republic is opposed. In other words: Sade's ideal society is a reactive reality in the sense that it takes shape specifically in reaction to something external.

This does not mean, however, that there will ever be a moment in the future in which the country will be able to rest and focus on itself. Indeed, the attacks from the outside will never stop, and in consequence, the country may never weaken its resistance against its opponents. Sade's republic will need to stand up continuously in the face of attacks that never cease imposing upon the country from the outside. One should thus conclude, Blanchot holds, that Sade's vision of the republic is not really expressed by the title 'Français, encore un effort si vous voulez être républicains'. Indeed, for Sade, being a republican does not entail that one last effort must be made: there is no final act of resistance through which the republic can be constituted from within. The truth of the republican, rather, lies both in the effort against modes of social organisation that are based on a stable internal point of reference and, more importantly, in the fact that such an effort will be undertaken endlessly.[16]

When Blanchot discusses the content of Sade's oeuvre, he does not only focus on Sade's political diatribe. In 'La raison de Sade' and 'Quelques remarques sur Sade', in particular, Blanchot quotes extensively from Sade's various novels. More specifically, he draws attention to four aspects of the theoretical reflections of the libertine novelist. What are these four aspects? And what is their relation to that which we have discussed in our first paragraphs?

The first aspect that Blanchot focuses on is the premise of the Sadean universe, namely, selfishness.[17] This term, he stresses, should not be read in a moral sense. The fact that Sade's world is centred on the notion of selfishness does not mean that the libertine primarily wants to defend his own interests at the expense of others. Selfishness in Sade, according to Blanchot, has an ontological, and not a moral, meaning. Blanchot is referring to the fact that, in Sade's world, the essence of man is not a being-for-the-other, but rather a negation of the value of the other's existence and a destruction of the positive meaning other people have in normal life. Therefore, Blanchot stresses that murder, although apparently key to any understanding of Sade, is only of secondary importance in Sade's world. When a sadist kills his victim, this death only serves to double a more fundamental fact: namely, that for the sadist, the other is nothing more than a stupid object without any human value.[18]

A second aspect to which Blanchot draws attention is the fact that Sade very often gives his characters ample occasion to express themselves, specifically those who deliver extended theological monologues. Blanchot refers, for example, to the 50-year-old judge, Saint-Fond, who is presented in the second part of *Juliette*, wherein he talks about the *Être-suprême-en-méchanceté*.[19] Blanchot cites the passage in which the judge holds that virtuous people, such as Sade's best-known character, Justine, are mistaken if they believe that their soul reflects God.[20] Indeed, Saint-Fond argues that God is not in the first place generous love, but rather an *Être-suprême-en-méchanceté* whose essence is to cause disease, earthquakes and civil wars, all in order to destroy humanity. This is reflected in the idea that, in Saint-Fond's theocentric universe, human beings are not the crown of the Supreme Being's creation; in Sade's world they are, as Blanchot writes, nothing but lifeless matter, 'an atom of nothing.'

Thirdly, Blanchot refers to the fact that in countless scenes the Marquis' libertines do not speak about God very positively. What is less known, Blanchot recalls, is that these blasphemous passages are somehow related to Sade's specific philosophy of nature.[21] Therein, like many of his contemporaries, Sade states that the assumption of God's existence is superfluous because the reference to nature is enough for a proper understanding of reality. This is evident from the following rhetorical question in *Dialogue entre un prêtre et un moribond*: 'Why are you searching for a man for her [nature], when it is possible that nature has created everything that you attribute to your god?'[22] According to Sade's libertines, in order to properly understand reality it is not necessary to refer to God, and Blanchot thus concludes that the Sadean universe is characterised not only by the negation of the other and humanity, but also by the negation of God's existence and principles.

Finally, Blanchot also pays attention to Sade's conception of nature, which understands nature as not only creating life, but also destroying her own products.[23] As we have seen in chapter 1, the reason is that nature aims at realising her productive capacities fully, and that through destruction she recycles the material required to create. The problem, however, is that nature's products themselves create life, in such a way as to preclude nature's ability to maximise her productivity. The result is that nature, by virtue of her desire for optimum production, is forced to destroy her products continuously. Blanchot points out that several of Sade's libertines hate this idea of nature as the endless cycle of creation and destruction. The reason is that, from this perspective, every type of destruction always ultimately serves nature, thus implying that nature escapes destruction and that she herself cannot be destroyed. This makes clear, Blanchot explains, that as a last resort some of Sade's libertines aim at a kind of destruction that also annihilates nature.

Blanchot thus explains that in the Sadean universe, the other, humanity, God and, at last, nature itself will ultimately be negated. These four aspects, which recur in several places throughout Sade's oeuvre, are placed side by side in Blanchot's reading. According to him, bringing together these passages clarifies the essence of Sade's world: namely, radical negation.[24] Indeed, although each individual negation involves affirmation, when Sade's work is considered as a whole, it is evident that this affirmation itself is also negated.[25] For example, the negation of humanity may lead to the affirmation of a positivity, namely the *Être-suprême-en-méchanceté*, but elsewhere in Sade's oeuvre this cruel deity is also denied by *natura naturans*. And this latter negation is finally unaccompanied by affirmation, as the sadist is characterised by the grotesque fantasy wherein nature is destroyed. Therefore, Blanchot concludes that through Sade's oeuvre there is a movement of radical negation at work, in such a way that it never affirms something and that it is nothing but its negative power.[26]

According to Blanchot, it is by reference to these two aspects – namely, permanent resistance, on the one hand, and radical negation on the other – that we must understand the link between Sade's oeuvre and the Reign of Terror. At first sight, this is somewhat remarkable. After all, there seems to be a more obvious similarity: namely, the fact that both in the Sadean universe and in the Reign of Terror a lot of people are killed. Indeed, an initial reading of Blanchot's essay could give the impression that he places this resemblance to the fore. For example, prior to the pages in which he addresses Sade's engagement during the French Revolution, he employs the following unallocated quotation: '"Nothing resembles virtue like a great crime".'[27] While Blanchot does not specify the source of this quote, his aim is to draw the reader's attention to the fact that both Sade and Louis Antoine de Saint-Just – who, along with Robespierre, was a key player during the Reign of Terror – might have said this. One could easily conclude then that the bond between Sade's oeuvre and the Reign of Terror lies precisely in the fact that during the famous September massacres, just as in Sade's work, thousands of heads ended up beneath the guillotine.

However, this rather superficial resemblance is not central in Blanchot's interpretation of the Marquis' work. The link between the content of Sade's oeuvre and the Terror is based on a more fundamental characteristic. In order to understand this relationship, we need to look at Blanchot's interpretation of the Terror.

In his Sade studies, Blanchot does not present his theory about the French Revolution and the Terror extensively. In order to gain an understanding of his thinking about these events, one can rely on, among others, 'La littérature et la droit à la mort', wherein Blanchot's interpretation of the French Revolution and the Terror is based on Hegel's analysis of this same phenomenon in his *Phänomenologie des Geistes*.[28] This is clear from the fact that Blanchot maintains that the French Revolution does not break with the *Ancien Régime*, but is an extension of the period preceding the Revolution. The reason lies in the notion of freedom, understood here as the ability to break free from what is given. Indeed, while the French Revolution may overtly aim towards the extermination of the clergy and theistic belief, this does not imply that the freedom once attributed to God also disappears. What happened during the Revolution is that freedom, which was formerly situated in a divine sphere, operates from a purely immanent perspective: it inserts a break in the sense that it destroys what is given radically. The French Revolution, according to Blanchot, presupposes the efficacy of the freedom that deposes the old regime.

At the origin of the fact that the French Revolution led to the cruel Terror is the fact that this immanent freedom was understood absolutely, and that figures such as Saint-Just and Robespierre demanded that the new French citizens lived out their pure freedom in a radical way.[29] This manifested itself in the requirement to break free from highly personal pleasures and personal affairs. Anyone, however, who is suspected of not being able to detach himself from his personal life and pleasures will be led to the guillotine. But more important for our purpose here is that the requirement not to alienate freedom in something other than itself also implies that one cannot use one's freedom to establish a new political order. Thus, because absolute freedom presupposes that it is not contaminated by a particular creation, the Terror remained 'between' the overthrow of the old and the establishment of the new regime.[30] As freedom, in its absolute sense, may only be used to destroy and may not be involved in creation, it remained between the old and the new. It is in this 'in between' that the Reign of Terror, on the one hand, and the continuous resistance of Sade's republic and radical negation, on the other hand, reflect one another.[31] In other words: the relation between the content of Sade's cruel oeuvre and the Terror lies in the fact that both endless resistance (which does not lead to an enduring constitution) and negation (which is not accompanied by affirmation), just as in the Reign of Terror, are effectively 'hanging' between two positive instances.

Terror, Writing and Language

In his third Sade study, Blanchot discusses the *inconvenance* caused for the reader by Sade's oeuvre. Indeed, there is probably no one who is not overwhelmed by a feeling of *inconvenance* when he reads through the literature of the Marquis. The question that is central in Blanchot's study is what the origin of this feeling could be. In the beginning of his essay, he argues that the unpleasant feeling springs from what he calls 'Sade's madness'. Blanchot uses the term 'madness' to denote three aspects of Sade's work, and thus distinguishes between three different forms of *inconvenance*. What are these three forms?

First, 'the madness of Sade' refers to these aspects that are well known among the general public, namely the cruel *tableaux vivants*.[32] Reading the passages in which these scenes are described causes what can be called 'emotional *inconvenance*'. The cause of such *inconvenance*, which is also the reason why these passages are insane, is that the violence is contrary to the requirement, central in normal life, to cause no harm to another's body.

Second, Blanchot again refers to the pamphlet 'Français, encore un effort si vous voulez être républicains'.[33] In the first part of this text, Sade holds that, in the new Sadean republic, religion should be abolished. The putative reason for this is that a religious life is deemed to hinder the capacity for a republican man to be a good husband and father.[34] While this argument is based on the protection of the family, in the second part of the very same pamphlet it is argued that the family itself should be destroyed. Indeed, Sade argues, since all women belong to all men, a woman cannot be a man's exclusive possession. This kind of contradiction is a second form of madness, here understood as 'unreasonableness', and provokes an intellectual *inconvenance* in the reader who generally expects the writer not to contradict himself.

Blanchot, however, is interested primarily neither in the emotional nor in the intellectual *inconvenance* caused respectively by the scenes of horror and the various contradictions in Sade's oeuvre. There is, he holds, a third and more fundamental form of *inconvenance*, and it is this form that most interests him. According to Blanchot, this *inconvenance* is related to what he calls 'the all saying of Sade' (*le tout dire de Sade*).[35] With this expression, Blanchot is not referring to the fact that Sade discusses what, in ordinary life, mostly remains unspoken. Certainly, Blanchot confirms, Sade's oeuvre is full of meticulous descriptions of acts about which normally nothing is said. That Sade breaks the rules of decency, however, is of secondary importance.[36] The fact that he transgresses the rules of common decency is an effect of 'the all saying of Sade' that reaches beyond the bringing out of what remains unspoken in everyday life.

'The all saying of Sade' refers to the fact that Sade aims at describing the whole of reality, seeking to say the last word about reality.[37]

This grotesque goal leads to what Blanchot calls 'the fury of writing'.[38] Thus, Blanchot conceives of Sade not as a corrupt aristocrat but rather as an abundant, prolific writer. Blanchot is referring primarily to the man who is chained to his desk and whose writing hand, sliding over the many sheets of paper, follows an excessive movement which does not come to rest.[39] On that basis, Blanchot suggests that Sade's madness is not so much related to the fact that he often blames his mother-in-law or that he has extramarital affairs. Nor does Sade's madness lie in his cruel scenes, or the fact that he contradicts himself in his reflections. No, as Blanchot argues, Sade's real madness is that he writes in an exuberant way, for example during his stay in the Bastille and in the prison of Vincennes, where he completes 7,200 pages of writing at the rate of one and a half sheets per day.[40] What, then, is the *inconvenance* associated with this madness?

Sade's fury of writing, the fact that his writing activity continues unabatedly, results in a very comprehensive oeuvre. The reader who is able to read this work – and it is this kind of reader that Blanchot has in mind – is overrun and blown away by the sheer multitude of pages, effectively effacing the distance necessary for one to read the last word about reality that Sade pretends to say. Consequently, Sade's reader is not able to remember the content of his literature. Although Sade's goal is to say everything, the consequence of his prolific writing activity is that the reader does not retain a word of what Sade wants to say.[41] Put differently: anyone who takes the time to fully read Sade will not become wiser; spending hours wading through his oeuvre will not bring new content to light, nor will it clarify the so-called dark side of sexuality. Rather, it will put the reader in touch with Sade's abundant activity of writing.

According to Blanchot, the *inconvenance* caused by this activity is not only emotional or intellectual, but can be rather defined as 'anaesthetic'.[42] It may be the case that one feels uncomfortable when reading the cruel or unreasonable passages, but for anyone who is reading Sade's whole oeuvre it is impossible to be touched by a shock caused by either cruelty or unreason. Thus, it is not only that the cruel passages or many contradictions are shocking, but also that the reader cannot perceive a shocking content. In other words: the emotional and intellectual *inconvenances* are minor compared to the *inconvenance* caused by 'the revolt of writing'. Sade's work, like the republic he has in mind, is constantly in revolt: it arises incessantly without settling down into a stable, persistent content.

The fact that in the title 'L'insurrection, la folie d'écrire' Blanchot associates Sade's writing with rebellion and resistance suggests that Sade's oeuvre is closely linked to the Terror not only in terms of its content but also in terms of Sade's writing activity and his enormous oeuvre. This suggestion is strengthened by the fact that Blanchot first understands that 'the all saying of Sade' is an 'intermediate-saying',[43] and then states that this 'intermediate-saying' corresponds to the interval or the 'in between', where, as we have seen, the Reign of Terror, resistance, and absolute negation intersect.[44]

In order to understand what Blanchot means by Sade's 'intermediate-saying', let us turn once more to 'La littérature et le droit à la mort'. The second part of this essay deals with the question of how everyday speech acts must be understood. Speaking, Blanchot holds, implies the efficacy of death. The explanation of this puzzling thought will show in what specific sense Sade's writing is an 'intermediate-saying', and will also explain why Sade's extensive literature is so closely related to the Reign of Terror.

The link between the daily use of language and death can be illustrated with the help of some examples.[45] Blanchot focuses, for instance, on talking about a cat. This speech act makes use of the three-letter word 'cat', which is composed of 'c', 'a' and 't', all of which are part of what Blanchot calls 'the materiality of language'. Important here is the fact that one's use of this materiality to talk about a cat will change one's relationship with the animal. While dealing with a cat is normally physical, speaking about a cat puts the existence of the cat at a distance. Speaking implies the negation of the particular existence of what is referred to with language. Just as we have seen in the case of the Revolution, speaking places reality 'between brackets'. Or, to use Hegel's oft-cited expression: language is the murder of the thing.

Normal speech acts such as talking about a cat, however, presuppose more than just the material, completely meaningless, inscriptions 'c', 'a' and 't'. Everyday speech about a cat is meaningful, and this is made possible by the fact that the three-letter word 'cat' expresses some content: namely, the idea of what a cat is. Thus, speaking about a cat implies not only the metaphorical death of the reality of the cat, but also that the cat arises from that death and lives on as an idea. In other words: a meaningful conversation presupposes a double death: the negation of the thing by language (first death), on the one hand, and the negation of the materiality of language by the idea (second death), on the other.

By Sade's 'intermediate saying', Blanchot means that the Marquis' language, like any language, withdraws reality from its actual presence – but, at the same time, Sade's stretching of writing ensures that it gets stuck in the moment before the expression of content. It is in this 'neutral' space between the first and second death that Sade's prolific writing activity focuses the reader's attention on the excessive writing itself and on the fact that this very activity communicates nothing beyond the fact that the libertine aristocrat wrote a lot.[46] Thus, Sade hangs in a 'neutral' interval between the absence of both reality and meaning, and it is through this hanging-in-between that Sade's writing itself is additionally related to the Terror.

The Materiality and Autonomy of Language

Blanchot's 'La raison de Sade' privileges an analysis of Sade's content while his 'L'insurrection, la folie d'écrire' focuses more on the writing of Sade's oeuvre. Nevertheless, one can perceive a resemblance between the two interpretations: in both cases, Blanchot reads Sade in a non-dialectical way. Resistance and absolute negation, on the one hand, and writing, on the other, are based on a negation which founds nothing positive.[47] In order to answer the question of how Sade is an 'ideal writer', only Blanchot's reading of Sade's prolific writing activity is important. This reading tells us two things that are not mentioned explicitly by Blanchot, but which are important in order to explain in what sense Sade, according to Blanchot, fits the image of the ideal writer.

The first aspect follows from the fact that we should not understand Sade's oeuvre in an intellectual way, meaning that, after reading Sade's oeuvre, one is not able to remember the specific content. In this sense, reading Sade is a superficial experience. The expectation that one can find in Sade's writing a central message, insight or lesson turns out to be nothing more than wishful thinking. Sade's literary work suffers from a deflation of meaning: while reading normally presupposes forgetting the materiality of language, reading Sade's oeuvre revolves around the fact that the content extinguishes the words. Thus, reading Sade does not tend towards idealism, precisely because the spirit is detached from the material. Rather, reading Sade tends towards materialism, which means the disappearance of meaning in the materiality of language. In other words: the death of content results in the appearance of what the linguist Ferdinand de Saussure famously described as 'the signifier'. Anyone who reads Sade accesses the rough, meaningless materiality of language itself.

The second aspect is closely related to the first. Since Sade's oeuvre is not sustained by content, it should not be understood as a reflection of an authentic self or, as Henri Bergson calls it, *un moi profond*. Certainly, the cruel and erotic scenes arise from the peculiar sexual preferences of the person Marquis de Sade. The result of the progression of the narrative, however, leads to the fact that not only the content but also Sade as a person disappear into the background. Consequently, the language of Sade's work cannot be understood as an instrument he uses to express content. In Sade, language can be perceived as an independent reality which cannot be reduced to the use that is made of it. The power of Sade's work lies not in Sade as a master of language, but in the autonomy of language that imposes itself incessantly. It may be the case that Sade's oeuvre springs from the hands of Sade who makes use of language in order to say the last word about reality, but Sade's madness is that, while writing, language itself becomes detached from his hand and continues to express itself unabatedly. Can't we already see here that, according to Blanchot, Sade as a writer prefigures the idea of a decentred subject?

In order to get a good idea of both aspects, namely the materiality and independence of language, it is also illuminating to look at Blanchot's reflections on the corpse.[48] Central to these reflections is the distinction between the first and the second version of the corpse.[49] The first version to which Blanchot refers is the dead body, stored in a coffin and located in a cemetery under a gravestone. That state of tranquillity, Blanchot holds, enables the relatives to form a stable image in which the characteristics of the deceased person are knotted together. While standing before the grave of my grandfather, for example, the image of a robust, hard-working man comes to mind. In short, the fact that a dead person lives on in his image presupposes that the corpse is transferred to a domain that is separated from the place where everyday life occurs.

Blanchot, however, is interested not so much in the dead body in all its peacefulness, but rather in a lesser-known experience of the corpse. Suppose, for example, Blanchot writes, that the dead body was laid not in a tomb but in the house of the family. The consequence would be, firstly, that the relatives lacked the physical distance necessary to form a good image of the deceased. This means that, due to its proximity, the physical presence of the corpse would come to the surface. When a corpse is kept in the house, one is not able to group the traits of the deceased person into an overall picture and only sees, due to the absence of the image, the corpse itself as meaningless material. Secondly, Blanchot points out that the presence of the dead body in the house would result in the fact that no one could enter a room without being reminded of the corpse. The dead matter would be, for the relatives, a ghostly, ubiquitous appearance which left no life in the house unaffected.

Just like Sade's language, thus, the second version of the corpse is also 'hanging'. Indeed, unlike the first, the second version remains hanging in the moment before the corpse is stored in the cemetery, the rest that enables the deceased to live on in his image. What announces itself in this interval between the life and the serenity of the buried body is the materiality of the body that does not cease to insist. In short, Blanchot not only looks at the many bodies with which the cellars in the Sadean universe are filled, he also stresses the similarity between the content and the language of Sade's oeuvre. As an intrusive physical presence, the language of Sade's oeuvre is similar to the second version of the corpse.[50]

This explanation, mainly based on 'L'insurrection, la folie d'écrire', allows us to understand why Sade, according to Blanchot, is the perfect writer. That it is this explanation we need – in other words, of Blanchot's statement from 'La littérature et le droit à la mort' that Sade meets the image of the ideal writer – becomes clear when we read in the same text his ideas about what literature should *not* be.

In order to indicate this, Blanchot refers, in the first part of the text, to a paragraph from *Phänomenologie des Geistes*, wherein Hegel discusses the phenomenon of working, a phenomenon he describes as consisting of three moments.[51]

The first moment is the activity of working, in which a product is manufactured. The second moment is the realisation of the product as a result of the activity. Whoever is at the origin of the action is interested in the objective reality of the product because his own person is reflected in the object. According to Hegel, this recognition, however, is hindered by the fact that others, who are also interested in the product, obliterate the traces of the creator of the product. This problem is solved during the third moment, because one perceives in the concrete object the content that the creator wanted to express in the product.[52]

Besides Hegel, Blanchot also refers to Jean-Paul Sartre's *Qu'est-ce que la littérature?* from 1948. In this text, Sartre attacks *nouveaux romanciers* such as Alain Robbe-Grillet, Jean Ricardou and Eugène Ionesco, who were quite popular at that time. Indeed, according to Sartre, literature should not be a free, open-ended play with words, as these avant-garde writers believe. Literary works must instead be engaged and should express the author's involvement with reality.[53] The writer Sartre has in mind needs to be someone who thinks about the current course of the world and who wants to change the world with his literature.

According to Blanchot, Hegel's and Sartre's reflections on literature are based upon the same conception of language. Both thinkers conceive of language as 'a loaded gun'.[54] This expression means that a writer first fills words with a message, idea or belief, and then fires these words into reality in order to communicate some content. This implies that literature should be understood in the first place by reference to the message the writer wants to convey to the reader. It also implies that language is nothing but a mere tool of which the materiality, as it were, should be forgotten so that it cannot hinder the expression of the content. For both Sartre and Hegel, therefore, literary language is subordinate to the primacy of its content.

In 'La littérature et le droit à la mort' Blanchot questions the secondary role language has in the view of both Sartre and Hegel. In literature, Blanchot states, language should not be a mere 'fleeting passage' and should rather present its 'physical tangibility'.[55] He then states: 'And in this way language insists on playing its own game without man, who created it. Literature now dispenses with the writer.'[56] Writers, Blanchot argues, should not use language as a means to express content; instead, they need to put the reader in touch with the materiality and the autonomy of language itself. According to Blanchot, it is precisely this goal that Marquis de Sade meets, and it is for this reason that Blanchot calls him the ideal writer. Indeed, Sade's literature brings the materiality of language to the fore, and seems to be the product not of Sade *qua* literary artist, but of the autonomy of language that expresses itself continuously. In summary: Sade meets the image of the ideal writer because he reveals both the 'outside' of language, namely the materiality of language that communicates no content, and language in all its glorious independence.[57]

III The Culture of the Book and Humanism

As already mentioned in the introduction, Blanchot's third Sade study is included in four different editions. The third time that the text was published was in Blanchot's extensive main work *L'entretien infini*, which contains thirty-nine other texts in addition. In this volume, Blanchot not only writes about the themes for which he became known – *le Neutre*, fragmentary writing, etc. – but also enters into discussion with Albert Camus and Nietzsche, among others. He also devotes a few pages to some considerations within the domain of philosophy of culture. He writes, for example, about the central role of the book in our culture and searches for the conditions and limitations of modern humanism. The fact that Blanchot included in the volume both a study on Sade's writing and cultural philosophical texts is odd at first sight. Nevertheless, it suggests that the two are not completely unrelated. To conclude this chapter, we turn to their relation.

Sade as Testimonial Literature

In the opening paragraph of 'La raison de Sade', Blanchot emphasises that the Sadean universe, in which mankind is denied access to heaven, is the hell par excellence. It is therefore for literature like that of Sade's that the section *L'Enfer* in the Bibliothèque Nationale was created around the beginning of the nineteenth century.[58] Blanchot thus reminds us that the authorities hid Sade's oeuvre from the eye of the people during and after his lifetime. This is also the case in the twentieth century, as witnessed by the affair of the French publisher Pauvert, who had to appear in court in 1956 because he had dared to publish some of Sade's writings. Blanchot draws attention to the fact that Sade's literature has a long history of prohibition and censorship. On this basis, it could be concluded that Blanchot's studies would like to abolish the forgetting of Sade's literature. The reason for this could be that Blanchot believes that the enormous oeuvre of 'the divine Marquis' deserves to be remembered in our culture. However, Blanchot's reading should not be understood as a reaction to something that has been forgotten. Decisively, the fact that Blanchot comments upon Sade's work ensures that his oeuvre still has a cultural role to play, but this fact is nothing but a mere by-product of Blanchot's interest in writing and in Sade's writing in particular.

On the basis of 'L'insurrection, la folie d'écrire', I wonder, however, whether Blanchot does not understand Sade in terms of 'remembering' and 'forgetting'. Therefore, I rely on 'L'absence de livre', the last text from *L'entretien infini*.[59] The starting point of this essay is that our culture is closely linked to books and that they are understood as the building blocks of our culture. As a physical medium of knowledge, the book makes it possible to store knowledge and therefore also to transfer knowledge to future generations. In other words, the book ensures that knowledge is not lost and can continue to circulate. According to Blanchot, books are also building blocks because of their role in the longing for an absolute knowledge. Because they are able to retain knowledge, that knowledge can then be expanded. In doing so, they contribute to the pursuit of knowledge that discloses reality in general. Our culture is thus strongly related to the book because these bundled piles of paper make it possible to pass on knowledge and respond to aspirations for the completion of knowledge.[60]

Blanchot not only measures the functional value of the book but also examines the assumption that goes with extracting knowledge from books. In this context, he refers to the first incisions in stone and wood.[61] According to Blanchot, these inscriptions were rather coincidental and did not respond to the search for a sign. Nevertheless, these scratches greatly altered the perspective from which, until then, reality was viewed. They led to the fact that, from that moment on, any acquisition of knowledge has been regarded as the immediate expression of a prior content. According to Blanchot, that is the idea behind the acquisition of knowledge. The acquisition of knowledge from books is accompanied by the assumption that every line drawn by man is in itself the expression of an original presence. Our knowledge culture, supported by the book, presupposes a metaphysics that asserts that inscriptions are the direct expression of a primary presence.

In his essay, Blanchot shows that this metaphysics is not true. The title 'L'absence de livre' does not refer to a future in which there would no longer be books available. Nor does Blanchot allude to a time when the episteme in which every line is understood as a sign referring to something else would have disappeared. After all, this paradigm is so deeply rooted in our culture that it cannot be deleted, even if all the books disappeared. In the title of his essay, Blanchot is referring primarily to the intention to demonstrate that the book is not an immediate expression of a previous presence or origin.

To show this, Blanchot goes back to the Judaeo-Christian monotheism of the Book, among other things. More specifically, he refers to the story from Exodus about the creation of the ten commandments on the basis of which God enters into a covenant with the people of Israel. These provisions are engraved by Him on two stone tables and given to Moses on Mount Sinai. When Moses then returns to the people who await him at the foot of the mountain, he tells them about the Decalogue. We read: 'And Moses gathered all the congregation of the children of Israel together, and said unto them, These are the words which the LORD hath commanded, that ye should do them.'[62] The people thus hear the divine law not on the basis of what God has engraved on the stone tables, but by way of Moses, who tells them God's precepts in a speech. It is this oral communication to which Blanchot draws attention and to which he attaches great importance. He states: '[it is] as if writing requires language (discourse) in order to become generally readable.'[63] Although the impression may be created that Moses' speech only repeats what can actually be read without Moses, more is happening here. It is only after he has said that the stone tables are the written precipitate of the Torah that one can read the commandments. Moses' speaking may occur after God's writing of the Decalogue, yet his intervention is not incidental. Without his verbal explanation, the people would only see meaningless scratches and the traces referring to a divine origin would be missed.

It is partly on the basis of this recalcitrant reading that Blanchot shows that the metaphysics of our book and knowledge culture are not correct. After all, Blanchot's analysis reminds us that the assumption associated with reading books and acquiring knowledge – that every line refers to a content – forgets something. What is forgotten is that every incision needs an addition, namely a set of conventions that determine which inscription expresses what content. It is only after this addition that the meaningless scratches can be interpreted as the expression of a primary presence. In other words, material inscriptions themselves are completely meaningless and do not express any original content themselves.

This fact is recalled by, among other things, the scene from Exodus about the stone tables. Blanchot states that this is also expressed by certain forms of literature.[64] Although he never explicitly mentions Sade in 'L'absence de livre', it is clear that Blanchot has Sade's literature in mind, among other things. The discussion of 'L'insurrection, la folie d'écrire' revealed that whoever, according to Blanchot, flips through Sade's oeuvre gets in touch with the materiality of language. Reading Sade, according to Blanchot, does not mean the resurrection in the idea of the thing killed by language, but the death of the content in meaningless materiality. In short, although Blanchot is primarily interested in Sade because he incarnates the ideal of the writer, Blanchot also uses his reading in a general reflection on our book and knowledge culture. According to him, Sade's literature is one of those literary forms that reminds us that inscriptions are not signs that automatically refer to something else and that they are not an unmediated expression of an original content.

The Death of Man as a Subject

In 'La raison de Sade', as we have seen, Blanchot states that egoism is the starting point of the Sadean universe. For the sadist, the existence of other people has no meaning whatsoever; others have already undergone symbolic death even before they have died a biological death. Elsewhere in Sade's oeuvre, Blanchot notes, not only the other man but the whole of humanity is ignored. The Supreme Being (*L'Être-suprême-en-méchanceté*) creates life for the sole purpose of killing mankind through floods, epidemics and earthquakes. From a certain point of view, it might be expected that Blanchot would refer to 'La raison de Sade' in 'L'athéisme et l'écriture: L'humanisme et le cri', which is included in the second part of *L'entretien infini*.[65] In that essay, in which Blanchot explicitly enters into dialogue with Michel Foucault's *Les mots et les choses* from 1966, Blanchot looks at humanism from a cultural, philosophical and historical perspective.[66] First of all, he reflects on the connection between humanism and pre-modernity, in which not man but God is central. Blanchot is also looking for the traces that lead to the death of humanism. He discovers these in the experience of writing, among other things. In what follows, I show that he has Sade's experience of writing in mind here. Blanchot, thus, does not find the first traces of the disappearance of humanism in the Sadean universe where human dignity is neglected completely. No, the end of humanism is heralded in Sade's writing drive. In order to understand that, we first have to find out what Blanchot means by humanism.

The starting point of Blanchot's text is a deconstruction of the opposition between humanism and Christianity. According to Blanchot, humanism does not so much break with Christianity as continue it. Humanism is a theological myth, he says at the beginning of his essay.[67] Conversely, it is not the case that God dies only in modernity, while before he was a living presence. According to Blanchot, God is also dead in pre-modernity. How exactly should we understand this deconstruction of the Christianity/humanism opposition?

With the assertion that God is already dead even in a pre-modern worldview, Blanchot refers to the break between Christianity and the age that is referred to by the term 'myth'. While in a mythological world the gods are citizens among the citizens and live near mortals, in Christianity the relationship between man and God is characterised by distance. This distance is made evident, for example, by a passage from Deuteronomy in which Moses addresses the people of Israel:

> And ye came near and stood under the mountain; and the mountain burned with fire unto the midst of heaven, with darkness, clouds, and thick darkness.
>
> And the LORD spake unto you out of the midst of the fire: ye heard the voice of the words, but saw no similitude; only ye heard a voice.[68]

This passage marks the distinction between Christianity and the epoch of myths. In Christianity, God is not among men, as in a mythological world, but is high up in heaven, at an immense distance from the earth, and speaks from a place where fire is located. That image symbolises that God is not allowed to be captured in images and that he has always been veiled in smoke, even when he is present in the world. According to Blanchot, this distance between God and the world means that God's death is not a consequence of secularisation. God's withdrawal from immanent life is part of Christianity as such. God, says Blanchot, has already left the world in Christianity and it is from this distance from the world that he grounds the world. That humanism, according to Blanchot, does not break with Christianity but is in line with it is expressed in the fact that in modernity mankind occupies the place of God. It may well be that in modernity the world is no longer supported by God, but that does not mean that the place from which the world is built is left open. In modernity, says Blanchot, it is man who, as a Cartesian subject, distances himself from the world and grounds the world from a point transcendent to the world.

Blanchot brings this analysis in 'L'écriture et l'athéisme' into connection with *Les mots et les choses*. In it, Foucault exposes the a priori structures in which knowledge is possible within a certain period of time.[69] During the Renaissance, or the pre-classical period, according to Foucault, knowledge is governed by the category of likeness. In the classical period, in the seventeenth and eighteenth centuries, however, attempts are made to provide a representation of the world based on analysis and synthesis. Characteristic of the episteme of the classical period is that those who represent themselves are not portrayed. This changed in the nineteenth century with the rise of the humanities. It is mainly this rise of representation that arouses Blanchot's interest. The reason for this is that the human sciences introduce a break with the theological basis of humanism. From a certain point of view, however, the modern, post-classical period is still an extension of humanism. As an object of scientific research, human beings are, as in humanism, the centre of the world. That same research, however, also brings to light the fact that man himself is embedded in and supported by what escapes his grip: society, nature, time, etc. Well, this means that in the nineteenth century the human sciences undermined the place that man had inherited from

God at an earlier time, namely a point outside the world from which the world is built and from which it acquires meaning.

According to Blanchot, this decentralisation also takes place in literature. He is thinking of writers such as Paul Valéry, Mallarmé and Sade, although he does not quote the last of these in 'L'écriture et l'athéisme'. The fact that Blanchot undoubtedly has Sade in mind in this context and that, thus, during the writing process, Sade destroys humanism is evident from Blanchot's reading of Sade in 'L'insurrection, la folie d'écrire'. According to Blanchot, the weight of Sade's literature, as I have shown, lies not with the writer as the subject of language, but with language that claims its independence and makes Sade disappear as a writer, as in the well-known image from the final sentence of *Les mots et les choses*, 'like a face drawn in sand at the edge of the sea'.[70] Thus, Blanchot already recognises, in the literature of the writer Marquis de Sade, the first traces of the anti-humanist structuralism of the twentieth century which argues that man is not the subject of reality, but that he himself is supported by something else, namely language. In short, in 'L'athéisme et l'écriture', Blanchot is reflecting upon the philosophical consequences of his Sade reading. The conclusion he draws from this reading is that Sade is the precursor of a movement that leads to man's death as far as he is the subject of reality.[71]

IV Conclusion

Among the French philosophers who commented on the literature of the writer Marquis de Sade, Blanchot occupies a special position from a certain point of view. For him, literature is the theme par excellence on which his entire oeuvre is built. However, it is not the case that he kept inventing new concepts in order to map out a certain form of literature. His thinking about literature is indeed accompanied by an ideal, and his interest is in a specific kind of writer, namely the writer who feels closely related to revolution. Blanchot was interested in Sade because his literature both illustrates a certain ideal and gets stuck in the revolutionary moment of radical negation, both in terms of content and in terms of writing.

3[1]

Apathy, Energy and Transgression

I Introduction

In the context of Sade reception in French post-war philosophy, 1947 stands as a turning point. In that year, the first version of Klossowski's collection of essays *Sade mon prochain* was published, as was Blanchot's first comprehensive Sade study 'À la rencontre de Sade'. Also in 1947, the philosopher and novelist Bataille became part of a small group of early Sade commentators, when on Monday 12 May, he gave a talk at a conference at the *College Philosophique*, titled 'Le mal dans le platonisme et dans le sadisme'.[2] Moreover, in the same year, Bataille wrote 'Le secret de Sade'. The occasion for this piece, published in two parts in *Critique*, was the recent publication of three texts: *Les infortunes de la vertu* and *Les 120 journées de Sodome* from Sade, and Klossowski's volume *Sade mon prochain*.[3] However, this is not to say that Bataille merely summarises Sade's text or that he criticises Klossowski's reading in any detail. In fact, 'Le secret de Sade', especially the second part of the essay, presents Bataille's own Sade interpretation for the first time. The second part of that essay would also form the basis of his later article 'Sade', which was included in *La littérature et le mal* in 1957.[4] Bataille's third text on Sade, 'Le bonheur, l'érotisme et la littérature (II)' from 1949, was published in response to another study on Sade, namely Blanchot's 'La raison de Sade'.[5] This essay contains the first sketches from 'L'homme souverain de Sade', the second additional study from *L'érotisme* (1957).[6] Bataille's final text on the novels of the Marquis was published first as a foreword in *Justin*. Three years later, this text was also included, albeit in a slightly different form, in his volume *L'érotisme*.[7]

In those Sade studies Bataille repeatedly comes back to two themes. First, he draws attention, just as almost all French Sade interpreters of his time do, to the libertines' apathy, which means that Sade's characters reflect in some way the Stoics of ancient Greece. Therefore, one cannot argue, at least not from Bataille's point of view, that Clairwil, a character from *Juliette*, is Sade's true hero. Indeed, when she kills, she has a twinkle in her eye and a blush in her cheeks. She is too enthusiastic, according to Bataille, to be an example of a true Sadean hero. In real libertinism, on the contrary, no trace of passionate emotion can be found. Sade's libertines are apathetic, and their enjoyment relates directly to their apathy. For example, whenever Juliette takes pleasure in killing, her enjoyment, as Bataille argues, has to be understood as an apathetic kind of enjoyment. Second, Bataille regularly mentions, without discussing in any detail, the formal characteristics of Sade's works. For example, he distinguishes repetition as Sade's main literary technique and draws attention to the icy character of the prose, which seems to indicate that the Marquis wrote without having had any readers in mind.

The reason why it is interesting that Bataille mentions both aspects is that they are usually overlooked when one reads Sade. First, readers of Sade do not usually link the sadist's enjoyment with apathy. Sadistic enjoyment is more commonly understood from the vantage of the sadist's jubilant cries, which suggest his enjoyment is nothing but an extreme version of the more common sexual sensations and experiences. Second, readers of Sade usually pay little or no attention to the literary qualities of Sade's works. Perhaps certain formal literary characteristics are noticed, but they are usually considered as secondary to the more fundamental content, namely the sadist's sexual enjoyment when committing a crime.

The fact that Bataille stresses the link between apathy and enjoyment is also remarkable from another point of view. Indeed, one would expect him to emphasise that the libertine transgresses moral prohibitions explicitly and that his enjoyment is evidently connected with this transgression. The reason we expect Bataille to interpret Sade in this way is that Bataille is known as 'the philosopher of transgression', who understands enjoyment as intrinsically related to transgression. Is it not he who holds that enjoyment presupposes the law and that one's enjoyment intensifies when this law is being transgressed? Yet somehow when discussing the enjoyment associated with apathy, transgression seems to play, at first glance, only a secondary role. Based on the same characterisation of Bataille as 'the philosopher of transgression', it is also surprising that he pays so much attention to the monotony of Sade's literary style. A philosopher in whose thinking the notion of transgression takes a central place would be expected to emphasise not formal characteristics like repetition or monotony, but rather those aspects of the literature that undermine conventional literary characteristics.[8]

How should we understand the strange yet intriguing thesis that sadistic enjoyment is related to apathy? How does Bataille interpret the sadist's apathy? What exactly are the differences and similarities between this and the *apatheia* of the Stoic? In what sense is the enjoyment connected with the apathy? Is the notion of transgression completely absent in Bataille's interpretation? If not, what then is its relationship with apathy? The second part of this chapter will take up these questions. The third part will then turn to Bataille's comments on the formal characteristics of Sade's literature. Proceeding in this way, it will be shown that there is a link between the texts in which Bataille addresses apathy and the texts in which he mentions certain literary aspects. In other words, it will be shown that, for Bataille, the form of Sade's oeuvre reflects the content.

II Sadism as an Expression of Energy

To gain an understanding of the relationship between apathy and enjoyment, I first look at the way in which Bataille understands Sade's apathy, irrespective of his own technical vocabulary (although it is not always clear whether Bataille's technical reformulation helps to clarify the phenomena he seeks to understand). I then sketch Bataille's framework comprehensively, since in the third part it will become clear that Bataille conceives Sade's apathy in relation to that particular framework. Finally, I clarify Bataille's notion of sadistic enjoyment, showing that this kind of enjoyment is quite similar to mystical enjoyment and that transgression has an important place in the sadist's enjoyment, albeit not in its moral but rather in its metaphysical form.

Apathy and Involvement

Normally people live in mutual commitment to each other, which means that people care about the welfare and happiness of others. This implies, among other things, that one assesses whether or not his acts will be harmful to others. Thus, one takes into account the possibility that he will not be able to continue his behaviour unhindered. If the behaviour is harmful to others, he will in fact change, slow down or stop that behaviour. This personal involvement with others is also expressed in an emotionally reactive attitude, meaning that in normal life people react and respond to the other's emotions. In concrete terms: people normally feel pity when their actions have harmful or hurtful consequences for others.

In ordinary life, however, one is involved not only with the other but also with oneself, which becomes clear if we look at some of the emotions that arise spontaneously in our lives. Indeed, a large part of our emotions cannot be understood without looking at the attachment we have to our 'self', in the broadest sense of the word. Such is the case, for example, with shame at our own brute nakedness, fear of an imminent danger, or distress resulting from a narcissistic injury by a close friend. This self-involvement is reflected not only in our emotions but also in our behaviour. Here, at least two aspects can be distinguished. First, people often have a personal connection with their action, meaning that human beings are involved in what they do and that they express via that involvement their interests and preferences. Second, persons are not only sensitive to the consequences of their actions for themselves; they often act because of the positive impact that these actions have on themselves. This implies that self-involvement can also have an inhibitory effect on action. If the consequences prove to be detrimental, then the action will be adjusted or stopped altogether.

Things work very differently in Sade's literature. When we look at his libertines, it appears, as Bataille rightly observes, that they are insensitive to, or do not take into account, the sorrow, the pain or the fear of others.[9] In *Les 120 journées de Sodome*, for example, we read the following: '"We are deprived of any sense of compassion, Duclos," [. . .] "We do not know these feelings here [. . .]. Leave the tears to the imbeciles and children, but never let them stain the cheeks of a reasonable and respectable woman."'[10] And when Eugénie asks in *La philosophie dans le boudoir* whether we should stop an action if it turns out that it can hurt others, Dolmancé answers: 'No, not even then, for no comparison can be made between what others undergo and what we feel ourselves; the greatest pain experienced by others must not be of any weight to us.'[11]

Apathy in Sade, however, does not only entail that the sadist has no emotionally reactive attitudes or that he is simply insensitive to the suffering of the other. His insensitivity has deeper roots; his absence of emotion is an expression of something more fundamental. More specifically, Bataille argues, echoing Blanchot, that the sadist is characterised primarily by what he calls the sadist's 'unicism' or 'absolute solitude'. This attribution should not be taken to imply that the sadist possesses a trait that others lack. Neither should it be taken to imply that the existence of the sadist is not intertwined with others. Bataille rather refers to the fact that the sadist is in no way related to the other and that he does not participate in the daily interpersonal circuit in which people are committed to and interested in each other. In short, one of the central features of Sade's world, according to Bataille, is the absence of a link with others. As we read in *Juliette*: 'One of the greatest prejudices in this respect is that we assume that there exists a kind of bond that connects us to others, – an illusion . . . , that bond does not exist.'[12]

When discussing the two aspects of the sadist's apathy, Bataille makes a small detour that seems to be a bit odd at first sight. Indeed, he links the insensitivity of the sadist with the attitude of a scientist.[13] This is remarkable, since the sadist's apathy seems rather contrary to, among other things, the curiosity of the scientist, the enthusiasm with which he recounts his professional activity, and the passion with which he conducts his research. While the sadist cuts off any form of relation with the other, the researcher seems to be deeply involved in the object of his investigation. Nevertheless, Bataille argues that it is precisely insensitivity and unrelatedness which the sadist and the scientist have in common. How then are we to understand this unexpected comparison?

According to Bataille, the scientist's apathy does not lie in the way in which he carries out his research, since he normally carries it out with enthusiasm; instead it lies in the attitude he takes towards the object of his research. That attitude consists in a neutralisation of the person-concerned attitude that characterises him as a moral being in daily life. While the scientist in everyday life responds to the emotions, desires and sensitivities of others, he now destroys this attitude and exchanges it for an objectifying, cold and neutral relation with the other. While in ordinary life he is touched by suffering, as a researcher he hardens himself and searches, for example, for a neurological explanation of the tears, or he considers the physical changes associated with the suffering.

However, the scientist is not only insensitive to humans when he himself is the object of research; he is also insensitive to the other's reactions to his research. His 'research drive' transforms him into an impersonal and ruthless individual who is insensitive to the emotional reactions that inevitably emerge when he reflects on topics around which there is a taboo or that question deep-rooted beliefs. In everyday life, anyone who were to adopt such a cold attitude would be regarded as cruel and inhuman. The reason we do not regard the scientist in this way has to do with the well-defined framework in which he operates – one which allows him temporarily to suspend his moral sensibility. On this basis, we can conclude that the sadist, 'the unmoved mover', recalls the scientist insofar as he is required to detach himself from the spontaneous tendency to be involved with others and to adapt to the reactions of others.

In the course of this discussion, it has become clear that the sadist's apathy is not an extension of the person-concerned attitude but, on the contrary, that it breaks with this attitude. Bataille stresses, however, that the sadist is characterised not only by the lack of commitment to the other but also by any form of self-involvement.[14] Sade's apathetic libertines do not just abandon their sympathy but also break away from emotions such as fear, shame and sadness that often spontaneously take the upper hand and that express a commitment to the self. This destruction of self-involvement also means that the sadist does not have the two aforementioned aspects of self-involvement. First, personal preferences and interests are completely destroyed in Sade's world. For example, while a heterosexual libertine might prefer a slender red-haired woman when not in the company of other libertines, this preference falls away as soon as he is in their company. From that moment on, anybody can satisfy his sexual desires: relatives, children, clothes, shoes, animals, etc. Furthermore, the sadist is in no way interested in the consequences of his actions for himself. Although he is fully aware of the consequences when he continues his atrocities (he will be put in jail), this does not deter him from further killing and torture. Nor is it true that the sadist commits crimes because this would bring him some kind of future benefit or advantage. In short, the sadist is not involved in what he does and does not focus on what is good in terms of his own self-interest.

General and Restricted Economy

Before we can fully understand the sadist's apathy, we must first look at Bataille's own specific vocabulary, which for the most part he developed during the 1930s and 1940s, and which provides the background against which he interprets Sade's literary works.[15] This framework is dualistic, in the sense that human existence can be separated into two systems each operating according to a different economy: on the one hand, the secular order which functions according to what he calls *l'économie restreinte* ('the limited economy'); on the other hand, the sacred order following the logic of *l'économie générale* ('the general economy'). How does Bataille understand the secular world, where daily life takes place, and the sacred order, which one enters only exceptionally?[16]

Bataille regularly refers to the Palaeolithic or the Old Stone Age. This is not only because it was in this period that funeral rituals and the first forms of art arose, but also, and above all, because it was in this period that the first durable implements and tools were constructed. This transformation of reality through the making of instruments evolved in the course of history and came to form the basis of secular life. This means that ordinary or secular life came to be thought of in terms of 'labour' and 'work', and that the man who lives this life came to be the *homo faber*. This implies that in secular life one relates to reality in a rather instrumental way: the things that are available and exist in the world are always part of a chain of means leading to the production of an end. Take the example of metal being used in order to construct a hammer. In the next step, this instrument is used to transform some wood into a piece of furniture, for example a chair, which helps a human being to sit while, for example, reading the newspaper. This relation of means and ends has a specific philosophical consequence, namely that the value of something does not lie in the thing itself but rather is derived from the intended purpose for which the thing is a tool. In other words, in the ordinary secular sphere, things have a meaning or value only insofar as they are useful or instrumental.

However, this does not mean that in the Palaeolithic period people replaced a more basic relationship to reality with an instrumental relationship. After all, it is only when one begins to work that for the first time a specific relationship to reality is established. Thus, work introduces, above all, not an instrumental relationship, but a relationship to the world as such. This implies that during this period one breaks with a certain experience of reality. From that time on, reality is no longer perceived as a continuum in which no distinctions appear to exist and in which everything seems to overlap with something else. Indeed, when humanity begins to transform reality, a distance is installed and a line is drawn between the world on the one hand and those who work in it on the other. In other words, it is only with the secular sphere of work that man begins to experience himself as distinct from the world. Only when one begins to manufacture does one begin to experience oneself as an isolated entity. The secular order is characterised by the fact that it is populated by people who experience a boundary between themselves and the environment, and to whom Bataille refers as 'discontinuous entities'. Moreover, that order remains as such only to the extent that man can attribute a distinct ego to himself and so long as he is able to differentiate between himself and the world.

Thus, in everyday life, man is related to reality in an instrumental way, a relation that is accompanied by an experience of discontinuity. According to Bataille, that does not mean, however, that human existence can be reduced to this instrumental relationship or that it cannot adopt another posture in life. For the greater part of his life man may put the world at a distance and experience things in the world as distinct from himself, but that does not mean that this is the only possible way he can experience reality. Another possible experience of reality is found in the way that non-human animals experience it. Animals, Bataille holds, do not take a transcendent position in relation to the world and are not related to the world as discontinuous entities. The world of the animal is a world in which everything seems to be superfluous and in which there seem to be no limits that separate bodies from each other. It is as if there is a fluid transition between the part and the whole, just as there seems to be no limit, to use one of Bataille's favourite metaphors, between a drop of water and the sea. Such an experience is not totally foreign to man; in fact it leads him directly into a sphere that Bataille describes as 'sacred.' At these sacred moments man experiences a continuity between himself and the world that is accompanied by a suspension of the instrumental relationship to the world. This experience can be aroused by the animal world, precisely because there, according to Bataille, the boundaries are confused.

The sacred moments to which Bataille refers are delineated in time and space because they are perceived as dangerous, in the sense that they could arouse the desire for continuity, and thus disrupt secular life. That, according to Bataille, is also the reason that lies at the basis of our attitude towards death, namely that the dead are removed from our ordinary life.[17] The dead are covered with a sheet, stored in a coffin, and carried to a place that is clearly separated from the space where daily life takes place. The reason why the dead are separated is that they remind man of his own death, which is the most radical form of self-loss. Death needs to be banished from the secular order because our culture has to protect itself from the experience of continuity and the loss of self that accompanies this experience. Indeed, death presupposes that every singularity disappears and that the differences are obliterated. The danger is that this could create a desire in the survivors for an experience in which all differences are flattened out. Whoever sees death at work, according to Bataille, might begin longing for an experience that blurs the boundaries and that destroys the ego as a discontinuous entity. It is good, according to Bataille, that human culture protects itself from this possibility of continuity and stores the dead apart from daily life.

The framework just outlined is translated by Bataille into an energetical terminology.[18] The starting point is the observation that on earth a high quantity of energy is circulating that survives and transcends the existence of man. That energy flows continuously in every human organism, meaning that man is at all times filled with energy he then invests in something else. He uses this energy, for example, for his productive activities or invests it in personal relations, that is, relations with himself and others.[19] However, the amount of energy that is required for involvement in oneself and others is smaller than the available energy. Man always receives more energy than he invests in work, in himself or in others. He thus contains an excess of energy which continues to grow incessantly. Because the production of energy never stops, there is a growing surplus that is not invested and that continues to be built up. This surplus is not used by anyone, but at the same time it would not be true to say that it has no effect. The extra energy leads to the growth of, for example, the human body or the many products resulting from labour. But, of course, this growth cannot be continued without limit. The increase of energy is well suited to domesticate the excess, but that solution works only temporarily because growth is limited. The consequence is that energy, because it continues to increase without being invested in something else, is built up until the moment that the boundary separating the person from the outside world breaks down. What follows is an explosion of energy in which the person disappears. This is accompanied by the suspension of labour and any form of involvement in people.

That burst of energy is very different from the energy handled by man in secular life. While energy is normally directed towards the person himself or towards others and is used for work, the explosion of energy now leads to nothing. When the person's ego is overwhelmed by the flow of energy, this energy is not invested in anything else. From the limited human perspective, in which the emphasis is on involvement and the use of power, this stream of energy is merely waste and extravagance. The excessive energy that breaks through the limits of the person as a discontinuous entity is what Bataille calls *la part maudite*; it is the remainder that does not fit into the worldview of man since in this view energy is primarily invested in and used for something else. From a more general non-human perspective, however, the same phenomenon can also be approached in a more positive way. From that perspective, reality is understood as the superhuman flux of impersonal and goalless energy that circulates continuously. Although man invests the stream of energy in himself, others and work, this energy is of itself not directed to something beyond itself. In other words, from this 'general' perspective, the burst of energy is not a loss. The unbounded and free flow means that the energy is consistent with itself. From this point we can now describe the sacred experience of continuity positively. Although the experience means that boundaries are blurred and that the person's ego is lost (which is a negative description), that loss of self is an effect of the energy that crosses the border between the self and the world. In short, during a sacred experience, humans are driven by non-human energy that is first saved by the person and then passes through him.

Energy and Apathy

In 'L'homme souverain de Sade', which highlights the role of apathy and wherein Sade is read from an energetical perspective, Bataille refers to eroticism, which he argues has nothing to do with sexual reproduction.[20] In fact, according to Bataille, the two are opposite to each other. While sexual reproduction is about the creation of new life, eroticism, following one of Bataille's central theses, is closely linked to death. Although during erotic moments people may whisper sweet words to each other, these things are only of secondary importance. Eroticism, Bataille says, primarily revolves around death.

However strange and provocative this may sound, it is in line with a common-sense conception of eroticism, as Bataille believes that eroticism causes the temporary disappearance of the person's ego and of the experience of a boundary between the person and the environment.[21] According to Bataille, eroticism is a sacred experience in which the transition from discontinuity to continuity takes place, a transition that is initiated by the act of undressing. This needs to be understood from the fact that the meaning of clothes is not reducible to their functionality. Clothes not only protect the body against the cold, they also highlight distinctions, which can be seen from the fact that several professions require a certain dress code, that some styles of clothes express the values of a social class, or that a person is identified by a distinctive garment. When someone is undressed at the beginning of erotic play, this causes the disappearance of interpersonal differences. Eroticism begins with observing the nudity that obliterates differences and wherein the beloved, as Bataille says, 'is sinking into a void' and 'loses himself in the nothingness of death.'[22] This arouses in others the desire to take off their own clothes and to lose themselves in a movement that ends in what the French call '*la petite mort*'. Formulated in Bataille's energetical vocabulary: observing the continuity of the other causes an excess of energy that then explodes in the person. The erotic experience can then be described as an explosion of energy in which the person's ego is dissolved, and that, unlike labour, is not directed towards a goal. In other words, Bataille addresses eroticism from *l'économie générale*, meaning that in erotic play man lives in accordance with aimless energy.

It is precisely upon these ideas that Bataille's Sade reading is based, which immediately makes clear that the apathetic sadist does not really break with normal eroticism. Certainly, it is the case that the relationship between the sadist and the victim differs at several levels from the relationship between lovers. However, the differences are not of such a nature that we can speak of a radical break between the two. Although the *tableaux vivants* seem to be totally different from what we know in normal life, Bataille argues that, in a certain way, Sade is in line with the sacred erotic experience.[23] This means that, according to Bataille, we must also understand Sade's apathy from a 'general' perspective. This rather unfamiliar interpretation needs some further clarification.

Above we have seen that, from Bataille's perspective, the ordinary world consists of marks that distinguish various entities. Eroticism is one of the experiences that erases these distinctions. This experience of continuity begins with the erotic fact of being undressed. The removal of clothes takes away what makes the other person unique. When the sadist abuses his victim, those atrocities have the same effect. Via extreme violence, just as with the act of undressing, the discontinuity of the other disappears.[24] More specifically, the discontinuity disappears, according to Bataille, through the fact that severe pain is expressed in the face of the victim.[25] With the cry of the victim, the mouth is opened wide and the face is contorted in a tense and strained expression. The result of that spastic cramp is that those aspects of the face that distinguish the individual – the colour of the eyes, the size of the nose or the shape of the lips – fade into the background. With the contraction of the facial muscles, the traces of the other begin to disappear. Therefore, severe pain, just like nakedness, destroys the discontinuity of the person. Normally people are recognised and distinguished on the basis of some particular facial features, but when someone suffers violently those features fade away, and the individual disappears in anonymity.

So too in the case of the sadist, the contemplation of the destruction of discontinuity leads to an experience of continuity. When the other disappears in pain, a violent move is triggered that ends in the mortification of the person's uniqueness. Formulated more precisely, the intense pain of the other and the loss of the self cause a stream of energy in which the boundary between the ego of the sadist and the outside world disappear.[26] It is exactly at this point that, as an effect of observing the continuity of the other, Bataille situates Sadean apathy. As we have seen before, this apathy breaks with the attitude of personal involvement, meaning that no energy will be invested in oneself or in others. This does not mean, however, that the energy as such disappears. No, the energy is disconnected from any kind of involvement, which means that a large amount of energy can be accumulated.[27] When the other as a discontinuous entity disappears in pain, then the energy, which was hitherto invested in the ego and in others, is no longer related to something; it becomes a large quantum of energy that puts that sadist's ego under pressure. When finally the person can no longer hold the pressure, they disappear in an explosion of energy, and the boundary that separates the sadist from the outside world implodes. That sacred experience of continuity is the outcome of a flow of non-human energy that breaks into human existence and for which the sadist is a vehicle. The latter echoes in the following passage from *Juliette* wherein a certain Madame Delbène describes the effects of a brutal crime: 'Then it is as if a new world opens up for you; a delightful, all-consuming glow then flows through your veins, which will ignite that electrically charged fluid on which the whole principle of life is based.'[28]

Based upon this analysis, we can now determine in what sense this conception of apathy differs from or is similar to the apathy of Stoicism.[29] Indeed, as is well known, apathy is central not only in Sade but also in the philosophical movement that flourished during the fourth and third centuries BC in Greece. First of all, it is important to notice that, in Stoicism, *apatheia* is a moral ideal which is based on a cosmology. The Stoic apathy needs to be understood from a certain conception of the universe, a conception that sees the universe as optimally rationally ordered by God. Although human reality is often chaotic or the product of mere coincidence, the cosmos is totally rational. The highest good, then, which leads to happiness, is that man lives in accordance with this rationally ordered cosmos, meaning that he structures his life following the rational lines of the non-human universe. This view implies that man is morally virtuous only if he makes his choices based solely upon a power which God gave to humanity: reason. Of course man does have sensuous desires but, as the Stoics argue, he cannot be reduced to these affects. But besides aspirations, he is also equipped with rational faculties, and it is only via living in the light of this divine spark in him that he will be able to achieve moral perfection. The moral good, in other words, lies only in man, namely in his rational mind. It follows then that emotions, which are seen by the Stoics as the opposite of reason, fall under the heading of moral evil. Indeed, according to Stoicism, emotions arise when a value is attributed to affairs that are external to the human mind, and that, thus, are actually morally indifferent. In other words, whoever is angry because his money has been stolen makes a moral mistake. The reason is that he is then determined by externals which have no moral value. He would only be morally virtuous if he were left untouched by the loss of his money. In short, apathy, which means that one is freed from emotions, is a necessary condition for moral virtue. The one who reaches that state of mind, and thus who makes decisions based on rational understanding, is good in a moral sense and lives in accordance with the cosmos.

This shows that Stoic apathy is embedded in a broader perspective. The one who is not affected by morally neutral external things is tailored to the rationally ordered cosmos. This means that the life of the Stoic is consistent with what transcends human life, which is also the case for the sadist. This is the key point. When the energy which in normal life is invested in the self or in the other is not so invested, and instead goes through the sadist, then the sadist is in fact obsessed by a stream of non-human energy that transcends 'limited' human life. In this respect, Sadean apathy is similar to that of the Stoic.

Despite this similarity, however, one can perceive at least four differences between the sadist and the Stoic. The first difference is that apathy in Stoicism is a moral ideal, while the Sadean apathy does not have a moral meaning, at least not in Bataille's analysis. Within the perspective from which Bataille reads Sade, the apathetic sadist does not incarnate the highest good. Just like eroticism, he is nothing but an illustration of a reality that falls outside of ordinary life and that, seen from the viewpoint of *l'économie restreinte*, is pure waste.[30] Second, for Sade, unlike for the Stoics, apathy is not a goal, as the sadist does not explicitly aim at the destruction of personal involvement. The fact that this attitude is destroyed is rather an effect of the fact that the sadist perceives that the other disappears in pain. This experience of continuity fuels the energy that then both breaks away from any kind of personal involvement and triggers a cruel movement wherein the sadist's ego will be dissolved. The third difference lies in the fact that in Stoicism the extension of the concept of apathy is larger than in Sade's case. While the concept of stoic *apatheia* refers to something that breaks with any externality – body, money, property, etc. – the concept of Sadean apathy refers only to the destruction of any kind of personal involvement. Fourth, other than in Stoicism, the apathetic person is characterised not by the use of the capacity of reason, but by the fact that he is overwhelmed by an energy which has as its consequence the destruction of any capacity of rational thinking.[31]

Sadistic and Mystical Enjoyment

According to Bataille, sadism and the activity of undressing have in common the destruction of the discontinuity of the other. Both destroy the distinction between the other and his surroundings. This means that the sadist enlarges, and in that sense recalls, what is always present in eroticism but what at the same time normally stays in the background, namely the fact that eroticism is associated directly with violence. Both sadism and eroticism also share the idea that the destruction releases an amount of non-human energy wherein the ego disappears. That energy, Bataille holds, is of itself not involved in anything else beyond itself. It occupies neither itself nor the other, and does not focus on a preconceived *telos*. The energy is impersonal and purposeless. In the ordinary erotic experience man lives in accordance with this a-teleological energy. Therefore, eroticism can be described as follows: it is an expression of a stream of energy in which the person's ego is dissolved and which is not directed to a future goal. This also makes clear that Bataille's Sade interpretation is completely in line with postmodern thinking, at least in the sense that, according to this kind of thinking, man is not the centre of the world.

The sadist, Bataille argues, lives fully from that stream of energy. The emphasis, however, lies not on the fact that the cruel actions lead to nothing. The sadist is characterised primarily by the fact that he is not hindered by emotions, such as remorse, that would betray a personal involvement.[32] Therefore it is not merely that a quantum of energy forms in the sadist that overwhelms him and dissolves his ego, it is also that that energy feeds – following the title of one of Bataille's Sade studies, namely *un érotisme sans limite* – a way of acting that can continue unperturbed, immune to hindrance from any form of involvement.[33] Put in other words, the impersonal energy is expressed in the uninhibited series of crimes. This implies that the sadist's activities are not based upon the sadist's will. The sadist's cruel act is an act without ego and is the expression or conductor of non-human energy. This is echoed in the following sentence from *Juliette*: 'But take it from me that the whole theory of free will is just a delusion and that a force stronger than ourselves encourages us to do what we have to do.'[34]

We can thus hold that Bataille understands Sadean apathy not only in a negative way but also in positive terms: negatively speaking, apathy is an effect of energy that detaches itself from any form of personal involvement; positively, apathy is the expression of a force that continues imperturbably. Furthermore, it appears that, according to Bataille, a turnaround can be perceived. While the collection of energy first is the effect of the crime, the apathetic crimes then become an expression of a large quantity of impersonal energy.[35] The sadist is thus not only characterised by the accumulation and explosion of energy that no longer circulates within the secular order. Due to the uninhibited concatenation of crimes, the sadist also lives truly from the flux of non-human energy that breaks down in its pure form into the human condition, and thus deforms that condition into something inhuman, in the sense that it transcends human characteristics.

Bataille holds that the sadist's enjoyment is rooted in the latter.[36] Sadistic enjoyment follows from the fact that the apathetic sadist lives in accordance with impersonal energy. The sadist enjoys the fact that his actions express the power of energy that transcends ordinary life and that, seen from the viewpoint of *l'économie restreinte*, is nothing but pure waste. In other words, the sadist's enjoyment is an effect of the fact that via his cruel deeds he is geared to *l'économie générale* according to which energy circulates freely and is not invested in something other than itself. Thus, sadistic enjoyment has nothing to do with pleasant sensation.[37] Indeed, that sensation presupposes immediate self-involvement – the sensations are always *mine* – while the sadist suspends any form of personal involvement. It also follows from Bataille's reasoning that it is not true that the sadist enjoys looking at the pain of others or that he likes to inflict pain on others. Indeed, if he enjoyed the other's pain, then this would imply that the sadist, although in a negative way, still depends on the other. This cannot be the case, however, as the sadist is characterised by apathy.

Thus, sadistic enjoyment, at least following Bataille's analysis, seems to be at first sight a rather special kind of enjoyment. Indeed, it is clear from the foregoing that the sadist's enjoyment is not physical and that it also differs from enjoying, let's say, a nice talk with significant others. Furthermore, sadistic enjoyment does not equal the joy that is associated with activities in which personal interests can be expressed. Bataille, however, suggests that the sadist's enjoyment is similar to at least one other type of enjoyment. In this respect, he connects the sadist with the mystic at least twice.[38] Just as with his comparison of the sadist and the scientist, this comparison is unexpected. Nevertheless, it suggests that there is a link between sadistic and mystical enjoyment. How ought we to understand this?[39]

Hermits are not characterised by the will to converse with others. They don't travel around the world to convince others of the idea that mankind was created by God and that man is part of a divine plan of salvation. Nor do they want to save the world or try to purify the world from evil. Mystics don't travel around the world but withdraw and separate themselves from it. They live isolated in monasteries where they get rid of their personal interests and ambitions via intensive prayer and meditation. Although mysticism cannot be reduced to this negative attitude, a mystical life begins with discipline.[40] However, this first stage can also be described in a positive way, since the emptying of self and of the world is supported by a love for God and by an intense desire for union with God. The fact that the mystic breaks with his individual life and with the world must be understood in terms of the upward movement to God as the object of desire.

However, the mystic is not continuously stirred up by his desire. The mystical life is interrupted, sometimes for a long time, by periods in which the love of and desire for God fade away. If that is the case, what then comes to the fore is what was at first nothing but a step towards union with God, namely the annihilation of the self and the world. When the focus on God is lost, the mystic falls back into a world in which nothing touches him and in which all life is drawn away from all sorts of things, just as in Hegel's obscure night where 'all cows are black'. This period is accompanied by a destruction of the will: the mystic no longer has any personal goals and destroys all sorts of desires. In that phase, known as 'the dark night of mystical suffering', the radical emptying of the self and the world leads to a deep apathy. Every force has left the mystic, which means that in the end he is unable to act.

In the final stage, one can perceive a spiritual union with God, meaning that the mystic disappears as a person and becomes the expression of a divine force that lives through him. This unification has as its effect the transcendence of the mystic's apathy, the state that had characterised the mystic after losing his desire for God. Thus, on the final stage of the mystical road, this apathy disappears. The mystic is taken away from his depressive state, and this is made possible by the divine power that expresses itself in him. God expresses himself in the mystic, and this 'incarnation' throws the mystic back into the world. God's expression in the mystic is the cause of the fact that the mystic starts working and living again. That worldly behaviour, however, breaks with the sorts of actions that characterise normal life. Indeed, the mystic's actions are no longer driven by personal goals and are no longer affected by what is happening in the profane world. This means that one can describe the mystic's behaviour as follows: when the mystic acts, it is as if he slides indifferently over things in a movement that leads to nothing.

It is precisely this unification with God, and the apathetic actions resulting from the expression of God in the mystic, that arouse the mystics' enjoyment. In other words, according to Bataille, mystical enjoyment is an effect of the fact that the mystic's behaviour is an expression of the divine power in him. On this basis, we can now understand the twofold similarity Bataille perceives between Sadean enjoyment on the one hand, and mystical enjoyment on the other. First, in both cases, enjoyment is not a goal, as is often the case in everyday life. Here it is rather a consequence or effect of something else. Both Sadean and mystical enjoyments are a non-intended effect of a unification with what transcends the person. Second, the enjoyment of both the mystic and the sadist results from the fact that they are unified with what transcends human life. In other words, both enjoy the unification with a non-human force that expresses itself in humanity.

Enjoying Transgression?

In ordinary life, people judge each other's actions, attitudes and statements on the basis of, among other things, moral categories, namely the distinction between good and evil. Nothing of what happens in Sade's world, from murder to incest to torture, falls under what we understand as good. The Sadean universe is on the other side of the moral boundary. Based upon another finding, that the experience of enjoyment is the only 'inner experience' which the sadist reports, it is not unlikely that some will find sadistic enjoyment to be about the transgression of the moral law.[41] Because the sadist continually behaves in an immoral way and also never seems to stop enjoying, it should not be surprising that some conclude that what the sadist really enjoys is exceeding the moral boundary. Sadistic enjoyment, following a popular understanding, is all about enjoying radical evil.

One would expect this interpretation to return in Bataille's Sade studies. After all, the term 'transgression' is a basic concept in Bataille's thinking. To see this does not require a thorough study of his entire oeuvre; it is enough to take a quick glance at that oeuvre and to browse through Bataille's books and articles quickly. For example, whoever opens *L'érotisme* sees that the title of the first theoretical part is 'L'interdit et la transgression' and reads in the introduction that, according to Bataille, we should think of eroticism as a transgression.[42] It is therefore not surprising that the introductions to, and commentaries on, Bataille's work often circulate around the notion of transgression. This is the case, for example, in the famous study that Foucault wrote about Bataille in 1963, one year after Bataille's death, whose title is 'Préface à la transgression'.[43] Therefore, it is also not surprising that in studies referring to his work Bataille is often presented as the 'philosopher of transgression'.

Based upon these findings, one might expect that in Bataille's Sade studies the term 'transgression' would be used repeatedly or that the French philosopher would understand his characters' enjoyment as related immediately to transgression. From what we have seen in the preceding paragraphs, however, this does not seem to be the case. Also, in none of his texts on Sade does Bataille regularly employ the term 'transgression'. From this point of view, it is somewhat surprising that, on the last pages of both 'L'homme souverain de Sade' and 'Sade et l'homme normal', he sometimes refers, either explicitly or implicitly, to transgression.[44] In this reference Bataille indicates that he does indeed interpret Sade's work with the help of the notion of 'transgression'. How should we understand this? And what is the connection between transgression and sadistic enjoyment?

In the previous sections we have seen that it is not pain as such that has an effect on the sadist, but what is happening in the pain, namely the destruction of discontinuity. That destruction, Bataille maintains, raises a desire for continuity and self-loss. Formulated more specifically, the loss of the self of the other causes the accumulation of a large amount of free energy in which the person's ego is dissolved. The sadist, however, is not only characterised by this accumulation of energy. That energy also expresses itself in the cruel acts, which are not inhibited by any form of involvement. The sadist is an expression of free and unbound energy which by itself is not aimed at anything other than itself. As we have seen, from the 'limited' human perspective, in which energy is normally bound, that apathetic behaviour is merely waste, but from the perspective of the general economy, on the other hand, the apathetic act indicates that the sadist lives in harmony with free energy.

It is precisely from that distinction between the 'limited' and 'general' economies that transgression in Sade must be understood. Thus, in the dualistic framework in which Bataille reads Sade, the emphasis is not on exceeding the moral boundary. Bataille's interpretation does not turn on crossing the boundary between moral good and evil. However, that does not mean that Bataille reads Sade without using the notion of transgression. Bataille does understand Sade from the notion of transgression, but the border that is exceeded by the sadist is a boundary that erases the moral distinction, namely the difference between the human and the non-human. Indeed, if the sadist is not hindered by any form of personal involvement, then he exceeds the 'limited' human perspective in which people are involved in themselves, and thus lives in accordance with non-human energy. This means that Bataille also understands sadistic enjoyment in terms of 'transgression', since the sadist's enjoyment arises from his alignment with the non-human flux of energy. In short, the sadist, Bataille holds, enjoys not the transgression of the moral law, but rather the transgression of the 'limited' perspective from which life is normally understood.[45]

III Literature as an Expression of Energy

As is well known, the surrealists were also interested in the life and work of Sade. In addition, figures such as André Breton and Paul Éluard saw in Sade an ally in their opposition to the existing power structures and in their desire for freedom. However, Bataille, who was first involved in surrealism, came into conflict with the surrealists from the late 1920s and early 1930s onwards.[46] He did not agree with the surrealists' use of Sade, and he opposed their interpretation on which that revolutionary use of Sade was founded.[47] Years later, in the foreword to the publication of *Justine*, Bataille repeated his criticism of the surrealists.[48] That criticism was based on the idea that the Sadean universe is detached from any human reality. However, when one relies on Sade, as the surrealists do, the libertine writer is engaged in a project of human concerns, implying that Sade is neglected as *das ganz Anderes*.[49]

According to Bataille, things are totally different in the case of the nineteenth-century literary critic Jules Janin, whose reaction to Sade's literature is identical to the way in which *l'homme normal* – to borrow a term from the later title of the Bataille text – reacts to it.[50] When Sade's works are spread among a broader audience, they are initially received with curiosity and excitement. Both disappear soon, however, once they have become more thoroughly known. Curiosity and excitement turn into horror and disgust. When the everyday reader goes through Sade's work, he distances himself from the world described in it. This reaction is not an indication of a lack on the part of *l'homme normal* to open up to a form of literature that deviates greatly from the easy reading of more conventional literature. Bataille actually believes that this reaction is more warranted than the surrealists' easy admiration. This is because the radical disgust regarding Sade testifies to the correct insight that the Sadean universe is incompatible with any form of human existence.

The fact that the Sadean universe contradicts profane life has to do not only with the presence of physical violence, but also with the sadist's apathy. Indeed, this lack of emotion breaks with the normal involvement that people have with themselves and others. The latter, namely the involvement with others, also characterises authors, whose writing normally results from the intention to communicate a content to a readership. Anyone who writes and uses language, Bataille emphasises, shows involvement in the sense that he or she wants to make something clear to someone else.[51] However, in the further continuation of my argument, it is not so much writing in general that has to be kept in mind. Rather we should distinguish between two distinct forms of writing, each of which is characterised by a specific form of involvement. First, the emphasis is on texts in which a thought or theory is defended. The writer of such texts shows involvement not only because he wants to share a certain content, but also because he has a sensitivity to the reactions of other people. He feels stronger when readers endorse the content, or he may revise his text when they present criticisms. Second, the emphasis is on literary texts, whose author also shows a special form of involvement: he speaks to the reader; he appeals to shared knowledge; he allows space for imagination, etc.[52]

Those forms of involvement contradict the fact that those who live in Sade's world are unrelated to each other. Nevertheless, the sadist is brought up as a character in an oeuvre that originates from the mind of the real person Marquis de Sade. As is known, this oeuvre consists of passages with philosophical speculations on the one hand, and non-philosophical literary passages describing the cruel erotic scenes on the other. One would expect that Sade, as a writer of those passages, first, would be sensitive to the reactions of others to his philosophical speculations and, second, would show a commitment to the reader by, for example, appealing to his imagination. If that were the case, one could then perceive a tension between the apathetic sadist as a personage on the one hand and the writer as a person on the other. In other words, if it is correct that the Marquis shows involvement with the reader, then Sade, insofar as he writes and apart from his characters, is not *das ganz Anderes.*

In 'Sade et l'homme normal' Bataille contests the presence of any such tension. Therefore, he relies on the philosophical passages in Sade's oeuvre. These passages often repeat the idea that nature strives for balance. This, according to the libertine heroes, is expressed in the fact that nature does not just create new life but also causes death and destruction through earthquakes, famine or disease. The fact that nature strives for a natural balance means, thus, that man must not only listen to the law but also transgress the law. In *La philosophie dans le boudoir,* for example, Dolmancé says to Madame de Saint-Ange's brother: 'I have told you a thousand times that nature, [. . .] in order to properly enforce the laws of its equilibrium, sometimes needs virtues and sometimes vices.'[53] From the perspective of nature, the acts that are usually regarded as crimes should not be penalised. Indeed, the tortures, rapes and murders are in accordance with nature's plans and must even be encouraged. That view originates from Marquis de Sade's brain and, according to Bataille, follows from his intention to justify his own cruel acts, such as the torture of the 36-year-old widow Keller in 1768.[54] The same view, as we have seen before, can be read in Sade's oeuvre at countless points. According to Bataille, the writing and making public of that view can therefore be seen as an attempt to change society's judgement about his cruel actions. The life of *la cour* may be loose, but society does not tolerate Sade's actions at all. The Marquis experienced this more than once after being caught. It is on the basis of society's punishment that Sade writes a philosophical system. Via this he wants to convince the world that his actions are not crimes; they are justified, precisely because they are in line with nature's will.[55]

Insofar as Sade, via his philosophical passages, wants to justify his actions and to convince the public that his deeds are not crimes, he shows an involvement with his readers. Nevertheless, Bataille holds, these same passages also express Sade's apathy with respect to the outside world. The reason is that the philosophical reasonings that Sade's characters develop are very long and comprehensive proofs.[56] The fact that those characters, during their conversations, want to prove all kinds of allegations is evident from the following: 'Do you realise, Dolmancé, that in this way you will even be able to prove [. . .]?'[57] And in *Juliette* we read: 'I will now, Juliette, the Pope then said, give you some examples to prove to you that [. . .]'.[58] Thus, in the philosophical passages, a thesis is always put forward that must be proved. For this purpose, one starts with an axiom or a definition from which the allegation is validly derived. That correct deduction guarantees the truth of the claim. Otherwise formulated, the truth of the conclusion is guaranteed by the truth of the foregoing statement and fact that the conclusion obeys an ironclad logic. This implies that the dissertations cannot be affected by the reader's reactions. They do not need his agreement to be true, and they are not affected if he rejects them. The statements are surrounded by an aura of inviolability and turn their head away from those who want to touch them. It is precisely in this regard that the dissertations should be understood as an expression of the apathy of the Marquis.[59] It may be the case that the philosophical passages indicate an involvement and that the content of those passages is an expression of his insensitivity regarding the reader. In other words, the brute fact *that* Sade writes is an expression of involvement, but *what* he writes is an expression of non-involvement.[60] When the Marquis writes about nature and shows that it needs evil, then, Bataille holds, he is moved by the reader as much as rocks are moved by lovers of nature.[61]

In addition to the philosophical dissertations, Sade's works also contain descriptions of erotic and criminal scenes. Bataille draws attention to the fact that reading these passages requires a lot of effort. Indeed, Sade's prose is extremely boring, as Bataille stresses.[62] Curiosity and excitement may first turn into horror, but those who are able to go through the many pages of Sade's literature are soon overwhelmed by boredom. Any form of affectivity disappears, and the reader quickly enters into an atmosphere of disinterest. That boredom, Bataille writes, is an effect of repetition, and moreover, this endless repetition is an expression of Sade's apathy.[63] How should we understand this? What is the link between repetition on the one and apathy on the other hand?

In the introduction to *La philosophie dans le boudoir*, just before one of the dialogues in which Dolmancé and Madame de Saint-Ange take the floor, it is the Marquis de Sade himself who is speaking. He claims that he commits his lustful literature to the 'lascivious women', 'young girls' and 'loving servants of slatterliness'.[64] Further, in the long introduction to *Les 120 journées de Sodome*, the Marquis does not directly addresses the reader, but meets the terms of the tacit narrative pact between the writer and the reader, namely that the former guides the latter. This means the writer makes sure that the reader can imagine what the story is about, making the reader somewhat familiar with a world that does not match the world in which his own life takes place. Therefore, he outlines the characters, daily life, the time schedule, etc. This fact, and also the fact that he appeals in *La philosophie dans le boudoir* to the reader and that he assigns the work to him, shows Sade's involvement.

After the introduction, however, no narrative is started that ends with all the pieces coinciding. What follows instead is a serial alignment of scenes and narratives that does not seem to end and does not lead to anything. That repetitive, monotonic rhythm changes the reader's reception of the text. That change is not an exceptional phenomenon, but is consistent with the following recognisable experience. Take, for example, a man who has loved a novel for years as if it were his own child: he insists that the pages are not creased, does not leave the book lying around, is angry when the book is given to someone else without his knowledge, etc. The reason he cherishes the book is because the content is in line with what has concerned him for a very long time. The novel unveils answers to the questions that obsess him. It is as if the author of the book had this specific reader in mind when writing. That fact urges the reader to reconsider the novel and to reread it several times. At the same time, however, this specific process also has a totally different effect. When he repeatedly rereads the novel to which he is so strongly attached, then the novel becomes an autonomous object that is no longer adapted to the particularity of that person. While the text seems to move to the reader first, it seems that the next moment the novel turns into itself and looks away from the reader who saw his soul first reflected in the text. Although the man reopens his favourite book because it seems to reveal the secret of his own being, it is exactly the repetition of his reading that causes the book to close and ossify.

Sade's novels also cause that apathetic effect. It may be felt after repeated reading, but it may also be felt even earlier. It is enough in this respect to open a book like *Les 120 journées de Sodome*, in which the four *narratrices* read and combine the cruel and erotic narratives. In the repetitive rhythm with which those narratives progress – according to Bataille – they seem to move away from the reader and follow their own movement. In the endless repetitions of the same, the text withdraws back into itself and closes to an *en-soi* that is hardened towards the reader. According to Bataille, this expresses the apathy of the writer Marquis de Sade. When he has written down the first scenes and narratives on paper, the writing of those passages is separated and the engagement with the reader as other is suspended via this becoming independent of the passages. Although he first appeals to and guides the reader, once the writing begins to lead his own life, Sade detaches himself from the reader and sacrifices the reader to the repetitive writing. Thus, according to Bataille, it is not true that only Sade's characters live in harmony with impersonal energy. There is a formal analogy between the sadist and Sade as a writer. Just like his characters, Sade develops the movement of non-human energy of which apathetic literature is the crystallisation. When focusing on the process of writing, Bataille says that writing is not a matter of shocking or witnessing, but of energy.[65]

IV Conclusion

Almost all the concepts from Bataille's binary thinking can be deduced from the tension between what he calls 'the profane order' and 'the sacred order'. By the first order he is referring to ordinary life in which man is concerned about his self-preservation, develops a morality, is productive, aims at controlling reality, etc. The sacred order includes some rather rare activities, experiences and figures that put the familiar world in a state of disarray. More precisely and expressed in Bataille's energetic terms: the sacred order stands for that part of reality in which energy breaks into in a pure non-human form. It is that area *au-delà* the ordinary life in which Bataille is interested and which he thematises in his texts. That interest also led him to a figure like Sade. More specifically, he is fascinated by the apathy of the person Marquis de Sade and of the characters who inhabit Sade's literary world. After all, this apathy expresses a reality that transcends the profane order and that cannot be explained by the terms in which ordinary life is mapped out. In other words, Bataille's interest in Sade has to do with the fact that his literature reflects the theme of 'transgression', in the sense of exceeding the 'limited' perspective.

4[1]

Ethics and Modernity

I Introduction

On 29 October 1974 in Rome, two days before the start of the four-day congress of the École freudienne de Paris, Lacan claimed in a press conference that what philosophers say is often considered uninteresting by most people. When they are able to captivate an audience, the number of interested parties is usually very small. This also applies to one of his own texts in which he talks about several philosophers and in which he links up with, among other things, an age-old philosophical theme. For example, in his answer to a question from an Italian journalist, he said the following:

> Moreover, no one has paid the slightest attention to this article. There is one good man that has commented on it somewhere; I do not even know if it has appeared. But no one has ever answered me on this article. It is true that I am incomprehensible.[2]

Lacan was referring here to the negative reactions to the first version of his text 'Kant avec Sade' in which he reformulates, in a more concise way, some of the thoughts that he had presented at his seminary on the ethics of psychoanalysis in 1959 and 1960.[3] The original intention was that this text, written in September 1962, would appear a year later as a preface to *La philosophie dans le boudoir* in the third part of Sade's collected works, published by Éditions du Cercle du Livre Précieux. However, when the third part of Sade's oeuvre appeared in December 1963, Klossowski's text 'Sade et la révolution' took the place previously reserved for Lacan. Lacan's own text was published in April of the same year in *Critique*. According to Élisabeth Roudinesco,

Lacan's biographer, the reason why his text is not included as a preface is that Jean Paulhan, who was a member of the editorial board of Éditions du Cercle du Livre Précieux, found his contribution unreadable and incomprehensible. Paulhan did not like 'Kant avec Sade' very much because of the baroque and allusive style, and the absence of references to sources consulted. Claude Tchou, the editor-in-chief of the publishing company, however, stated that Paulhan had nothing to do with the refusal to include Lacan's text in Sade's collected works. Tchou wrote in a letter to Élisabeth Roudinesco that he himself was responsible for this. The reason he gave was that this text does not adequately display Lacan's level of thinking.[4] This did not prevent Éditions du Cercle du Livre Précieux from including a slightly modified version of Lacan's text in the second edition in 1966, three years after the first edition, albeit not as a foreword but as an afterword.[5]

As the title indicates, Lacan in 'Kant avec Sade', just as in his seminar a few years earlier, reads the work of Sade and Kant together. To put it mildly, that is striking. However, this link is not new. After all, other writers before Lacan had already linked the work of Kant and Sade. This is the case in de Beauvoir's text 'Faut-il brûler Sade?'[6] and in a lecture by Bataille.[7] However, the reference to Kant in those texts is only indirect. This relation is treated differently different in 'Juliette oder Aufklärung und Moral', the second supplement from *Dialektik der Aufklärung* (1944) by Max Horkheimer and Theodor Adorno.[8] In this essay, the two main figures of the Frankfurt School connect Kant and Sade extensively with each other.[9]

Although various thinkers preceded Lacan in this, it remains surprising that he juxtaposes the oeuvre of Kant and Sade. At first glance the two are antipodes. While the philosopher from Koningsbergen leaves his home only for his daily walk shortly after lunch and dies a virgin, Sade is known for his debauched life and his many travels through France's neighbouring countries. More important than these biographical anecdotes is that the Sadean universe seems to be diametrically opposed to what Kant is aiming for. Are the libertines not characterised by the fact that they use every opportunity to blatantly violate the law, while Kant focuses on obedience to the law? Is the oeuvre of the Marquis not known for its countless blasphemous passages, while Kant also frees up a place for religion within the limits of enlightened reason? Finally, is it not the case that Kant writes about the conditions for the contemplation of beauty, while some libertines only become excited by exposure to the ugly?

Already on the first page of 'Kant avec Sade' it appears that Lacan focuses neither on Kant's criticism of pure reason nor on his criticism of aesthetic judgement, but on his second criticism. When Lacan puts Sade's oeuvre next to that of Kant, he also indicates that he reads Sade mainly from an ethical perspective.[10] On the same first page, Lacan also makes clear how we should understand the fact that he places Kant beside Sade. Thus, he launches the provocative proposition on which his text centres, namely that 'it [*La philosophie dans le boudoir*] gives the truth of the *Kritik* [*der Practischen Vernunft*]'.[11] Nowhere does Lacan explicitly explain what exactly he means by this thesis. In the second and third sections of this chapter I show that Lacan's thesis can be explained in two ways. I then argue that, on the basis of what Lacan writes, one can also read his thesis the other way around. On the basis of a few passages, I show that, according to Lacan, Kant's thinking is the truth of Sade. According to Lacan we should not only read Kant with Sade but also Sade with Kant. I will conclude the chapter with another surprising suggestion by Lacan. I suggest that Sade's literature brings some underexposed aspects of moral experience to the attention of the public.

II Lacan's Criticism of Kant

In his *Ethics of the Real: Kant, Lacan* from 2000, Alenka Zupančič argues that Lacan's ethics is a continuation of Kant's ethics.[12] Lacan, according to Zupančič, is a Kantian. She is supported in this by well-known Lacan interpreters such as Bernard Baas and Slavoj Žižek.[13] In the following section, I will show that Lacan's alleged Kantianism cannot be perceived in his essay 'Kant avec Sade'. The first explanation of Lacan's thesis that Sade is the truth of Kant is, after all, a criticism of Kant's moral philosophy. In order to gain a good understanding of this criticism, we first need to take a closer look at Lacan's reading of Kant.

Nature and Reason

When Lacan, in *L'éthique de la psychanalyse,* discusses Kant in detail for the first time, he explicitly places Kant's ethics in a historical context. The Kantian ethics, according to Lacan, are an extension of the crisis that modern science has caused.[14] Contrary to expectation, this crisis is primarily not about the fact that sixteenth-century science broke with the classic belief in the immediate access to reality through thought. In Kant's terms, the scientific is not primarily a result of its claim that we can only reason about appearances (*Aanschauungen*) of a reality that, in itself, is unknown (*ein Unbekanntes*). What is so shocking about modern science is its insistence on nature's morally neutral character. From the perspective of modern science, nature is neither good nor bad. According to Lacan, this normative neutrality has a disorienting effect on the individual. This is because, until the sixteenth century, nature was always the ground or compass for moral decisions. Kant's ethics, like the science of his time, refuses to attribute any moral qualities to nature. This means that we ought to understand his position as strictly opposed to that of a philosopher like Aristotle, who approaches ethics as though it were a practice of refining the goodness that is already found in nature. In Kant's modern ethical system, 'ought' does not follow from 'is' but is rather a law that the individual himself legislates. Nature is no longer what makes man good in Kant's time; the *ratio essendi* of the moral law is now a question of human freedom. Seen in reverse: the moral law is the ground of the *ratio cognoscendi* of freedom. Even though man cannot have knowledge of his freedom – because it exceeds the theoretical boundaries of knowledge that Kant erected in his first critique – he becomes conscious of the fact of his freedom when he freely imposes laws upon himself.

If Kant argues that nature can only function as an ontological ground for ethics, it follows that he would be opposed to any theory of moral sentiment upheld by philosophers like David Hume. These theories argue that morality ought to be grounded in our spontaneous feelings of sympathy and aversion.[15] According to Hume, for example, the moral good is defined as what sympathy strives towards, namely, *das Wohl* or well-being; immorality refers to that group of things to which we have an aversion, namely, *das Übel* or unhappiness.[16] In this system, good deeds are good whenever they lead to the state of well-being that we all spontaneously strive to achieve; deeds are bad if they are the cause of unhappiness, which everyone naturally wishes to avoid. This direct anchoring of ethics in sensory-based strivings means, according to Kant, that its practical prescriptions apply in a hypothetical or conditional sense. After all, they are not good in themselves, but only in so far as they act as a condition for the realisation of the spontaneously coveted states of mind. The reason why Kant does not consider this provision to be ethics is that *das Wohl* is morally neutral. The problem is not that human beings are determined by pathological objects, the pursuit of well-being and the avoidance of accidents.[17] Kant does acknowledge that man strives for happiness and avoids misfortune, but he does not accept that ethics should be anchored in empirical strivings.

Since Kant refuses to ground ethical behaviour in sensuous desires, Lacan reasons that the former must prize apathy or *Affektlosigkeit* as a necessary condition for ethics.[18] We must be morally indifferent to all phenomenal objects and feelings, even *Neigungen* or impressions if they are not to pollute the purity of an a priori ethics. This does not mean, however, that Kant's ethics is absolutely arbitrary. He may have freed ethics from its ties to natural goodness and sensuous objects, but he did not leave it entirely without direction. At the very moment that Kant severed the bond between ethics and nature, Lacan argued, he made room for something else to emerge: a law with the power to determine the moral will.[19] All that is left of ethics after one rejects empirical considerations is an unconditional law, a categorical imperative whose aim is *das Gute* – not *das Wohl*. All individual moral choices, Kant argues, must be undertaken on the basis of a universal principle of ethical behaviour; they should never take into consideration one's personal feelings or preferences. Kant's first formulation of the categorical imperative states: 'Act only on that maxim by which you can, at the same time, will that it should become a universal law.'[20] If you want to know what you ought to do, then you must determine whether or not the maxim of your action meets the demands of universal validity.[21] Kant's answer to the question about the good is, therefore, a priori determined by reason. The fact that we can determine whether a maxim can be made universal or if its generalisation would lead to contradictions, after all, is proof of reason's power. In short, Kant argues that the core of ethics lies in reason and its formal-logical principle of non-contradiction.

To conclude his introduction of Kant's ethics, Lacan refers to a passage from 'Die Analytik der reinen praktischen Vernunft', the first book of *Kritik der praktischen Vernunft*. He cites an example that Kant uses to clarify when a maxim is not suitable for general legislation.[22] Take, for example, a pledgee who wants to expand his assets in all possible ways. One way would be to take possession of a property of which the owner has died and of which there is no evidence that he has transferred his property to the pledgee. Kant wonders whether it is permissible for the man to increase his assets in this way. This means that he wonders whether the maxim can, at the same time, serve as the starting point of a universal law: can anyone deny that a building has been given to him if no one can prove that this is the case? The answer to this question is negative because the extension of the maxim to a law leads to a contradiction. After all, the pledgee wants to make use of the practice of keeping a pledge, whereas this practice would disappear if everyone took possession of the goods that had been given to him as a pledge without first being put down on paper. On the basis of reason, Kant therefore concludes that the extension of the maxim to a law is contradictory, and formulates the law that the property must be returned to its owner.

Lacan does not merely refer to the case of the pledgee to illustrate how Kant determines which maxims we cannot count as ethics. In addition, he uses this example to criticise Kant's ethics. Lacan states that the example shows that it is problematic that Kant's formal ethics are not based on a concrete social reality.[23] Lacan does not explicitly mention why precisely this is a problem for him. He makes his point clear by referring to *Ubu Roi ou les Polonais*, a surrealistic play *avant la lettre* from 1896 by the French novelist and poet Alfred Jarry. More specifically, Lacan quotes the main character Père Ubu's last sentence at the end of the play. Père Ubu says: 'Long live Poland, because if Poland were not there, there would be no Polish people either.'[24] What does Lacan mean by this?

The Polish people, says Père Ubu, must honour and be thankful for their homeland. This imperative seems to be based on a superficial observation: the existence of the country, Poland, is the necessary condition for the existence of the Polish people. One can hardly speak of a Polish people, one reasons, if Poland does not exist. Lacan, however, draws our attention to the factual invalidity of Père Ubu's logic.[25] In the eighteenth and nineteenth centuries, Poland was divided and came under the rule of, amongst others, the Prussians. Nevertheless, the Polish people continued to exist and continued to oppose foreign rule. History, therefore, teaches us that Père Ubu's speech in praise of Poland is baseless: the existence of Poland is not a necessary condition for the existence of the Polish people. What seemed, at first sight, to be true, therefore, is contradicted by reality. In other words, reason cannot guarantee the truth of its claims; it must test them against reality.

Lacan refers to Père Ubu to clarify the problem that he sees in Kant's ethics: an ethical system that does not refer to reality cannot guarantee the good. This is evident from the example of the pledgee who ought not to increase his wealth by keeping money that was not explicitly bequeathed to him.[26] Kant's method, while it might arrive at the morally correct maxim, misses the real reason why stealing is wrong. He focuses, instead, on the abstract idea of property and forgets that property only has meaning – and can only be called good – within a certain context. Kant, therefore, forgets that property is not intrinsically good. It could be that, in another context or in a different time, property was not considered to be a good thing. If that were the case, then it would entail that Kant validates a practice that goes against the good. In other words, the problem that Lacan points to is that Kant's ethical system is too empty and formal. Whenever ethics is grounded not in concrete reality but only in reason, it can be filled with any content whatsoever. In such a situation, it is difficult to distinguish the good from the bad.

Ethics and the Possibility of Evil

Lacan's critique of Kant is that the latter's ethics cannot guarantee the good and that it can, therefore, lead to evil. This is exactly what Lacan illustrates in his reading of Sade. Sade's universe, Lacan claims, is the radical consequence of Kantian ethics. This is because, according to Lacan, Sade's universe meets the two conditions that Kant tells us are necessary to make a maxim or action morally viable. What are these two conditions?

The first condition, Lacan says, is 'the radical rejection of the pathological (that is, of every preoccupation with goods, passion, or even compassion'.[27] Human, sensuous nature is not a guideline for the sadist. He is characterised by the fact that he distances himself from the quest for well-being and the avoidance of unhappiness. The sadist also denies feelings like empathy, remorse, anxiety and disgust. In short, the sadist is beyond *das Wohl* and his will is not grounded in phenomenal reality.

Second, Lacan claims that the sadistic universe is bound by universal laws.[28] Although the sadist has freed himself from every pathological determination that results from sensuous desires, there is a law beyond freedom that has the power to limit the sadist's cruel behaviour, a law that the sadist must submit himself to without question. What is more, the core of the law for the sadist, as it is for Kant, is founded not in a belief in God or in nature but in the form of these two things. Lacan claims that, for Sade, form is the substance of the law.[29] This means that the law owes its validity to its universalisability and that it is the ground for a universal morality.

The sadist is thus characterised, in Lacan's view, by an apathetic obedience to a categorical imperative.[30] In order to properly understand this law, let us turn to Lacan's first formulation thereof in the first version of 'Kant avec Sade' from 1963: '"I have the right to enjoy your body", I can say to anyone, "and I will exercise this right without any limit to the capriciousness of the exactions I may wish to satiate with your body".'[31] The second half of this law is a clear rejection of what Kant calls 'pathological' nature. The libertine does not allow himself to be limited by, for example, the anxiety of a victim with whom he might otherwise spontaneously empathise. Most important, however, is the first half of the maxim: the assertion that the sadist has the right to enjoy any and every body. According to Lacan, this is the most extreme consequence of what is implied in the 1789 'Déclaration des Droits de l'Homme et du Citoyen'.[32] Lacan reconstructs Sade's reasoning as follows: if no one has the right to enslave anyone else and everyone is free, it follows that no woman could ever belong to just one man; instead, she belongs to all men. Sade himself says:

> Never may an act of possession be exercised upon a free being; the exclusive possession of a woman is no less unjust than the possession of slaves [. . .] a woman existing in the purity of Nature's laws

> cannot allege, as justification for refusing herself to someone who desires her, the love she bears another, because such a response is based upon exclusion, and no man may be excluded from the having of a woman as of the moment it is clear she definitely belongs to all men.[33]

At first sight, therefore, Lacan's formulation of sadistic law seems to be a categorical imperative. Lacan translates Sade in terms of Kant's principle of universalisability: everyone can always be the sadist's object of pleasure. This conclusion, however, is premature. There is someone who escapes from Lacan's formulation of the law: the sadist himself. The law states that *I* (the sadist) have a right to enjoy anyone's body but not that they have a reciprocal right to enjoy mine. The one who speaks the law is, therefore, an exception to the law that he himself has made. This is clearly incompatible with Kant's universalisability condition. It is without a doubt for this reason that Lacan slightly modifies his formulation of sadistic law in 1966. The following is the version of the law in 'Kant avec Sade' from the *Écrits:* '"I have the right to enjoy your body, anyone can say to me, and I will exercise that right without any limit to the capriciousness of the exactions I may wish to satiate with your body."'[34]

The modification of 'I can say to anyone' into 'anyone can say to me' is crucial. This reformulation allows Lacan's law to better stand up to the test of universalisability and this makes sadistic law a law in the Kantian sense of the term. This new law recognises not only that 'I' (the sadist) can call upon the right to pleasure, but also that 'I', at the same time, am subjected to the right to pleasure that others can exercise.[35] Put differently, the fundamental rule of sadism is that everyone has the unlimited right to get pleasure from everyone else.[36] This coincides with the passage quoted earlier from *La philosophie dans le boudoir.* While Sade first states that all women belong to all men, he later states:

> If we admit, as we have just done, that all men ought to be subjugated to our desires, we may certainly allow then ample satisfaction of theirs. Our laws must be favorable to them as we know [. . .] that all women must submit to our desires, we naturally also allow them to freely express their own desires. [. . .] I say that women, having been endowed with considerably more

> violent penchants for carnal pleasure than we, will be able to give themselves over to it wholeheartedly, absolutely free of all encumbering [. . .] ties.[37]

The above quotation reveals what Lacan finds so philosophically relevant about Sade's literature – even despite the fact that it does not question our moral intuitions. To read Sade, in Lacan's view, is to do mental gymnastics.[38] Although Kant and Sade are opposed to one another on a superficial level, the sadistic universe is based upon the same criteria as those that, according to Kant, moral actions must meet.[39] Kant and Sade both reject sensuous nature as a guide for action and both insist upon universalisability as a criterion for action. Sade's writings, therefore, stretch the reader's mental capacities and demand that one rethinks the grounding premises of Kant's moral philosophy. This intellectual exercise forces Lacan to conclude that Kant did not fully consider his starting point.[40] Kant's formal ethics, after all, entails the possibility of what we intuitively consider to be evil.[41] In other words, the correct employment of Kant's fundamental law brings his ethics into a sphere where 'good' and 'evil' become confused with one another.[42] (Would Lacan's conclusion have been entirely different if he had taken into consideration Kant's second formulation of the categorical imperative?) Expressed in terms of Kant's first critique: Lacan's reading reveals that the good only ever appears to be transcendental.[43] While it might be an unavoidable tendency for practical reason to seek out the universal good, it is ultimately never found. The good is nothing but a mental representation whose material substrate is *Unbekanntes*. To summarise, the first interpretation of Lacan's famous thesis that Sade is the truth of Kant is that the latter's literature gives us a picture of what Kant never foresaw. This interpretation shows us, to the chagrin of many commentators, that we cannot read Lacan as a Kantian on the basis of 'Kant avec Sade'.[44]

III An Ancient Theme in Moral Philosophy

We can also understand Lacan's thesis that Sade is the truth of Kant in other ways. It is with this in mind that I refer to the fourth paragraph of 'Kant avec Sade' in which Lacan claims the following: 'Here

Sade is the starting point of a subversion, of which [. . .] Kant is the central point.'[45] Just before stating this thesis, Lacan refers to the relationship between the good and happiness, and how it is traditionally thought by philosophers. This shows that, for Lacan, Sade also reads against the background of a theme about which philosophers have always thought. Sade, Lacan seems to say, subverts the way in which thought is given to goodness and happiness classically, and Kant plays an important role in this subversion. Although Lacan does not explicitly explain this in his essay, there are at least two passages in which he alludes to what he may mean. In what follows, I will rely on these passages to answer the following questions: in what sense does Sade's oeuvre undermine the relationship between the good and happiness? What role does Kant play in this? In what respect is Sade Kant's truth?

Evil and the Supreme Good

Although Lacan does not refer to it himself, we can introduce his reading using Kant's text from 1792, *Die Religion innerhalb der Grenzen der bloßen Vernunft*. For my explanation it is not so much the central idea of this key text in the philosophy of religion that is important, namely that ethics ends in religion, but rather the part in which Kant thinks about evil. In this, he distinguishes four forms of evil.

The first form is radical evil. In this concept, Kant is referring not to an excessive form of evil, but to an evil that, in addition to goodness, is rooted in human nature. More specifically, he understands this form of evil as consciously giving into passions when they arise and tempt the renouncing of moral duty. Radical evil therefore does not stand for being overwhelmed by all kinds of drives and tendencies that put freedom under pressure. Rather, this form of evil is rooted in the freedom that chooses to reverse roles – which is why Kant calls this evil *perversitas* – and to let the passions take precedence over the observance of duty. *Fragilitas* is the second form of evil. This form means that the law is not followed due to the weakness of the human character. Anyone who perpetrates this evil, while endorsing the law and aiming to comply with it, remains in default of its implementation. The third form of evil, *impuritas*, means that the reason why the law is adopted is not purely moral. The law, as it stands, meets the criterion for the good, but the implementation of the law is contaminated by non-moral motives. In addition to perversity, weakness and impurity, Kant also gives a fourth form of evil, namely the devilish or diabolical. By this Kant means that one assumes maxims that are contrary to the law. The reason for this is not that passions take the upper hand. After all, this would mean that the violation is only a consequence and not a goal. Diabolical evil means that contravening moral law itself is the motive for adopting maxims that are contrary to the law. Kant, however, states that diabolical evil is impossible. After all, since man traces his freedom through the law, it is impossible for this law to be deliberately violated by man at will.[46]

Although, according to Kant, diabolical evil is an anthropological impossibility, figures regularly appear in Sade's literature that are strongly reminiscent of it. The most striking figure is the *Être-suprême-en-méchanceté*.[47] As we have already seen in the first and second chapters, this being is mentioned by Saint-Fond in *Juliette*. When Juliette and Clairwil meet him, he explains his theology to them in a grotesque exposé. The point of departure for his presentation is the observation that torture, death and rape dominate the universe. Reality is nothing but evil, which leaves no possibility unexploited. However, this evil is the result not of human inadequacy or contingent factors but of the *Être-suprême-en-méchanceté*. We read:

> When I consider the universe, I see that everywhere evil, disorder, and crime reign supreme. What conclusion does this lead to? . . . there is a God, one hand or another must have created all that I see, but he created it only for evil, he lurks only in evil.[48]

In Saint-Fond's hallucinogenic theology, the world is not a product of God's love, but is created by a deity so that he can enjoy the evil he causes on earth. Evil is therefore not the result of the weakness of the human character, or of the choice to give priority to passions over the law. According to Saint-Fond, evil is devilish in a Kantian sense because there is a Supreme Being that experiences pleasure in evil for the sake of evil itself. In other words, Saint-Fond's God enjoys torture, murder and rape precisely because they are against the law. It follows, Saint-Fond states, that God's creatures are even better off when committing evil themselves. After all, God's malice manifests itself not only in the fact that He consciously contravenes the law, but also in the fact that He addresses those who submit to the law in a compliant manner. Anyone who nevertheless wants to live a virtuous life, according to the criminal judge, will later be ruthlessly punished for it.[49]

Lacan refers to Sade's Supreme Being in the first passage to which I refer to show that we can also understand his thesis in a second way.[50] In this passage he not only mentions the *Être-suprême-en-méchanceté* but also states that Kant must exclude the existence of an evil deity.[51] What Lacan means by this is that Kant, although he indicates in his *Religionsschrift* that the existence of devilish evil is impossible, must in the first place avoid the existence of a diabolical Supreme Being. Kant may well argue that a diabolical deity *cannot* exist, but according to Lacan that deity *may not* exist for Kant. To understand the reason for this, we must briefly return to Kant's *Kritik der praktischen Vernunft*.

In the first book, 'Die Analytik der reinen praktischen Vernunft', Kant dissociates ethics from sensuous nature. According to Kant, lust and displeasure, natural strivings or happiness should not act as pointers to moral action. In the second book, 'Dialektik der reinen praktischen Vernunft', Kant states that moral law nevertheless necessarily invokes a supreme good, the *Summum Bonum*. That good, more specifically the combination of virtue and happiness, is not a ground that precedes moral intention but is presented as that in which the completion of moral action is crowned with happiness. While in his analysis Kant distinguishes between phenomenal and noumenal nature, in the second book he links virtue and happiness. According to Kant, however, the *Summum Bonum* is not attained during earthly life. The reason for this is that no finite creature is capable of perfect virtue, namely the conformity of the will with the law. This forces Kant to postulate the immortality of the soul, which enables man to reach full conformity with the law beyond finitude.[52]

It is important for what follows that virtue makes man worthy of happiness, but that virtue by itself does not guarantee happiness. Although Kant thinks happiness and virtue together as the highest good, they are, based on the distinction between phenomenal and noumenal nature, unequal. There is no 'analytical' connection, according to Kant, between virtue and happiness. Living a virtuous life does not in itself lead to happiness.[53] It is on this basis that Kant inserts the postulate of the existence of a good, trustworthy God. Such a God guarantees to the virtuous man in the afterlife the happiness he deserves on the basis of his moral actions.[54] Because Kant thinks the good and happiness together but at the same time states that we cannot deduce one from the other, he needs a God who bridges the gap between the good and happiness. It follows that Kant must exclude the existence of a Sadean *malin génie*. After all, a devilish Supreme Being that punishes the good for the sake of the good would not close the gap between the good and happiness but would widen the gap further.

The reason Kant must avoid the existence of a devilish Supreme Being indicates that Lacan understands the Sadean universe from the existence of a Supreme Being that destroys the connection between good and happiness. The destruction of this bond is shown in the first place in *Justine*. In it, the punishment of the good is the central theme on which the narrative is built. Thus, in the preface, Sade states that the intention of his novel is as follows: 'to show Virtue as his victim, to sketch an unfortunate person who ends up in one disastrous situation, the means of crime, the target of all possible wickedness.'[55] Virtue is expressed in the pious Justine. She is presented as virtue in the flesh whose fresh, flawless appearance reflects her life, which is not contaminated by vice. Everyone Justine meets, however, inflicts the most brutal violence on her: they break Justine's limbs, burn her eyelashes and pull out her nails. Justine, however, is not the object of these acts because she is committing a transgression. No, those devilish figures abuse Justine precisely because she lives perfectly in accordance with the law. Precisely because she embodies virtue, the 'missionaries' of the *Être-suprême-en-méchanceté* push her into misfortune. Justine's moral perfection therefore offers a guarantee, but it is not happiness but rather unhappiness that is ensured by the libertines. Happiness, on the other hand, is only guaranteed to those who do wrong. An example of this is the history of the life of Juliette, Justine's sister.[56]

Virtue and Happiness

In the previous section we saw that in Sade, moral virtue leads to unhappiness while in Kant a trustworthy God assures the reward of virtue with happiness in life after death. As a result, Lacan positions Kant and Sade as opposites of each other. This seems to be in contradiction with the passage from his essay that was mentioned earlier. On the one hand, Lacan states that Sade primarily undermines the classical view of the relationship between virtue and happiness. On the basis of the above, however, it appears that Sade also subverts Kant. From this we can deduce that, according to Lacan, Kant still fits with the classic ethical systems in a certain way. On the other hand, Lacan claims, in the same passage, that Kant also prepares for Sade, which means that Lacan, who sees Sade breaking with classical time, also understands Kant's ethics as modern. According to Lacan, Kant is located between classical time and Sade. What Lacan exactly means by this middle position is made clear in this passage: 'the ancient axis of ethics: it is nothing more than the selfishness of happiness. It cannot be said that any reference to it was eradicated in Kant.'[57] Kant's position in the middle has to do with the fact that, in his ethics, happiness is present – which means that he still has one foot in classical times – but that this is the case in a different way from in a traditional view of ethics – through which Kant's ethics prepare for Sade. How should we understand that?

By pointing to the fact that happiness is still present in Kant's ethics, Lacan does not mean that there is still a negative reference to happiness. What Lacan means is that, according to Kant, moral law necessarily refers to a supreme good in which true virtue and sensuous longing for happiness come together. According to Kant, good and happiness are related, and it is in this respect that his ethics are still in line with classical times. According to the classics, according to Lacan, the moral law does not run counter to natural strivings. The moral categories graft on to nature and actualise the good that is already potentially present in natural strivings. This actualisation is accompanied by happiness. From a classical perspective, happiness indicates that the development of the *causa finalis* is on the right track. Happiness accompanies becoming a good person, the actualisation of the possibility of the good.

The connection between virtue and happiness also characterises Kant's ethics. The difference between Kant and classical time, according to Lacan, has to do with the fact that, prior to Kant, it was assumed that good by itself leads to happiness. According to a classical view, the development of and the excelling in virtue are in themselves accompanied by happiness. Kant, on the other hand, must postulate a God to ensure the *Summum Bonum* because living in accordance with moral law is not in itself a guarantee of happiness. Kant's ethics may therefore still be partly classical, but it also expresses the typical modern thought that a virtuous life, in itself, does not guarantee happiness. After all, in modernity the connection between virtue and happiness is completely contingent. With the disappearance of the gods in the sky, the certainty that morality will be crowned with eternal bliss has also disappeared. Modernity is Kant without God.

It is from that perspective that we must understand Kant as a preparation for the Sadean diabolical universe. Sade's world, we have seen, may be a subversion of Kant in the sense that in that world virtue leads to misfortune, but Kant has also made Sade possible because in his ethics doing what is good does not make someone happy. The destruction of the traditional guarantee that the good in itself leads to happiness has paved the way for a new guarantee expressed in the Sadean universe, more particularly in Justine's life. The new guarantee is that anyone who lives a morally virtuous life will live in unhappiness. It is because Kant has cut through the 'analytical' bond between the good and happiness that it has become possible for the good to culminate in unhappiness. In other words, according to the second interpretation of Lacan's thesis, Sade is the truth of Kant because he is the extreme twist in the modern gap opened by Kant between the good and happiness.

IV Law and Desire

At the end of 'Kant avec Sade', Lacan refers to the film *El* from 1953 by the Spanish-Mexican director Luis Buñuel.[58] This film is about the aristocratic bachelor Francisco, who by chance meets the young girl Gloria and then marries her. During the honeymoon Francisco begins to imagine that his new wife is being chased by her ex-lover. Francisco's jealousy takes on ever greater forms and ends in the closing of Gloria's vagina.

Lacan recalls that also at the end of *La philosophie dans le boudoir* yarn and needles are used to tie the labia of Madame de Mistival together.[59] Lacan refers to this passage when he responds to a question he raised a few paragraphs earlier. He wonders whether Sade's libertinism succeeds in radically overthrowing all laws and allows the libertine to soar towards the enjoyment it promises.[60] While Sade's literature may at first glance appear to be a fabrication of a pleasure no longer bound by the law and freely available, perhaps, as Lacan wonders, the freedom of libertinism is nothing but a naive illusion, and the truth of Sade's heroes is that they too are irrevocably bound by the law. Lacan expressly states that this is indeed the case.[61] According to Lacan, this idea is depicted in the final scene of *La philosophie dans le boudoir*. The sewing up of Madame de Mistival is interpreted by Lacan as blocking access to the mother. In the end, as the scene shows, the ultimate object of desire – from Lacan's psychoanalytic background, the mother is the first representative of this – is radically forbidden and inaccessible, even in the Sadean universe.[62] Thus Lacan indicates that, although he does not formulate this explicitly anywhere, he considers Kant to be the truth of Sade. In Lacan's vocabulary: Sade illustrates how desire is subject to the law of the signifier and does not reach its real object. In Kant's terminology: the sadist does pretend to enjoy indefinitely, but in the end, he is entangled in a transcendental illusion. What the sadist enjoys is nothing more than a performance that throws a veil over the real object that ultimately remains unknown. In order to know exactly what Lacan means by this, we first have to find out what the sadist wants. Then I will show that according to Lacan beauty reveals what the final scene from *La philosophie dans le boudoir* represents, namely that Kant is the truth of the Sadean universe.

First and Second Death

In Revelation, the last book of the New Testament, it is explained that, after the descent of the new Jerusalem from heaven, the dead will rise from their graves. They will overcome their first death and enter a new life. It is, however, also possible that a few of them will be barred from entering heaven on earth. We read: 'But the fearful, and unbelieving, and the abominable, and murderers, and whoremongers, and sorcerers, and idolaters, and all liars, shall have their part in the lake which burneth with fire and brimstone: which is the second death.'[63] In short: to suffer 'second death' is to be killed once more after arising from the first, biological death.

Without referring to this passage explicitly, Lacan uses the expression 'second death' – which Sade himself does not use – to put Sade's world into perspective.[64] More specifically, Lacan feels justified in using this expression because of a passage from *Juliette* where Pope Pius VI, or Braschi, gives an account of his natural philosophy to Juliette and Clairwil, her *compagnon de route*.[65] As we have already seen more than once, the core of Pius' system lies in the fact that nature is a force that aims at the greatest possible production of new life. In order to achieve this, nature must, curiously enough, eliminate some of her creatures. The reason for this is that nature's creatures also produce life and are, for this reason, in competition with her. If nature wants to freely exercise her creative and productive power, then she must regularly destroy the life that actually exists. Nature does this, according to Pius VI, by causing wars and hunger. Nature is, therefore, both a creative and a destructive force.

More important than this for Lacan, however, is what Pius says about death: what we call 'death' is actually, from the perspective of nature, a new beginning. What nature kills only loses its current form but is then repurposed to create new life. This 'fruitful' death is the 'first death' that Lacan presupposes when he introduces 'second death'. But, the Pope tells us, the first death is ultimately not sufficient. Nature does not want to continue creating and destroying ad infinitum. Nature wants to be free of the never-ending cycle of coming and going; she wants to put an end to her creative and destructive activities. In order for this to come about, it is not enough for the sadist to simply kill the other. What nature wants from the sadist is that he faces death a second time. Indeed, this would prevent death from producing new life. This is how Sade phrases this demand:

> In order to better serve her (nature) we must be able to prevent the buried corpse from regenerating. Murder only takes the first existence from the person that we have met, we should be able to give him the second in order to be even more useful to her.[66]

Attacking the body a second time, this time as a corpse, which puts an end to the cycle of nature, is what Lacan calls 'second death'.[67]

Thus, just as in the New Testament, second death has an eschatological meaning in Lacan's Sade reading. For Lacan, however, second death is not the sinners' death, but rather the end of the cycle of rebirth. To say that the sadist aims at his victim's second death is to say that he wants to reduce him to an object that can no longer be taken up in nature's rhythm, an object that is excluded from nature's cycle of regeneration.[68]

In order to fully grasp Lacan's reading of Sade, we must examine how he translates Sade's natural philosophy into his own vocabulary. We will, therefore, turn to Lacan's seminar on the ethics of psychoanalysis. Shortly after reading the key passage from *Juliette* which states that death must be met a second time, Lacan says: 'there is somewhere – though certainly outside of the natural world – which is the beyond of that chain [of signifiers].'[69] Here, Lacan informs us about what he calls 'the chain of signifiers' and places it on the same level as nature in Sade. Arguing that Sade aims at something that is beyond 'the world of nature', where the law of destruction and creation no longer reigns, is to say that he aims at a place beyond the signifier, *au-delà* the symbolic order. What does Lacan mean by this?

Lacan explains the symbolic order as a historically developed and culture-dependent structure that gives meaning to an inherently meaningless reality. It does this by making strict distinctions in reality by way of signifiers. This is the basis, for example, for the strict distinctions between man and beast, and woman and man. This, however, does not mean that the symbolic is completely independent of natural reality. The differential structure generates meaning in reality but grafts itself onto reality according to the places that are already indicated in reality. Consider, for example, the fact that some human beings have a penis and others do not. In itself, this distinction generates no meaning. The presence or absence of a penis only acquires meaning from the perspective of the distinction between 'woman' and 'man' that is attached to this real, natural difference. According to Lacan, we must understand life on the basis of the primacy of the symbolic that creates meaning by using signifiers making absolute distinctions.

The symbolic order, however, does not only create differentiations in life; it also distinguishes between life and death. Just as in the case of the presence or absence of a penis, the distinction between life and death has no inherent meaning; life and death can be placed alongside one another without any difficulty if the symbolic order does not come between them. It is only through symbols and rituals that we separate life from death, and give any meaning to this natural distinction. This explanation reveals why Pius VI's 'fruitful' death presupposes the existence of signifiers. The Pope can only think of death in relation to life if both are not indifferent to one another, but rather distinguished by the signifier's work. Sade, therefore, does not understand nature as 'pure nature', namely, a meaningless material exchange that operates independently of the primacy of the signifier. Sade's nature is, according to Lacan, always in the grip of the symbolic. This explains the sense in which the sadist wants to go beyond the symbolic when he kills his victim for the second time. The second attack attempts to dismantle the work of the signifier that is responsible for thinking of death as a basis for life. In sum, the sadist wants to reduce its object to a stupid thing – a rotting body that disturbs the cycle of nature.[70]

Beauty and 'Between Two Deaths'

According to Lacan, the sadist is after an object that escapes the endless circle of life and death, an object that must be tortured a second time after his body has died to prevent it from ever being able to generate new life. The object of the sadist's desire is, therefore, something that is utterly useless. What is more, Lacan holds that the eschatological desire to kill the victim twice encounters a limitation. The libertines do not succeed in their project of turning their victims into stupid, meaningless things. The cause of their failure lies in the incredible beauty of their victims. How ought we to understand this? What does Lacan understand by beauty?

Shortly after Lacan addresses second death in *L'éthique de la psychanalyse*, he makes what seems to be a detour. He refers, once again, to Kant, but this time to the latter's analysis of beauty in the *Kritik der Urteilskraft*.[71] More specifically, Lacan refers to Kant's summary of aesthetic judgement, which is reflexive, according to Kant, because it only makes pronouncements about the viewer's feelings of pleasure. These feelings are disinterested. By this, Kant means that the physical presence of an object is not important for the experience of beauty. According to Kant, the viewer is not interested in possessing the object and enjoying the material benefits of his possession; instead, he is satisfied by the perception of the pure appearance of the object. In aesthetic judgement, the feeling of pleasure that one gets from observing something beautiful is related to a representation rather than a real, tangible object. In other words, the viewer separates the beautiful representation from the real object that he rejects as raw, meaningless material.

According to Lacan, we must understand the victim's beauty in this Kantian sense, namely, as a pure representation without *res extensa*. This means that the victim, like an angel or a ghost, is an appearance without substance or material weight. The Sadean universe is, therefore, not populated by physical bodies. Lacan's suggestion is that the victims are already biologically dead. Sade's world is occupied by an immaterial appearance of beauty that is freed from the dead matter of the body after the first death. After this physical death, the victims, as it were, leave their bodies behind and live on as pure, immaterial beauties. This survival suggests that the victim has not been taken up by the symbolic circle of coming and going, and that he has entered a sphere beyond the first, biological death. The body can, therefore, be destroyed, but the suffering victim lives on in the pure immaterial representation, or as a symbol, of the beautiful.[72]

Lacan then turns his attention to the fact that the beautiful in Sade is also untouchable.[73] The victims always appear picture-perfect in their coffins, no matter how cruelly they had been treated. No matter how deeply they are buried in the ground, they remain beautiful. Just like the cat and the mouse in the cartoons of Tom and Jerry, they always emerge untarnished from the debris. This indestructible beauty is the limit of the sadist's desire. It is because he is faced with a beauty that will not allow itself to be tarnished that the sadist is not prepared to attack his victim a second time. The sadist does succeed in killing his victims the first time around, but their beauty saves them from second death. The sadistic victim thus finds himself 'between two deaths'.[74] To use Lacan's vocabulary: although the victim falls out of the circle of life and death, he does not entirely escape the symbolic order because he is beautiful.[75] The fact that beauty eternally returns without a scratch is an expression of the power of the symbolic order that will not allow itself to be destroyed. The beautiful is that piece of the symbolic that the cadaver holds onto at the very moment that it is about to step out of the symbolic order. This is what prevents the body from falling into meaninglessness. Completely in line with Kant's aesthetics, Lacan, thus, states that beauty in Sade creates a distance with respect to real material. In Sade, therefore, the beautiful and the true do not fully coincide. The beautiful is the last outpost of the symbolic that hinders our ability to see the true object of sadistic desire: the stinking, rotting body.[76]

The desire to get rid of all meaning is not particular to the libertines in Sade's novels. The Marquis himself cherished this desire.[77] According to Lacan, this desire reveals itself in the famous will that Sade wrote on 30 January 1806, eight years before his death.[78] Sade's will is not just a list of his bequests; it is also a long description of how he wished to be buried.[79] Sade asks that acorns be sewn onto his gravestone so that he might disappear from our collective memory. According to Lacan, this would have been Sade's way of achieving his own second death.[80] Like his libertines, however, Sade does not succeed in dying a second time. He survived his death as a symbol. After all, the tomb presumes the activity of the symbolic order. It marks a distinction, namely between man and matter, where all other differences have already disappeared.[81] Lacan stresses, however, that Sade, even after his first death, is not able to disappear as silent, meaningless material but symbolically continues to exist.[82] His name, a primordial signifier that distinguishes him from others, lives on in the eponym of sadism; biographers such as Gilbert Lely and Jean-Jacques Pauvert describe his life extensively; in post-war France, Sade's oeuvre is extensively read by numerous leading philosophers; and in 1991 his oeuvre was included in the prestigious Bibliothèque de la Pléiade. In summary, Kant is the truth of both the sadist and the person Marquis de Sade: for both the real, meaningless thing around which their desire revolves is *ein Unbekanntes* and it is kept at bay.

V Sade and Moral Experience

In the opening paragraph of his essay 'Kant avec Sade', Lacan briefly refers to two of the three great Greek gymnasia that were located just outside the city walls of ancient Athens.[83] First of all he mentions the Akademeia, the school founded by Plato, the buildings of which were in an orchard dedicated to the demigod Akademus. Second, Lacan cites the Lykeion, which was also situated on a wooded site. There were not only several wrestling areas, a gym and a race-track, but also a covered walkway (*peripatos*) where philosophers liked to stay for hours. It was there that Aristotle founded his famous Peripatetic School.[84] Lacan also mentions Stoicism. This philosophical movement takes its name from the place where its founder, Zeno of Citium, taught its pupils, namely the colonnades (*stoa*) located on the north side of the Athenian Agora.

Lacan mentions these locations in order to remind us of the importance of concrete places in the creation of the classical ethical systems. According to him, there is also a specific place in modernity that has a special significance for moral philosophy. He is referring here not to the typical eighteenth-century salon, but to the *boudoir* to which the characters of *La philosophie dans le boudoir* withdraw.[85] Lacan places Sade's pernicious room on the same level as the forest, the walkway and the colonnade.[86] The importance of this specific place is that it recalls certain aspects of moral experience that receive little attention in modern ethical systems. Lacan thus uses Sade's literature not only to criticise Kant's ethics, but also to bring certain aspects of moral experience to light. Sade's *boudoir*, as Lacan holds, reveals a normally underexposed truth of moral experience. Although Lacan puts this thesis forward at the beginning of 'Kant avec Sade', it is not explicitly elaborated. There are, however, a few passages in which he suggests what he means.

First of all, we can recall that Lacan draws attention to some analogies between Kant and Sade. Lacan points out, however, that the two share not only apathy and the criterion of universalisability.[87] Kant also incorporates the feeling of pain into his ethics. At first glance, that seems strange. After all, Kant argues that a feeling should not function as a basis for determining morality. Nevertheless, according to Kant, there is also a positive relationship between morality and the phenomenal. This relationship is expressed in the experience of pain. Pain, according to Kant, is a positive feeling. Feeling pain indicates that the pathological nature is being eliminated as a guide to moral action. The experience of pain indicates that there is a transition from the phenomenal to the noumenal reality that is no longer guided by *das Wohl*.[88]

Also, in Sade's case, according to Lacan, pain reveals a reality beyond that of sensuous strivings. The fact that the pain does not end reveals to the victim that the sadist does not care about the fact that the victim wants to avoid pain and that he is concerned about his own well-being. That the sadist does not care about the other person's strivings means that he obeys the law, at least as Lacan formulates it. After all, we have seen that this law commands us to enjoy without limiting our enjoyment. The fear and pain of the victim should not inhibit the enjoyment of the sadist. While in everyday life people are involved in the desires of others, the sadist is required to be uninterested in the welfare of his victim. In other words, the suffering and the fact that it lasts forever show the victim that the sadist is beyond normal life and that he does not allow himself to be determined by the pathological nature of the victim.[89]

It is important for the continuation of our line of reasoning to underscore how Lacan understands the victim's attitude towards the cruel sadist. According to Lacan, this attitude is not characterised by passivity and submissiveness. The victim should not be understood as a mere, stupid object that passively undergoes the cruel actions of the sadist. In the universe of Sade, in contrast, according to Lacan, the victim is mysteriously fascinated by the sadist.[90] The victim attaches himself to and is under the spell of the apathetic sadist. In the idiosyncratic world of Sade, Lacan argues, the sadist is the one who stirs up the victim's imagination. This fascination with a figure who is not interested in the happiness and well-being of others shows that the natural strivings of the victim are eliminated. The fact that the victim has been mesmerised by the sadist, despite many sufferings, shows that the spontaneous desire for happiness, well-being or pleasure is neutralised. This also implies that one cannot explain the fascination oneself in terms of 'pleasure', 'lust' or 'happiness'. From the fact that the fascination is focused on what goes against one's own sensuous desires, it follows that this fascination does not meet a natural interest.

What is said here about the attitude of the victim also characterises certain moral issues. Take, for example, those situations in which special care, dedication or devotion is demonstrated. We cannot understand this from the point of view of the pursuit of lust, well-being, pleasure or happiness. In care and devotion, one can identify an involvement in a reality that matters and gives depth to life. However, such involvement is not a means whose value is determined by the extent to which it contributes to the realisation of a sensuous purpose. If that were to be the case, it would imply that things could be exchanged for other things that are expected to be more enjoyable. What a phenomenon like devotion shows, however, is a stubborn attachment to an object that transcends the daily circuit of interchangeable goods and therefore transcends sensuous strivings. In short, certain moral actions revolve around a reality in which a value is expressed that goes deeper than the concern for one's own well-being. This is related to the fact that a deep-rooted connection with matters with a surplus of meaning can also continue when one's own well-being is at risk. Attachment to items loaded with extra weight may be accompanied by a willingness to suffer pain and to deflect the sensuous striving for happiness, well-being or pleasure. Moreover, the absolutisation of things that do not fit in with their context can, in extreme situations, lead to one's own life being put at risk or sacrificed.

According to Lacan, moral philosophy often overlooks the fact that certain things cannot be traced back to sensuous strivings; that, in some circumstances, the striving for happiness is eliminated or even one's own life is sacrificed. To illustrate this, Lacan refers to a concrete situation from Kant's *Kritik der praktischen Vernunft*.[91] In it, Kant presents a man who claims that he cannot control his sexual desire for a woman in their encounter. The question Kant asks is whether the same man would share the bed with the woman if he was first told that he would be sentenced to death afterwards. According to Kant, the answer is easy to guess: the man will give up his sexual desire. By this Kant wants to indicate that man is able to control his passions, which, according to Kant, is a necessary condition for moral action. Lacan states, however, that Kant's example only applies to 'the ideal bourgeois', who bows his head to the law and reduces his desires when they call into question his self-preservation.[92] What Lacan means is that Kant overlooks the fact that the man might consider a wild but deadly night with the woman, not because he cannot control his passions but because she embodies a value that weighs more heavily than his self-preservation. Kant forgets that some aspects of moral experience cannot be understood from the reason its law imposes. Certain moral situations must be understood from the point of view of the weight of a heteronomous thing that makes its demands and suspends sensuous desires. Ethics, as Lacan reminds us, through the cruel *tableaux* of Sade's literature, revolves around an attachment to an object that gives weight to life and that is not given up for the sake of loss of lust or one's survival.[93]

This aspect of moral experience is recalled by the victim's attitude towards the sadist. Lacan not only discusses the fascination of the victim with the sadist, but also maps out the position of the sadist. To this end, he invokes theological concepts and religious metaphors. He indicates, among other things, that we must understand the sadist as a fetish.[94] In this context, Lacan refers to the first, anthropological meaning of the term 'fetish,' which originally refers to an object that is worshipped by African peoples. This worship does not take place on the basis of an objective characteristic. Any material object can be the object of worship. The surplus of meaning is derived from the fact that the fetish is an embodiment of the deity: it is a cult object in which divine power is incarnated. However, it does not follow from this that the fetish and the divine are interchangeable. Although the divinity expresses itself in a concrete, tangible thing and is closely attached to it, the divine does not fully become one with the material substrate into which it expresses itself.

The reason why, according to Lacan, we should consider the sadist as a fetish is that he does not participate in ordinary interpersonal life. The sadist, according to Lacan, is absorbed in a divine atmosphere. The cruel, apathetic sadist is completely imbued with a deity, namely the *Être-suprême-en-méchanceté,* which has descended and is expressing himself in the sadist. Nevertheless, Lacan asserts, the sadist and the Supreme Being do not coincide totally. While the sadist may be an expression of diabolical evil, he is only an instrument or an extension whose use is served by the deity, and with which the deity does not coincide entirely. What Lacan wants to make clear by means of the fetish is that the sadist moves between the profane, immanent life on the one hand and the divine, transcendental life on the other.[95] In the sense that the sadist is on a borderline, he is, according to Lacan, comparable to the voices that the psychotic person hears.[96] Although the voice is present in the psychotic person and can only be heard by him, it seems to come from a place that is alien to the life of that person. Another 'amboceptive' object to which Lacan returns several times elsewhere is the gaze.[97] Just like the voice, the sadist and the fetish, the gaze is situated in an intermediate area, namely on the edge of the visible and invisible. Although the gaze is inseparably bound to a material substrate, namely the eye, and appears in it to another person, it cannot be precisely determined and located in its carrier.

The fact that the sadist finds himself between the ordinary and the divine life reminds us that moral action too must be thought of from a relationship of tension. Lacan has two aspects in mind in this respect, among others.

First, contrary to Kant, Lacan argues that it is not reason but a phenomenal object that makes up the weight of moral experience, which does not mean that that object conforms to natural strivings. After all, moral experience reveals an attachment to an object that resists the changing demands of the pleasure principle. In other words, Lacan does follow Kant insofar as he does not want to reduce ethics to sensuous strivings, but he breaks with Kant because that does not mean that any object must be excluded from moral reality and that ethics must be thought of from the point of view of reason. However, the fact that moral experience revolves around things that transcend sensuous strivings does not imply that the value of those things can be precisely described. The things that are laden with an extra weight derive their dignity from a reality on the other side of the phenomenal whose history is difficult to determine. Matters that give life power and substance are often the expression of a past that continues to have an effect on the present through chance and unspecified paths, and that do not adapt our desires. In short, the fact that something is dear to someone does not mean that this special attachment can be explained. Can't we catch here a glimpse of a postmodern thinking about ethics?

Second, according to Lacan, the things that are separated from the whole of interchangeable goods derive their special value not from themselves but from a reality beyond the phenomenal. It cannot be deduced from this, however, that moral action is aimed at a conceptual, abstract reality. On the contrary, this action revolves in the first place around the concrete and particular in which this meaningful reality, which is difficult to trace, expresses itself. This means that what gives things a surplus of meaning is inextricably bound to 'dumb', material objects that have no meaning of their own. Consequently, the possibility of a loss of meaning is intrinsically linked to the structure of meaning. Since the meaningful is linked directly to the meaningless, it is always possible that the special value disappears and that what is now appealing no longer has any power over time any more.

VI Conclusion

Although Lacan later returned to the oeuvre of Marquis de Sade in other contexts, it was especially at the end of the 1950s and the beginning of the 1960s that Lacan, in the wake of his contemporaries, read Sade intensively. During this period, his interpretation moved against the background of his interest in ethics, which is also the theme of his famous seventh seminar. This reading shows that Lacan's interest in Sade was twofold. On the one hand, he read Sade's literature as an expression of one of his core ideas – namely, that ethics circulates around a heteronomous object that falls out of the symbolic order – and used Sade to draw attention to some underexposed aspects of moral experience. On the other hand, according to Lacan, Sade's work reflects an age-old moral and philosophical theme of which Sade is the radical offshoot. In this context, Lacan also understood the erotic passages as an illustration of the cruel consequences of Kant's moral philosophy.

5[1]

Sadism as Formalism

I Introduction

In an interview from 1973 Barthes said: 'If you will, there are certainly three writers who count a lot in my life, I can almost say daily, to the extent that I read them a little in the evening, not all the time, but I always come back to them a little like that. There's Sade, obviously, there's Flaubert and there's Proust.'[2] Barthes expressed his interest in Sade for the first time in 1954 in a study on the French historian Jules Michelet and in two discussions on the performance of *Dom Juan*.[3] In these texts, Barthes mentions Sade only incidentally. It is only in the next decade that he began to study Sade more extensively, beginning with 'La métaphore de l'œuil', in which Barthes relates Sade to Bataille.[4] The first text in which he focuses exclusively on the Sadean universe was published in 1967 as 'L'arbre du crime' in the avant-garde literary magazine *Tel Quel*, for which Barthes wrote more than one contribution.[5] This was republished along with two other essays – one about the French utopian socialist Charles Fourier and another about the Spanish theologian Ignatius of Loyola – in the volume titled *Sade, Fourier, Loyola*.[6] In addition to those three essays, the volume also contains *Sade [2]*, a text that, just like Barthes' *Fragments d'un discours amoureux*, consists of text fragments that seem at first sight to be unrelated to each other.[7]

According to the Barthes scholar Philippe Roger, it was during the 1950s that Barthes came under the influence of the Sade interpretations of other leading philosophers. Roger mentions, among others, Klossowski and Bataille.[8] However, it was mainly Simone de Beauvoir's existentialist reading of Sade that left its traces in Barthes' first interpretations of Sade. Nonetheless, this existentialist element has completely vanished by the time of 'L'arbre du crime' in 1967. In this text, the general tone of Barthes' reading changes. His emphasis becomes rather more linguistic than existentialist. The reason for this is his turn in the 1960s to structuralist linguistics, which from that time on formed the basis for his literary criticism and analysis. In this chapter, three issues that are central to Barthes' linguistic interpretation will be highlighted, and it will be shown how they oppose three popular views of sadism and the literary oeuvre of Sade.

First of all, Barthes opposes a moralistic reading, which sees Sade's oeuvre as a danger to culture because of its radical opposition to a generally accepted view of the good.[9] This reading, which has often been used as a pretext for banning the publication of Sade's work, implies that Sade's texts should be assessed primarily in terms of their content. According to Barthes, however, this is not the best way of reading Sade. His literature should not be understood in the first place as the expression of a content. Certainly, there are places in Sade's oeuvre where the content is still central, but in many other places, the focus has nothing to do with the expression of content. According to Barthes, this is indicated by Sade's use of repetition and his weaving together of a wide variety of literary genres, among other things. In the second section I illustrate some of these aspects, and I explain how they support Barthes' reading of Sade. Finally, based on this, I show that Barthes sees Sade's literature as the early precursor of what he calls the death of the author.

Secondly, Barthes opposes the reading that sees sexuality in Sade as a radicalisation of our more common sexuality. According to that reading, the overwhelming sexual pleasure of the libertine constitutes an elevation of normal sexual pleasure. So too, the infliction and suffering of pain are understood as heightened extensions of a more ordinary pleasure. The cruelty of Sade is understood as an exaggeration of the violence that is always a part of sexuality. However, according to Barthes, the difference between Sadean sexuality and normal sexuality is not a graduated, quantitative difference. Between them, there is a deep gap. In Sade's sexuality a new language is expressed that transgresses the codes to which love life normally adheres. Sade is the founder of a language.[10] According to Barthes, this also leads to a totally different form of enjoyment. In the third part, I first explain in what sense Sade can be said to have established a new erotic language. Based upon this, I elucidate Barthes' understanding of the enjoyment of the libertine.

Thirdly, Barthes opposes a certain common-sense view of Sade, which holds that the Sadean universe is lawlessness and unruly. Against this reading, Barthes emphasises that Sadean society is based on a tight order and perfect regulation. Every resident must strictly follow the well-defined daily format, and the hierarchical structure must be maintained at all costs. This image is not consistent with the popular belief that in libertinism the natural drives free themselves from the denominational power of society. In the fourth part of the chapter, therefore, I highlight Barthes' interpretation of Sade's society and demonstrate a surprising agreement between Sade's literature (second part), eroticism (third part) and society (fourth part).

II A Writer on the Border

In 'Flaubert et la phrase' from 1968, Barthes claims that a new form of literature was created by writers like Flaubert and Mallarmé.[11] He further claims that the first traces of this can already be discovered in Sade's literature. At the same time, he suggests that Sade's prose is still in part classically inspired. Thus, according to Barthes, Sade is a border case.[12] His literature stands at a pivotal crossroads in the long history of literature. In what follows, I will first show why Barthes sees Sade as belonging, at least in part, to the classical tradition. Then I indicate in what sense Sade can also be said to be an early precursor of modern literature. On this basis, I conclude that Sade, according to Barthes, initiates the so called 'death of the author'.

Traditional Literature

According to Barthes, there are two forms of classical literature.[13] While he claims that Sade belongs to the classical tradition, Barthes does not specify to which of the two forms he belongs. What are these two forms? And where in Sade's oeuvre do we find them?[14]

To indicate the first form, I turn to Sade's novel *Justine*, where we find the following episode.[15] When the merchant Saint-Florent leaves Justine alone in a forest, she hears two men making love behind a bush. The two men, Count Bressac and his servant Jasmin, abduct Justine and bring her to the castle belonging to Bressac's mother, who then employs her as a maid. Despite having been taken to the castle against her will, Justine serves Bressac's mother very calmly and without resistance. Bressac himself embodies a generation of young men who are bored and who no longer take pleasure in maintaining the social position of the family or in serving the king. In addition, he accuses his mother of keeping him away from the city life of Paris and for taking over his financial resources. Therefore, he asks Justine to help him poison his mother. The virtuous young lady refuses to cooperate and informs the female Marquis about her son's cruel plans. It doesn't help, however, because Bressac eventually succeeds in killing his mother. The episode ends in the woods, where Bressac and Jasmin, as a punishment for her betrayal, torture Justine.[16]

This episode indicates that the form of *Justine* is in line with one aspect of the classical literary tradition.[17] This is evidenced by the sudden appearance of the Count, who presents his plan to kill his mother, and also by the ending of the book in which the mother dies. Indeed, the conventional construction of a novel, according to Barthes, begins with a presentation of the protagonist and a description of the context in which the story takes place. Then, at some point and often unexpectedly, one or more characters are introduced that influence the further course of the narrative. They express a wish that shows some aim or purpose that they intend to carry out in the future. The bulk of the story occurs between the expression of the wish and the moment the wish is fulfilled. In this way, the story recalls the image of an upward stepping motion.[18] The story consists of a chronological sequence of episodes that build on each other. Each event is both a continuation of the foregoing and a carrier of new elements that contribute to the moment when the narrative finds completion. That moment, which is the culmination of the sequence of events, confers an internal coherence on the narrative. What is most important to note is that it is only from this internal coherence that the episodes derive their meaning. An episode, therefore, has no meaning in itself; it obtains meaning from its inclusion in a larger, integrated whole. In short, the first form of traditional literature is characterised by a structure that creates meaning. This meaning arises because the different parts go together in a harmonious whole.[19] It is that aspect that we find in the episode from *Justine.*

In addition, there is another form of classical literature that one can perceive in Sade. This is evident from, for example, 'L'auteur des Crimes de l'Amour à Villeterque, folliculaire', a letter written by Sade to the French literary critic Alexandre-Louis de Villeterque in 1801.[20] This letter is a response to Villeterque's review of Sade's *Les crimes de l'amour.* In this review, Villeterque states that Sade's novel is immoral and completely unworthy of the name of literature. Sade replies that this criticism shows that Villeterque did not understand the idea of his volume properly. After all, it is not evil, but rather good that takes centre stage. The crimes are ultimately always overcome by the power of the good. To show this, Sade points to the novel *Faxelange ou les torts de l'ambition.*[21] There we see the young Faxelange express a desire to marry Goé, while her parents demand that she marries the rich American Franlo. Faxelange obeys their will, and Franlo takes her on a journey. The destination is not America, as was promised, but a castle in a forest, where Franlo exposes Faxelange to the most horrible crimes. The novel ends with the rescue of Faxelange by Goé. The point of the novel, according to Sade, is that good always overcomes evil.[22] This shows that some of Sade's novels have an underlying message or idea. It is precisely in this sense that Sade's prose still belongs to the classical tradition. Indeed, certain forms of classical literature, such as the *roman à these,* are supported by a central message or an idea on which the story hangs. In summary, Sade's literature belongs to the classical tradition not only because certain episodes show a purposeful narrative structure, but also because some of his novels are structured by a message or idea.

Modern Literature

As noted before, Sade also already belongs to modern literature, according to Barthes.[23] The reason for this is, among other things, that Sade's literature does not produce meaning. The absence of meaning, according to Barthes, is a result of countless repetitions.[24] How should we understand this?[25]

In some novels, the solid space inside of a house functions as the fixed framework in which the monotonous life of the main character takes place. In other novels, however, rooms not only have a static function, but often also play a dynamic role. In this case, they act as passages that allow for the movement of characters. To this purpose the country road, sea or air also lend themselves well. The dynamic space acts as a transition between two opposing spaces. The country road, for example, connects the countryside and the city in many realistic novels. That transition from one space to another is an expression of the desire to give life a completely new turn. The main character gives up his life as a poor farmer and travels to the city in the hopes of gaining great wealth, or the hero of the story goes out into the wide world to come to repentance or wisdom, as in the *Bildungsroman*. From that point of view, the dynamic space responds to the structure of a classic purposeful narrative.

Barthes points out that Sade's characters often move from one region to another.[26] For example, the meeting between the sisters Justine and Juliette is preceded by a whole travel history, which goes as follows. The two meet for the first time after more than fifteen years in Montargis, located in the Loire region. Juliette is resting in a hostel with her husband, because they are too tired to return to their estate, when they see a handcuffed girl stepping out of a courtyard. They both go outside, driven by curiosity, and the prisoner turns out to be Juliette's sister Justine. She tells Juliette her life story from the moment their paths separated following the death of their parents.[27] She relates her fateful fifteen-year journey that stretches diagonally across France.[28] The journey takes her through the woods of Chantilly and Luzarches, both north of Paris, stops in a Benedictine monastery near Auxerre, and continues across Dijon to the province of Dauphiné. There, Justine stops in Lyon and Vienne, and also in Grenoble, where she intends to start a new life for herself. However, she is kidnapped by Dubois and later, at Lyon, arrested by six men. Those riders stop in Montargis, en route to Paris where they are heading to have Justine's condemnation confirmed, and it is there that she is reunited with her sister.

On this basis, one might think that Sade's prose is an example of the picaresque novel, an epic genre from the late sixteenth century and the beginning of the seventeenth century that is characterised by a series of adventures that connect the protagonist with all possible circles.[29] As a result, this kind of novel offers a varied look at the living habits and customs of a culture. However, according to Barthes, though Sade describes an extended journey, he is not writing in the picaresque genre. This is because the characters in a picaresque novel constantly experience new adventures, while Sade, on the other hand, describes only one event.[30] Barthes means that, while Sade constantly changes the context and characters, every episode is nothing but a repetition of the same. Wherever Justine is – Auxerre, Lyon or Grenoble – and whomever she meets – an earl, monk or schoolmaster – she always undergoes the same fate. In particular, a three-part structure is repeated again and again.[31]

In a first phase, a philosophical discourse on nature justifies the criminal acts. For example, Dubois, with whom Justine escapes from prison in Paris, holds that, in nature, evil is as necessary as good. Then, in a second phase, the libertine adds his deeds to the word. Coeur-de-fer, for example, fascinated by Dubois' speech, undresses Justine and rapes her. Finally, the episode often ends with either the departure of the libertine or the escape of the victim. However, the flight path travelled is not a dynamic space. It does not carry the traces of a new life, but only leads to a similar episode. Sade's literature is the continuous repetition of the same scene. That repetitive rhythm indicates that the episodes do not build on each other and do not work towards a goal. In the Sadean universe, the teleological structure based on a sequence of unique scenarios does not take a central place. Instead, there is a serial alignment of the same. That means, according to Barthes, that in Sade no meaning can arise.[32] The aimless repetition of the same precludes the maturation of a history or the inclusion of the parts in a coherent whole. One can therefore say that, unlike classical literature, Sade's prose does not recall the image of an upward movement, but that of a flat and broken line or a slow-moving stream.

Barthes draws attention not only to repetition but also to another aspect of Sade's literature. He notes that, as a reader of Sade, he is aware of the food that the libertines eat.[33] For example, we know that during the afternoon the libertines, on the first day of their stay in the castle of Silling, drink a lot of wine, eat meat, and drink madeira as dessert.[34] Not only is food central in Sade's literature, it is present in prodigious quantities. When the libertines move up to the table, their meal is not limited to an appetiser, a main course and a dessert.

A huge variety of food and drink is consumed. For example, Justine's meal – when she eats with a Countess called Gernande – includes two soups, five appetisers, eight dishes of meat, six kinds of wine and four kinds of liquorice.[35] Sade's menus are, in other words, exuberantly filled catalogues of food. The libertines use every opportunity to expand their food collection.

Although Barthes is the only post-war Sade interpreter who seems to notice the food details in Sade, he does not really go into them in any depth.[36] Nevertheless, it is and remains striking that Sade mentions the food. As with so many details of daily life, details regarding food are mostly excluded from the narrative, because they usually do not contribute to the progress of the story. If meals are discussed, according to Barthes in 'L'effet de réel' from 1968, the mention of details is normally intended merely to fill the gaps between the events that contribute to the structure of the narrative.[37] In the classic novel, food remains in the background and falls between the wrinkles of the narrative. However, in Sade's prose, it is clear that such details are not filling gaps. Since there is no purposeful narrative structure in Sade to begin with, one cannot talk about filling narrative gaps. In other words, the baroque lushness of insignificant details is an expression of the absence of a targeted action logic; the abundant presence of details emphasises that Sade's stories do not create meaning. The reason for this is that details in themselves are completely meaningless. Even when classical authors mention details, those details are in relation to the whole nothing but an excess. Details are, generally speaking, insignificant things without predictive or informative value. If, as is the case with Sade, the whole disappears and the nonsensical details come to the forefront, then this accentuates the fact that the literature is not presenting us with the unfolding of a history.

According to Barthes, in Sade's literature – where no history is ripening and the various episodes are repeated continually – it is not the unity but the becoming independent of the part in relation to the whole that takes a central place. In short, Sade evokes meaninglessness.[38] His literature is a reflection of 'a zero degree of meaning'.[39] It is, among other things, based upon this fact that Barthes considers Sade as a modern writer. In addition, he also states that Sade's literature is not supported by an underlying message or idea, as was the case with traditional literature. Although Bathes does not specify in what sense this is the case, he points both to the long dissertations and to the plurality of literary genres contained in Sade's texts.[40] For Barthes, these indicate that Sade's literature is not primarily based upon the communication of a message or idea. In what follows, we will take a closer look at these two aspects and explain their relation to Barthes' claim that content is only of secondary importance to Sade.

With regard to the first aspect – the presence of long dissertations – I return to the previously mentioned episode from *Justine*. When Bressac frees Justine from the forest where she has been left by Saint-Florent, he tells her the cruel deeds he expects her to do. These do not match Justine's expectations. After all, she has led a pious life, and so she hopes to be able to convince the Count of this. She states:

> Sometimes I sought refuge in religion; almost always I found comfort in it and tried to convey her refreshment to the soul of this wicked creature [. . .] but the Count did not let me use such weapons for long.[41]

Bressac responds to Justine's religiously inspired way of life and tries to convince her of the lies and true motives of the Christian faith. He asks the rhetorical question: 'So, according to these views, what are religions other than a bridle with which the strongest wanted to keep the weakest in power out of despondency?'[42] Further, he insults 'the leper Jew, born of a slut and a soldier'.[43] Although Bressac indicates that he wants to enter into dialogue with Justine and urges her to interrupt him, she never gets the chance to answer. Bressac's talk is a radical monologue and seems to be driven by rage. The unstoppable rhythm on which his speech thrives puts Justine's aside. Bressac cannot stop. He combines sentences at a high pace, repeats the main element of his exposition to the point of boredom and constantly adds new examples. The result is a long discourse that almost explodes due to the repetitions. As a result, Bressac's talk overpasses its goal. What attracts attention is indeed not the deception of which he accuses Christianity, but the continuous addition of the same elements to his blasphemous exposition. The expansion of his speech pushes the atheist message into the background. Although that message seems to be central, the weight of the monologue is elsewhere. In Sade's philosophical passages, in other words, the text is not subject to an idea, but characterised by a prolonged expulsion without any purpose.

In addition to the long philosophical speculations, Sade's literature is also characterised by the wide variety of genres that are placed next to each other. To illustrate this, we can go back to *La philosophie dans le boudoir*. At the beginning of this novel, Madame de Saint-Ange tells her brother Le Chevalier that they will be accompanied by a girl in the next two days. That girl is the fifteen-year-old Eugénie whom she had met a year earlier in a nearby monastery. When her brother asks for the reason for that unexpected visit, she answers: 'I will spend most of the time educating this young creature. Dolmancé and I will print in that beautiful little head all the principles of the most unbridled frivolity.'[44] The rest of the book takes place in a lush salon where Eugénie learns the secrets of sexuality. The didactic explanations are interspersed with erotic and criminal scenes. Sade also adds historical data, anthropological facts, travel stories, lyrical desertions, descriptions of nature and intrigues. Barthes emphasises that Sade's literature is characterised by the juxtaposition of diverse genres that usually do not coincide. That combination of genres, however, makes it impossible to read Sade in a hermeneutical way.[45] Due to the enormous quantity of genres, it becomes impossible to detect one central idea or message in the book. In Sade's literature, there is no underlying point that holds the book together or unifies it. Sade's literature is primarily a heteroclite mix of different genres that cannot be traced back to a centre.

The Death of the Author

Above, we have seen that Barthes distinguishes two forms of classical literature. The first form is characterised by the sequence of episodes that are meaningless in themselves but gain meaning from being incorporated into a harmonious whole. In the second form, the text is carried by an underlying message or idea. In spite of the fact that Barthes distinguishes these two forms of literature, the two have at least four characteristics in common.

First of all, both are characterised by the primacy of content. The key is the production of meaning and the presentation of a message or idea. Secondly, the content which is expressed in the text can also be disconnected from the text. As a result, the reader's attention is taken away from the text itself. This means that because of the emphasis on content, the reader does not consider the rhythm, style, language, etc. Thirdly, both are based on the difference between content and form. They rely on the distinction between what is expressed and the way in which the text is organised. This distinction means that what is expressed and the organisation of the text are not assigned the same value. The form is just a means or instrument for delivering the message. Fourthly, the literary critics of both the first and the second form of classical literature emphasise the author of the text. The emphasis on the author derives directly from the fact that a certain content is always expressed in classical literature. The fact that a text expresses a content raises spontaneously the thought of an author who brings the content into being. When a narrative produces meaning, it naturally leads us to the mind of the writer responsible for shaping the various components in such a way that they form a harmonious composition. The classical novel leads to an author who, through the text, wants to convey a certain message or idea to the reader.

The four similarities of the two classical literary forms contrast with the modern aspects of Sade's oeuvre. According to Barthes, in Sade's literature, at least in some parts, the distinction between the content and the form disappears. These places do not work out any formal principles that allow a content to appear in the text. Unlike with the reading of classical literature, therefore, the reader's attention is focused not on a content that shines through the text but on the text itself. Reading Sade is thus not accompanied by the disclosure of a content from the depth of the text. The repetitive rhythm of Sade's paragraphs, the expansion of passages, and the mix of diverse genres both distorts the search for a content that lies behind the text and directs the attention of the reader to the text itself. Sade's literature shows the text as text.[46]

This interpretation of literature, here applied to Sade, also returns in 'La mort de l'auteur' of 1968. In that well-known essay, Barthes refers mainly to Mallarmé, who is, according to Barthes, one of the first modern writers, and to the experimental literature of avant-garde authors such as Philippe Sollers and Pierre Guyotat, who belong to the movement of *nouveaux romanciers*.[47] According to Barthes, those writers share with each other, and with Sade, an approach to literature that does not express content. In this thesis he associates the proposition, as the title already indicates, that this modern form of literature marks the death of the author. Barthes means that modern literary texts seem to come into existence without the intervention of an author. Since they do not express content, the reference to a point outside of the text from which content is bestowed on the text also disappears. The text comes to refer only to itself and seems to originate from nothing but itself.[48] Although Barthes does not explicitly refer to Sade in 'La mort de l'auteur', his Sade reading must be understood against the background of the theme of the death of the author.[49] According to Barthes – the similarities between his Sade interpretation and 'La mort de l'auteur' indicate this – Sade's oeuvre is one of the first forms of modern literature announcing the death of the author.[50] In Sade's literature, one can perceive the first traces of the autonomy of the text that is not supported by a subject in the sense of an author, which implies that Barthes also interprets Sade as a decentred subject.[51]

III Sade's Erotic Scenes

Besides the literary characteristics of Sade's oeuvre, Barthes also explores the erotic *tableaux vivants*. In particular, he states that the scenes operationalise a new erotic language. Sade is not a pornographer, Barthes holds, but a language founder and a grammarian of pornography.[52] In what follows, I explain what Barthes means by that, and conclude that we should not understand Sade's eroticism in terms of the notion of transgression. Finally, I explain what it means to say that the enjoyment of the libertine is empty.

Pornography and Grammatics

Les 120 journées de Sodome, just like the *Decameron* of Giovanni Boccaccio, is a 'frame story', in the sense that the book is the framework for many other stories.[53] In Sade's book, four old women tell erotic and scandalous stories every evening over the period of a month. In December, it is Champville's turn. Barthes twice quotes the passage in which Champville is interrupted by an anecdote from the Duc de Blangis.[54] This passage, on which my explanation of Barthes' interpretation of the erotic scenes is based, goes as follows:

> The Duc then told [. . .] that he had known a man who had fucked three children he had conceived with his mother. One of the daughters was married to his son, so that the man in fact fucked his sister, his daughter and his daughter-in-law. He forced the son to fuck his sister and his mother-in-law.[55]

One could then conclude that the libertine is primarily interested in the deliberate violation of the incest prohibition. However, following Barthes' interpretation, the transgression of the prohibition in the cited passage is not central. This conclusion is based upon two arguments. In order to find them out, we must first look at Barthes' interpretation of Sade's eroticism.[56]

First of all, let's go back to *La philosophie dans le boudoir*. In the final scene of that book – which Lacan also focuses on, as we have seen in the previous chapter – Madame de Mistival wants to remove her daughter Eugénie from the escort of Dolmancé and Madame de Saint-Ange. Eugénie, however, refuses to join her mother. The mother reacts with shock to this resistance and is surprised that she cannot apply her rights to her daughter. Dolmancé helps Eugénie and answers Madame de Mistival, saying that the relationship between parent and child does not have a real foundation. Consequently, according to Dolmancé, the parent has no rights and the child no obligations:

> Learn from me, Madam, that there is nothing more imaginary than the feelings parents have for their children [. . .]. And you, children, who from now on, if possible, will be even more redeemed from the respect for your parents that is truly based on a chimera, are convinced that you too owe nothing to the people whose blood gave you life.[57]

That passage indicates that Sade breaks with ordinary life. Normally, on the basis of a blood relationship, people have a surplus of meaning that separates them from the daily impersonal circuit. That means, for example, that I have more interest in my brother than in the activities of my neighbour. In Sade, however, sharing a blood bond has no weight and family members have no more meaning than coincidental passers-by. And not only is there no distinction between family members and non-family members, with Sade there is no one who has a special meaning. Thus, the horror of Sade's world is not just about the many crimes; it is also about the fact that no one transcends interpersonal life. The Sadean universe is the destruction of a world of depth, in which things have differing weight; it evokes a flat reality without dimension. Based on this, Barthes describes the participants in the scenes as 'units,' stupid entities without particular significance.[58]

Deleting mutual differences in this way entails that the incest prohibition has no effective power. But that does not mean, Barthes emphasises, that the erotic scenes equal unrestrained liberty Rather, the opposite is the case. Sade's eroticism is characterised by the central role of several rules that require strict obedience.[59] This requirement echoes in the passage in which Madame de Saint-Ange talks to Dolmancé and Eugénie before entering the scene: 'I pray to you, let this orgy be well organised; even in the midst of rapture and awe, it is necessary that we are concentrated.'[60] In particular, the scenes are characterised by two rules that each break into two parts.[61]

The first rule implies that in each new scene the characters should change both object and role. By way of illustration, we can re-appeal to *La philosophie dans le boudoir*. After Eugénie has been deflowered by Dolmancé, she wants him to take her again. Dolmancé, however, refuses: 'Let's change, because I cannot hold it [the position] . . . Your back, Madame [Madame de Saint-Ange], I beg you . . . Here I have less trouble . . . My cock is so in it! But this beautiful anus is no less delightful, Madame!'[62] Dolmancé does not take Eugénie again; he instead takes Madame de Saint-Ange. In doing so, he meets the rule that requires the libertine to take another victim in every new scene. That rule also returns in *Les 120 journées de Sodome*: 'As in the case of animals, there will be a change of partner, a mix.'[63] Sade's eroticism, thus, always involves the repetition of the same treatment of a constantly varying object. However, the libertine must not only change his objects, but must also undergo – which is the second part of the first rule – in another scene what he first did with someone else. Duclos, the first narrator of *Les 120 journées de Sodome*, relates the following event: 'Immediately after he had closed the door he wanted to kiss my behind. I offered it to him and, and after sucking my anus three times, he loosened his pants and asked me to do to him what he had just done to me.'[64] The second rule requires the libertine to aim at achieving what Barthes calls 'the total figure'. This means first of all that every body part of every participant must be treated or play a role in the scene. An example of this is the following passage from *Les 120 journées de Sodome*:

> He is among six girls. One stabs him with a sting, the other squeezes him, the third burns him, the fourth bites him, the fifth scratches him [. . .]. Everything happens interchangeably without sparing any spot of his.[65]

In addition, participants will be asked to form a group in which everyone is in contact and acts simultaneously. The following scene meets this requirement:

> He fucks a girl's mouth after he had shat into her mouth. A second girl is above the first and pushes the head of the first between her thighs. A third girl is shitting on the face of the second. He himself fucks his shit in the mouth of the first and eats the shit of the third off the face of the second.[66]

In summary, the second rule implies that all body parts and all participants, or units, are involved in the scene. In this context Barthes repeatedly notes that it is impossible actually to perform Sade's total figures.[67] The reason for this is not so much that the actions exceed our moral limits. The impossibility has to do with the physical boundaries confronting the second rule. The combinations of characters in a scene and the bizarre constellations associated with that scene would only be possible for an acrobat; they transcend normal physical possibilities. In short, the scenes do not mimic reality. In this sense, the sketched figures are in line with non-figurative art.

From the foregoing it has become clear that the *tableaux vivants* are composed of two things: units on the one hand, namely the characters without particular meaning, and two specific rules on the other. Both things, according to Barthes, indicate that Sade is the founder of a new erotic language consisting of 'erotemes', namely the units, and 'pornogrammatic' rules. It is this language that is at work on the erotic scene.[68] In other words, the erotic scenes are the operationalisation of a new erotic language. They are the result of the continuous application of two grammatical rules and the continuous recombination of 'erotemes'.[69] Thus, according to Barthes, Sade's literature is characterised not only by the difference between theory and practice, speech and picture, but also by the fact that the scene itself has to be read as a text.[70] In other words, Sade's literature is more than a frame story, namely a triple narrative. The book is the framing of stories describing scenes that should be understood as a combination of 'erotemes' and 'figure-sentences'.

The fact that eroticism in Sade is an operationalisation of a language is accentuated in *Les 120 journées de Sodome*. In that book, the four founders of the libertine society gather together with their slaves in a semi-circular meeting room each evening. In the arc-shaped section are four glass niches with a couch in the middle for each of the four libertines. The naked victims are in the middle on stairs leading to an elevated platform with a throne lined with black velvet carpets and golden fringes. This throne is intended for the four *narratrices* filling the evening with stories.[71] The libertines interrupt these stories continuously. They mimic the episodes, and their practices closely follow the narratives. The central and elevated position of the embroidered throne does not symbolise the primacy of the erotic text about practice, namely the fact that the libertines perfectly mimic the stories. No, the throne highlights in the first place what is said in those narratives, namely that the described scenes, which are converted by the libertines into practice, should themselves be read as text fragments.

This interpretation sheds new light on the scenes from Sade's literature, and also on the passage from *Les 120 journées de Sodome* with which I introduced Barthes' lecture above. Therein it is said that Duc de Blangis knew a man who had sexual relations with his relatives. From the finding that the libertine has sexual relations with relatives, one could deduce that he is trying to break the law. The violation of the incest prohibition implies, one might think, that transgression of that law is also the purpose of his sexual activity.

Barthes' interpretation, however, leads us to the conclusion that we should not understand Sade's eroticism from the notion of transgression. This conclusion is based on two arguments.[72]

First of all, the Sadean universe is characterised by the fact that family ties have no weight and that therefore the incest prohibition has no meaning. Since the law does not obtain, it cannot be said that the libertine is trying to break the law. If one speaks of the libertine as violating the incest prohibition, one speaks from a standpoint outside of Sade's universe. From the perspective of the sadist, the incest prohibition has no power and thus its transgression cannot be a goal.

Secondly, I have shown that Barthes understands Sade's eroticism as the continuous application of strict rules to units. For example, Barthes understands the fact that the composition of the erotic figures always changes as an answer to the first rule requiring that the characters change their role at each new scene. This means that the sexual contact between what from the outsider's perspective are referred to as 'relatives' is not a goal but a side effect of something else. From the fact that the libertine on the scene first takes his 'wife' and then his 'sister' it does not follow that he intentionally aims at the transgression of the incest ban. Transgression in Sade is not a consequence of the 'pornogrammatic' rule that demands that victims be continuously exchanged.

Enjoyment Without Content

Earlier in this chapter, we have seen that Barthes does not understand eroticism in Sade as transgression, and that, consequently, he does not see enjoyment as an enjoyment of the transgression. However, Barthes does not then explain how we should understand enjoyment in Sade. Nonetheless, he suggests at various places that the enjoyment of the libertine is an empty pleasure.[73] In order to understand what Barthes has in mind with this suggestion, we must first take a short detour, starting with the cited passage in which de Blangis addresses his friend's sexual escapades.

If that passage were to be put in a scene without adding any further comments, it would probably cause little fuss. Some would no doubt be indignant about the sexually dissolute life of the Duc's friend. However, most would feel emotions of horror or disgust when it is reported that the libertine's partners are relatives. These emotions do not come into being spontaneously; they only arise upon discovering that the persons belong to the same family. That shows, according to Barthes, that emotions like horror and disgust are not in line with our nature and do not express spontaneous inclinations. The human experience is the effect of a cultural order or structure, in this case the family, which forms the background against which life moves. Two aspects of that order, which Barthes understands in terms of form and content, are important for the further course of my explanation.[74]

First of all, a cultural order constitutes meanings that are not present in nature. These meanings are created by the marking of formal distinctions that do not themselves reflect any distinctions at a biological level. In normal life, meaning arises because things are separated from each other and gain their own weight.[75] A cultural structure like the family does not emerge from nature. Nature itself does not distinguish parent and child from each other. Both are, seen from the perspective of nature, worthless products of a mere biological metabolic process. It is only when the community acknowledges parent and child that a constellation with distinct positions is created in which each member has a meaning that transcends biology.

Secondly, a whole of prohibitions and restrictions is both a confirmation and expression of the cultural order. This ordering is based on, and expressed through, rules. This implies that respecting formal rules is an expression of sensitivity to a meaningful reality. An example of this is the tone that someone uses to appeal to his father. The deference or reserve built into a conversation with a father shows that this man has a certain weight in life. The tone, however, is honouring not biological characteristics, but the man as the subject of a meaningful content, namely fatherhood. The same applies to compliance with the incest prohibition. The fact that relatives do not have sexual relations with each other shows that they all ascribe to each other a meaning that is not reducible to the biological.

Thus, in ordinary life, meaning arises because a form has been imposed on reality that distinguishes all kinds of things. All the rules are an expression of that meaningful reality. However, in Sade's literature, as we have seen, the characters don't belong to a family and do not represent any special value, which does not mean that there are no rules and regulations in the Sadean universe. The latter is reflected in the field of eroticism. In fact, according to Barthes, eroticism in Sade is nothing but the continuation of 'pornogrammatic' rules. Sadean eroticism is primarily characterised by the continuation of the two rules. Precisely because of the fact the Sadean characters are not supported by a particular order, these rules do not express a meaningful reality, unlike in ordinary life. The rules are purely formal requirements without any content. In short, the countless erotic *tableaux vivants* are the result of a continuous and endless reorganisation of stupid units according to empty rules.

From that perspective, we can link Sade's eroticism once again with modern art. Sade's eroticism and, for example, the supremacism of the artist and art theorist Kazimir Malevich are both nothing but a constant recombination of units and lines following solid patterns that do not express a content. In that regard, Barthes also notes that Sade's scenes can make the reader laugh. The reason for this is the meticulous care taken for the erotic scene that does not represent meaning. In this way Sade's scenes cause the same hilarity as the excessive attention to a ceremony that has lost its dignity. In summary, as an endless reproduction of contentless rules, Sadean erotic scenes lean on both abstract art and the hilarious.

Based on the foregoing, we can now understand what Barthes means exactly by what he calls 'the empty enjoyment' of the libertine. This thesis implies that the enjoyment of, for example, de Blangis' friend differs from the enjoyment associated with ordinary eroticism. To clarify this, consider the following situation. Suppose a man is told to go into a dark room where he will share a bed with his mistress who is waiting for him there. The day thereafter, however, he is told that the person in the bed was not his mistress but his mother. The result would be the transformation of what was initially enjoyable into something horrible. This reveals that sexual enjoyment in ordinary life is closely related and sensitive to the fact that individuals are the subject of a particular content. It would be completely different if the man were the Duc's friend. If one were to tell him afterwards that the woman who gave birth to him had participated in the erotic scene, then his pleasure would not turn into disgust; it would remain pleasure. The reason is that the bonds of blood have no weight in Sade's universe and the characters are not included in a family order that marks distinctions and thus establishes meaning.

Thus, while sexual pleasure is normally content-related, the enjoyment of the libertine is not bound to or dependent on content, and it is in this sense that Barthes understands it as empty. What then is Barthes' positive description of enjoyment in Sade? The enjoyment of the libertine is an effect of the unimpeded reconfiguration of meaningless units and the working through of eroticism on its own contentless rules.

IV Sade's Society

Barthes not only focuses on the literary aspects of Sade's literature and on the erotic scenes, he also describes Sade's society. In particular, he has an eye for the food, clothes and a tight time schedule. However, Barthes does not discuss these aspects in detail and only notes them briefly. In what follows, it will be shown that from Barthes' remarks one can conclude that Sade's world breaks with a classical universe. This analysis will be based upon Foucault's analysis of the difference between a pre-modern and a modern worldview (although it may well be doubted that there is such a clear-cut break between pre-modernity on the one and modernity on the other hand).[76]

From a Divine Order . . .

In 'La prose du monde', the second chapter of *Les mots et les choses*, Foucault deals with the worldview that characterised Western culture until the seventeenth century.[77] He refers, among other things, to *Traicté des signatures ou vraye et vive anatomie du grand et petit monde* from 1624 by Oswald Crollius.[78] The latter mentions the ancient belief in the medical power of monkshood, a herbaceous plant, to cure eye problems.[79] That belief is based on a resemblance between the seed – little dark balls in white pods – and the human eye. Another example from Crollius' work is the belief in the healing effect of the walnut for the head and the brain.[80] In particular, the hull or shell of the nut is used to heal wounds of the skull, and the nut is used to heal diseases in the head. This belief in the medical power of the walnut is also based on a formal similarity. The nut resembles the human brain, and just as the human brain is covered by a skull, so the nut is covered by its shell. Both monkshood and walnut show that the basis of the classically inspired universe is resemblance.

The similarities between different spheres of life imply that reality can be understood as a circle expanding outwards concentrically to the point that it forms a coherent whole.[81] This can also be formulated as the idea that the human microcosm is included in an all-encompassing cosmic order, which means that reality does not simply fall back on or refer to itself. In a pre-modern worldview, reality, as in the title of the second chapter of *Les mots et les choses*, has something prosaic about it. Foucault holds that in a classical view every part of reality refers to a vague, difficult-to-describe mystical body in which reality is participating. Moreover, the microcosm is also an expression or reflection of the macrocosm, which means that the order governing human reality is not arbitrary but can be traced to a superhuman order. This is expressed, among other places, in ethical issues. In a classical universe, the moral law is an expression of a natural law. The moral law is justified by reference to an order that expresses itself in the microcosm. This implies that in the case of a crime, it is not only the actual damage caused by the crime that is condemned. Transgressing the moral categories is also symbolically condemned, because a crime affects the cosmic order. In a classical worldview, reality is therefore full of meaning, in the sense that it refers to, and is an expression of, a higher order.[82]

. . . to a Divinisation of Order

As previously mentioned, Barthes emphasises the frequent descriptions of food in Sade's prose. This has to do with his interpretation of the composition and literary characteristics of Sade's oeuvre, but it also has to do with much more than this. His interest in food is also part of his concise ethnography of libertine society.[83] Barthes notes, for example, that food shows up in different contexts.[84] He refers, among other things, to Bressac, who explains to Justine how to kill his mother. She describes the plan as follows: 'I would put a small dose of poison, which Bressac gave me, in the cup of chocolate which the lady took every morning.'[85] Barthes also mentions that meals often precede or follow orgies. For example, in *Les 120 journées the Sodome* we read the following: 'Since there was the same abundance at every meal, it suffices to have described one. One resembled the other. Since almost everyone had an orgasm, it was now necessary to regain strength and consequently there was a lot of drinking.'[86] Third, Barthes points to another function of food in Sade's society. This function is evidenced by, for example, the passage from *Les 120 journées de Sodome* in which Duclos tells of the rime when she lived with a man called d'Aucourt. There, she was subject to a strict regime. Four times a day, she had to eat fish and dairy products, while bread and fruit were hardly served. Regarding this regime she says: 'As a result of this regime, I had to shit twice a day, as he had foreseen, softly and with a delicious taste, as he claimed.'[87] This shows that food in Sade's society is used for at least three purposes: to poison, to gain power, and to satisfy the coprophagic drift of the libertines. In other words, in Sade, the food is of functional or instrumental importance. Foods are nothing but a means of achieving a specific purpose.[88]

Barthes not only focuses on the functionality of the food, but also notes that the Sadean society is divided into different groups. This arrangement is visible in the fact, Barthes reminds us, that the different social groups have their own distinctive clothes.[89] In *Les 120 journées de Sodome,* for example, the young boys and the young girls are divided into four groups each with a particular style of clothing: Oriental, Spanish, Turkish and Greek.[90] Even when Justine ends up in the Benedictine monastery, the residents are divided into groups with their own dress code.[91] And not only the different types of clothing, but also the contrast between the clothes and the absence of clothes, indicate the difference between the several groups. For example, when in *Les 120 journées de Sodome* the inhabitants start to eat after the orgy has taken place, the slaves are nude, while the libertines are dressed. That order, however, as expressed in the clothes of the characters, has no ground.[92] Origin, age or gender are of no importance for the organisation of the Sadean society. The arrangement is completely arbitrary, meaning that the clothing has only a diacritical function. It only marks the distinction between the different groups. In Sade the clothing is a sign without content or a distinctive mark without further meaning, because the order it indicates is based solely on itself.

The arbitrary ordering is also unbreakable.[93] It is impossible to leave a group for a higher or lower group in the hierarchy. Neither promotion nor demotion is possible. The hierarchical order is irrevocably fixed: once sadist, always sadist; once a victim, always a victim. This emphasis on the indisputable order is reflected in the strict regulations and the punctual timetable.[94] Thus, in *Les 120 journées de Sodome*, at the beginning of their four-month stay in the castle of Silling, all residents are grouped in order to read the house rules. Three of the most important rules are: the name 'God' must always be accompanied by a curse; care for the body is forbidden and defecating is only possible after explicit permission; finally, every laugh is prohibited. Those prohibitions and commandments are set against the background of strict time regulation. All residents must get up at ten o'clock every day, eat at eleven, listen to the storytellers at six o'clock, and stop the orgies at two o'clock.[95] Thus, in Sade's universe, tight organisation is central. The following communication to the boys and girls in the castle of Silling is the motto of the libertine order: 'So what I recommend to you is punctuality, submission, and a total negation of yourself.'[96] Sade's society is organised according to an unwavering arbitrary order in which food is nothing but functional. What conclusions can we draw from this?

In ordinary life, the daily meal differs from the food that is served on public holidays. Take Christmas Day, for example. For Christmas dinner, the food is more sophisticated and extensive than on a normal day. The choice of a special meal expresses the special importance of this occasion. The food, thus, has an additional meaning, which cannot be reduced to satisfying hunger. This surplus of meaning, which adds to the function of food, is derived from a religious framework that gives more weight to certain days. In other words, the reservation of, for example, poultry for the Christmas dinner shows that social life has an order that, although vague, refers to and needs to be understood against a Judaeo-Christian background. The Sadean universe differs from this, in the sense that every extra meaning of food has been erased. What remains is its pure functionality. The emphasis on usefulness indicates that Sade's world does not refer to a larger unifying whole. The Sadean universe, as is indicated by the functionality of food, is not a sign of anything beyond itself; it is a world cut off from a higher signification. This is proven not only by the food, but also by the fact that the classification into groups is completely arbitrary. This indicates that the Sadean society has no subject or ground. Thus, when Barthes pays attention to functionality and arbitrariness, he points out that in the society of Sade a theological or cosmological foundation, which in earlier times gave meaning to reality, is absent. That does not mean, however, as Barthes reminds us, that the Sadean universe is out of order. Although unfounded, the Sadean society is characterised by a division between different groups. Moreover, in Sade, the disappearance of the ground of order is accompanied by an increase in emphasis on the meaningless order itself. In short, Sade's society is not an expression of a divine order but is characterised by a divinisation of order.

V Conclusion

According to Barthes, it is not only the case that in Sade's literature the theoretical reflections and the erotic scenes alternate with each other. Philosophy and eroticism, according to Barthes, are also interchangeable. This is expressed, for example, in a passage from Sade's work quoted by Barthes, in which a libertine reacts as follows to a colleague's speech: 'Saint-Fond's ejaculation was brilliant, bold, energetic, etc.'[97] According to Barthes, this interchangeability has to do with the fact that Sade's eroticism is structured as a language system. What is more, the eroticism and philosophical explanations correspond to the fact that their language does not express any content. We can take this thought further: Sade's literature (first section) and Sade's eroticism (second section) are characterised by the absence of any content. However, Barthes does not only point to the analogy between what happens in Sade on a textual level and his eroticism. Barthes also draws attention to the similarity between Sade's literature, eroticism and society. Even Sade's society, as we have seen in the third section, is meaningless, in the sense that it is not supported by and is not an expression of a higher reality. This reading, which Barthes presents in 1967, is an illustration of his interests during the 1960s. Whereas in the previous decade he wrote socially critical texts and from the 1970s onwards was more interested in the activities of reading and writing, in the sixth decade of the last century his thinking revolved around the theme of formalism. This is expressed, among other things, in the development of a formal analytical model for literary texts and in his interest in Japanese culture, which is characterised by fixed formulas, formal connections, etc. In short, Barthes is interested in Sade because his literature reflects the theme that revolves around the absence of a content.

6[1]

Literature and the Clinical

I Introduction

In the list of philosophers whose studies I discuss in the various chapters, Deleuze stands out. After all, his interest is more in the literature of the Austrian writer Leopold von Sacher-Masoch (1835–95) than in Sade's oeuvre.[2] This interest in Masoch is expressed in, among other works, 'De Sacher Masoch au masochisme' from 1961,[3] 'Mystique et masochisme' from 1964 and 'Représentation de Masoch' from 1993. Deleuze's best-known and largest study on Masoch is *Présentation de Sacher-Masoch: Le froid et le cruel*, published in 1967.[4] Although Deleuze mainly discusses the work of Masoch in this study, Sade is not absent. Especially at the beginning and the end of his studies, Deleuze's attention was focused on both writers at the same time.[5] This observation already offers a first insight into the thrust of Deleuze's text, since the fact that he juxtaposes the oeuvre of Sade and Masoch inevitably evokes the concept of 'sadomasochism'. In other words, Deleuze's *Présentation de Sacher-Masoch* is made primarily against a clinical background.

In order to get a clear picture of the structure of Deleuze's study, it is necessary to keep his interpretation of Sade and Masoch separate. In the first part of this last chapter, I will highlight Deleuze's surprising thesis that the Sadean libertines are not primarily perpetrators of violence – or dreamers, as Klossowski claims – but thinkers. This is related to the fact that, according to Deleuze, the sadist does not enjoy the countless atrocities in a sexual manner, but rather enjoys the unhindered development of thought.[6] In *La philosophie dans le boudoir*, for example, philosophising is not merely a stepping stone to the real work in the bedroom, but the thinking itself is eroticised.

According to Deleuze, just as the pain and humiliation of others are not central in Sade's case, Masoch's world too is not characterised by the passive variant of pain and humiliation. Being beaten and humiliated is only an expression of something else that is more central, namely the pregenital relationship between the masochist and a motherly woman. In the second part, I discuss Deleuze's interpretation of the masochistic universe as a world in which motherly figures are the leading ones. On this basis, we will be able to focus in the third part on the central argument of Deleuze's study. This study, it will be shown, is an explicit attack on a few figures for whom sexual perversions such as sadism and masochism are not two different realities but one and the same. I also show that *Présentation de Sacher-Masoch* is already paving the way towards Deleuze and Guattari's criticism of Freud's psychoanalytical theory in so far as the latter thinks of certain phenomena in Oedipal terms. The two criticisms have in common a foundational assumption that Sade and Masoch are symptomatologists and that their work refers to a clinical reality.[7]

II Sade and Reason

As we have seen several times in the previous chapters, Sade's literature is not only composed of erotic and cruel scenes; it also often contains lengthy passages of philosophical discussion. Deleuze gives greater weight to these passages than to the physical scenes. According to him, the libertine is characterised primarily by the activity of pure thinking, and the scenes are only a condition for that thinking. Before we can understand that, we must first examine how Deleuze interprets the scenes and the content of the philosophical statements. Finally, this will enable us to gain insight into Deleuze's seemingly peculiar statement that the libertine is sexually excited by thinking.

First and Second Nature

As an introduction to Deleuze's reading, let us begin with two passages from Sade's literature. The first passage is from *Les 120 journées de Sodome*, in which we find out that the favourite scene of a certain character, Saclanges, is a dinner with a woman. Sade describes that dinner as follows: 'The president arrives, the soup is served, both are drunk and lose their heads. Both vomited in each other's mouths.

Both swallow everything in and then do the same, one with the vomit of the other.'[8] The second passage is from *Juliette*. It describes how the woman libertine, Noirceuil, is killed: 'As soon as she stood this way, twelve burning candles were placed between her thighs, in such a way that the flames licked both her vagina and anus.'[9] Unusual scenes of this kind return in Sade's literature every now and then. They inevitably give rise to certain emotions in the reader. While the first scene evokes disgust, the second scene is followed by compassion and horror. According to Deleuze, the libertines in Sade's universe need scenes like this.[10] However, the sadist does not need them to highlight his involvement in human affairs. The gruesome and obscene scenes rather aim towards the opposite. They offer the sadist a platform on which he can learn to become insensitive. In doing so, the sadist examines what, according to Deleuze, is central in the Sadean universe, namely the requirement to be apathetic at all times.[11] The sadist must eliminate emotions including compassion and disgust and neutralise any kind of personal involvement. More positively formulated, the sadist aims at an activity that, precisely because every form of involvement is destroyed, can continue uninhibited and unhindered.[12] However, the absence of any involvement does not belong to human nature. In everyday life, individuals are spontaneously involved in themselves and others, and also take into account the effects of their actions on themselves and on others. It is from this point of view that, according to Deleuze, we must understand the multitude of such scenes. They offer the sadists the opportunity to learn to harden themselves. By repeatedly exposing oneself to extreme situations that evoke normal emotions, habituation occurs which ensures that ultimately the sadist can perform any activity in an apathetic way.[13]

Deleuze not only examines the scatological scenes, but also discusses the theoretical passages of Sade's literature with their natural philosophical speculations. His discussion of these speculations is based on the distinction between first nature on the one hand and second nature on the other.[14] What does Deleuze mean by this?[15]

What Deleuze means by Sade's 'second nature' can be grasped through a reading of *La philosophie dans le boudoir*. In the third dialogue, Dolmancé and Saint-Ange teach the young Eugénie the different parts and sexual functions of the human body. As the session proceeds, the subject changes and they talk about those acts which are conceived in our culture as morally reprehensible: theft, incest and murder. The fact that society prohibits these acts is based, Dolmancé says, on a wrong, anthropocentric idea. Dolmancé justifies murder by relating the act to nature: 'No destructive act can be described as criminal, because destruction is one of the most important laws of nature.'[16] From a non-anthropocentric perspective, Dolmancé argues, murder is not a crime because it is in line with nature's destructive law. Still, he indicates that nature is not only characterised by destruction, since creation is also fundamental to nature. The ratio between these two laws is defined as follows: '[Destruction] gives back to nature elements which her skilful hand immediately uses to reward other beings.'[17] In Sade, destruction of life does not imply that matter as such disappears. It is rather the case that by being dismantled, matter first loses its current form and then lives further in a new guise. Thus, at this stage of Sade's thought, destruction is understood as delivering formless material that enables nature to continue its creative activity. This explanation reveals what Deleuze means by 'second nature' in Sade's theoretical passages: that destruction is impure because it is related to something other than itself. More particularly, second nature refers to the endless cycle of life and death, in which destruction is involved in the production of life. This fact, namely that destruction is related to life, implies that the force of destruction cannot continue itself unobstructed.

In Sade's philosophical dissertations, Deleuze also discovers a different conception of nature. In it, nature, to which Deleuze refers by the expression 'first nature', is nothing more than pure destruction. To explain exactly what he means by this, Deleuze refers to two passages from *Juliette*. The first passage is that in which Juliette and Clairwil travel from France to Rome to visit Pope Braschi.[18] Shortly after their meeting, Juliette tells the Pope that she is well aware that for him too, religion is nothing but a mere mask that hides sexual instincts. Before she will offer him her sexual services, the Pope must also meet four conditions. The first is that he must give an account of murder. The central idea of the mockery that Braschi then gives is as follows: 'The murders [. . .] serve even to a certain extent her [nature's] intentions, [. . .] and it is certain that she does so only because she desires the total destruction of the creatures she has made.'[19]

According to the Pope, nature aims at total destruction. This means that in Sade's case, one can also find the image of a nature that is not a prerequisite for the creation of new life, as is the case in second nature. In first nature, destruction has detached itself from the focus on life and therefore continues unhindered until the moment that all life has been eradicated. That first nature, which continues unimpeded, echoes in the second passage from *Juliette* to which Deleuze refers: 'I would like, Clairwil said, to find a crime that would go on ceaselessly [. . .] and I would like it to spread so far that it followed a general destruction.'[20] In short, first nature is pure because the destruction is not contaminated by involvement in life, which means that it can continue uninterrupted.

This first nature, which, together with second nature, is developed in Sade's dissertations, is connected by Deleuze with the scenes in which the sadist learns to detach himself from every form of personal involvement. More specifically, Deleuze states that we need to understand the scenes in the light of speculation about first nature. How should we understand that?

If the sadist, like everyone else in everyday life, were to be struck by the pain of others, for example, this means that his actions would correspond to the idea of second nature. Just as destruction in the case of second nature cannot continue unimpeded because it serves creation, the activities of the non-apathic sadist could not continue unhindered. The reason for this is that the sadist would continue to hang on and be involved with others. The cruel scenes must be understood from the sadist's desire to transcend second nature and live in harmony with the idea of first nature. The sadist conjures up an activity that, just like destruction in first nature, is involved in nothing and can therefore unfold freely. In other words, the sadist seeks to be a reflection of the object of natural philosophical speculation, namely pure unconstrained nature, *in casu* destruction.

Thinking and Auto-Eroticism

Towards the end of his studies, Deleuze uses a different vocabulary: he goes back to Freud's terminology. The fact that Deleuze reformulates his reading in a psychoanalytical vocabulary does not mean that his reading fits in seamlessly with Freud's views on sadism. It is rather the case that he takes Freud's thinking as a starting point. One of the central concepts in this framework is the Super-Ego, of which Freud sketches the genesis in 'Der Untergang des Ödipuskomplexes' from 1924.

The origin of that Super-Ego is situated in the phallic phase. During this phase, Freud explains, the boy displays a special interest in his penis. Touching his penis is the effect of the erotic excitement generated by the Oedipal bond to the mother. At the same time, the boy notices that his parents reject the preoccupation with the penis. If the boy does not stop playing with his genital area, the father's threat is that the penis in question will be removed. At first, the boy does not believe in this threat of castration. It is only when the boy observes that the girl does not possess a penis that he takes the threat seriously. The Oedipus complex is then destroyed when the child introjects the ban on incest in the Super-Ego. That authority perpetuates the law of the father who claims the mother for himself alone and prevents libidinal impulses from returning to consciousness. The Super-Ego is thus the intrapsychic heir to the law of the Oedipal father.

In 'Das Ich und das Es' from 1923, Freud wonders where the Super-Ego derives the rigour from with which consciousness accuses the Ego. According to Freud, it is not only the father who lies at the origin of the power of the Super-Ego; the stringency of the Super-Ego also has another source: 'What is central in the Super-Ego is a pure culture of the death drive.'[21] The aggressive accusations with which the Super-Ego bombards the Ego are an expression of the cruel, amoral death drive. However, this is not the first manifestation of this drive. The aggression directed against the Ego is a reversal of the aggression that is first directed against the father as a rival during the phallic phase. The aggressive self-reproaches are an internalisation of the aggression that primarily has the father as an object because, like his son, he longs for the mother. The collapse of the Oedipus complex therefore means that the death drive no longer has the father as an object, but instead grafts itself on his heir, namely the Super-Ego. The Super-Ego may be an heir to the father, but it derives its strength from the death drive that expresses itself in consciousness. This death drive, as Deleuze emphasises, is considered cruel and amoral in itself, but does not allow itself to be known as such as far as the emphasis is on the conflict between his Super-Ego and his Ego.[22]

This changes in the case of sadism, which, according to Deleuze, is characterised by the omnipotence of the Super-Ego. The sadist, says Deleuze, coincides with the Super-Ego: 'One could almost say the opposite about the sadist: that he has a strong and destructive Super-Ego and that he is only that.'[23] According to Deleuze, the all-powerful presence of the obsessive Super-Ego does not mean, however, that the Super-Ego merely oppresses the Ego. No, says Deleuze, in sadism the Ego disappears from the psyche and is projected onto the victims. For the sadist, the victim is not a lust addict or inanimate object, but a reflection of himself. Therefore when the sadist is aggressively handling his victim, that means, according to Deleuze, that he is hurting himself. In other words, sadism focuses on the destruction of the Ego by the cruel Super-Ego. This interpretation means that, according to Deleuze's psychoanalytically inspired reading, sadism reveals what the Super-Ego is, namely an amoral destructive force. In other words, when the conflict between the Super-Ego and Ego is not intra- but interpsychic, the Super-Ego is not moralistic but sadistic.[24] In other words, in sadism, the Super-Ego is not an heir to the Oedipal law of the father who claims the mother for himself alone, but the representative of a father who closes the labia of the mother, as in the final scene of *La philosophie dans le boudoir*, or sets fire to them, as in the passage from *Juliette* quoted above.

The connection between Deleuze's assertion that in sadism the cruel Super-Ego destroys the Ego, on the one hand, and his discussion of Sade's scenes and the philosophical dissertations from the previous section, on the other hand, can be clarified by means of a passage from Freud's 'Das ökonomische Problem des Masochismus' from 1924.

In this text, Freud states that the non-sadistic Super-Ego, as the heir of the Oedipal father, will be transferred over time to a series of figures which, all the more so as the series shifts forward, transcend individual life history. The strictness of conscience is transferred to teachers, authorities or heroes, but also to less personal forms such as God and nature. According to Freud, fate is the last stage in the series of transfers.[25] The movement described by Freud means that an impersonal power like nature goes back to childhood. In nature, one discovers the contours of the figure of the Oedipal father. According to Deleuze, this personification of nature is opposed to the movement that takes place in sadism. We read that the father represents nature as an original and anarchistic force.[26] While nature, according to Freud, gets the traits of the father, sadism, according to Deleuze, implies the opposite, namely depersonalisation of the father.[27] The sadistic Super-Ego and the non-Oedipal *homo familia* go back to and get drawn by *homo natura*, more specifically, the first nature of pure destruction.[28] Just as destruction is not aimed at the creation of new life, so sadism is characterised by the fact that it eliminates all forms of involvement. This is expressed on the one hand in the destruction of the Ego, namely the neutralisation of self-involvement and the point from which involvement in the world departs, and on the other hand in the abuse of the mother who first introduces the child to the outside world and symbolises the movement of spontaneous natural involvement in reality.

Up until now, we cannot yet say that the sadist has succeeded completely in his plan, namely *vivere secundum naturam*. So far, the sadist has not yet lived in accordance with the idea of first nature. The sadist does tend to reflect nature, but he does not coincide with it. The reason for this is that the sadist is only similar to first nature in a negative sense. Just like pure destruction, he does break with any kind of involvement, but for the time being we have not yet seen how this break is expressed in an activity that continues unhindered. In this context, Deleuze points out the importance of thinking in Sade's universe. It is through the activity of thinking that the sadist becomes one with nature and not through the destruction of the Ego by the Super-Ego. Nevertheless, the fact that the Super-Ego is destroying the Ego cannot be separated from thinking. According to Deleuze, this has to do with desexualisation.[29] How should we understand that? And in what sense does Deleuze believe that the sadist becomes one with nature through the activity of thinking?

Deleuze understands desexualisation in a Freudian sense. To clarify this term, we can again refer to 'Das Ich und das Es'. In it, Freud states that his findings about melancholy reveal something about the psyche in general.[30] This syndrome is characterised by the change of the real occupation of an object into an identification with the lost object. After the loss, according to Freud, the object is interjected into the Ego. This identification, intended to compensate for a loss, is also an important part of psychological development. When the child gives up the first erotic wishes, the child will be able to overcome that loss by constituting the object in the Ego. This means that the Ego accepts the traits of the object and is now the love object itself. According to Freud, this deflection of libido from the mother to the Ego, or the conversion of object libido into narcissistic libido, is accompanied by desexualisation.[31] By this he means that the sexual purposes of the drives are being destroyed. At the same time, this also changes the quality of the drive. Desexualisation has a transformational effect on the drive, which loses the quality of sexuality and becomes indifferent energy. Deleuze discusses Freud's line of thought, since he explains that a certain amount of energy becomes replaceable and neutral.[32] In sadism, however, this neutral energy is not invested in Ego. Sadism means that the Super-Ego cuts the Ego out of the psyche. Sadism is characterised by this; namely that the Super-Ego releases an energy *not* directed at the Ego but rather t invested in thinking, which also shows that Deleuze's interpretation is an example of a postmodern way of thinking.

In order to gain insight into the central role of thinking in which the energy is invested, it is useful to return to Sade, and more specifically, to *Justine*. In it, a certain Dubois points out to Justine that in France, certain acts are regarded as vices that continue to be virtuous elsewhere. This is explained to be due to the difference in climatic conditions in which opinions arise: different living conditions lead to different views. For Dubois, the contingency of opinions, which she calls 'mere opinions', is the reason why she does not take them as a guideline for action. Ethical rules should not be based on erratic opinions but should take thinking as their starting point.[33] Unlike ordinary opinion-forming, reason does indeed have a necessity which enables it to serve as a basis for ethics. This necessary dynamic is evident in, for example, a passage from *La philosophie dans le boudoir* wherein Dolmancé delivers a long monologue. The content is less important than the way in which he begins every sentence with the following argument: 'Now then! If it is established that [. . .] has been proven that [. . .] has been demonstrated that [. . .] has been demonstrated if it is certain that [. . .]'.[34] Dolmancé concludes his speech as follows: 'if,

I say, all this is proven, and that is undeniable, do you think [. . .]?'[35] What does that passage teach us?

This passage shows that the conclusion is derived logically from the given axioms. If the truth of the premise is established, the conclusion must necessarily be drawn from it and it is guaranteed by the given starting point. It is in this geometric, Spinozistic argument that 'the apathy of reason' shows itself, according to Deleuze.[36] After all, the truth of a claim is determined by logical-deductive thinking, part of which is the 'geometric ideas' that causally distract and are insensitive to deeply rooted beliefs. Now, more important than the fact that reason is pure and separate from common opinions is that in the aforementioned passage, the image of reason as a spiritual machine emerges. It is important to note that from this passage, reason emerges as a spiritually moving body which, precisely because of its apathy with regard to convention, continues its operations of thought unruffled and unhindered. After all, it is through this uninhibited unfolding of insensitive thinking that the sadist becomes one with first nature. If logical-deductive thinking starts and then continues uninhibited, the sadist participates in the *natura naturans* which is expressed in thinking. The object of thinking, namely imperturbable first nature, occupies the thinking itself and therefore, through thinking, allows the sadist to participate in that which he had previously only imagined. This clarifies – and here I am again referring to Deleuze's psychoanalytical conceptual framework – the role that the sadistic scene plays in Deleuze's thinking. The libertines need young people so that they can project their Ego onto them and so that the Super-Ego can extract energy from the destruction, which can then be invested in the unfolding of pure thinking.

According to Deleuze, the sadist sexually enjoys this process of free thinking.[37] This connection between uninhibited thinking and sexual pleasure is also found in Sade's literature: 'This capricious part of our mind is of a licentiousness that knows no bounds; its greatest victory, its greatest pleasure, is achieved when it breaks all the chains in which it is held as prisoner.'[38] Deleuze does not specify exactly how we should understand the sexual pleasure of thinking. In what follows, I show that he means that the sexual pleasure of thinking has its roots in a sexual pleasure from childhood. Freud discusses this enjoyment in 'Drei Abhandlungen zur Sexualtheorie', written in 1905.

In this text, Freud writes about the activity of sucking by the child.[39] The first form of sucking involves the mother's breast as its object. The fact that the child falls asleep afterwards with red cheeks suggests that sucking is accompanied by sexual, pregenital enjoyment. According to Freud, this enjoyment is a consequence of the milk which flows from the breast to the child's mouth. Thus, the feeling of enjoyment is connected directly to the satisfaction of the need for food. Later, when teeth appear, and the child can chew food, the breast is no longer necessary. However, Freud notes both that the child continues sucking although it is no longer necessary for nourishment and that the experience of enjoyment does not disappear. Moreover, the arousal of enjoyment, Freud explains, remains sexual. The child continues sucking on parts of its body and the sexual enjoyment this arouses is described by Freud as auto-erotic. With regard to Deleuze's interpretation, it is important to note that this sexual enjoyment is generated independently of the need for gratification.[40] It is not the object of sucking, namely eating food, which causes enjoyment. It is sucking itself and the uninhibited continuation of this activity which arouse sexual enjoyment. In sadism, this auto-erotic drive source is reactivated. Just as in sucking, the activity of thinking is not focused on something that lies outside the activity itself. The sadist is directed to pure thinking and this activity is grafted upon a past from which sexual enjoyment arises. The sadist frees auto-erotic enjoyment which first accompanied sucking and now occupies the process of pure thinking.[41]

This conception of sadistic enjoyment is close to Deleuze's interpretation of the sadistic scene, which holds, as we have seen, that the sadist does not identify with the Oedipal Super-Ego. To put it differently: sadistic enjoyment cannot be understood Oedipally. The reason is that the relationship between repetition and enjoyment has been reversed.[42] Indeed, in Sade, thinking is not aimed at the reclamation of previously forbidden enjoyment, which has been repressed. Moreover, sadistic enjoyment does not repeat any enjoyment from the past.[43] On the contrary, in the sadistic universe enjoyment is an effect that goes along with the unleashing of pure, logical-deductive thinking.[44]

III Masoch and Imagination

Deleuze notes that Masoch's sexuality, in contrast to Sade's, is expressed in all domains of life.[45] Masoch's sexuality is a lifestyle which characterises his political, artistic and religious ideas. How should we understand this? What characterises Masoch's notion of sexuality? How is this sexuality related to the other spheres of life?

The Ideal of a Cold and Severe Mother

As is well known, Plato's Socrates is on a permanent search for interlocutors, whom he asks to define things like justice or virtue. Socrates then calls for a more precise description in order to come to a definition that indicates how things essentially are. The goal seems to be that the discussion partner should abandon his contingent opinion and direct his mind to the truth of the Idea. Thus, Socrates' partners seem to have a central role in the dialogue, while Socrates himself is merely a passive listener. Arguably, however, Socrates' ignorance is feigned. In reality the roles are reversed: Socrates is the one who leads the conversation actively. He discovers the other's errors by asking pointed questions and demanding clarifications of a definition until the Idea comes to light.

According to Deleuze, this method of irony also characterises masochism.[46] Masoch should be read from a Platonic perspective, since, just as in the Socratic dialogue, the relations between the masochistic characters are different from the way they appear at first glance. The beginning of *Venus im Pelz*, Masoch's best-known novel, illustrates this well.[47] The novel opens with the introduction of the two main characters, Severin and Wanda von Dunajew, and goes on to illustrate the relationship between them. Severin is described as throwing himself before Wanda's feet and saying solemnly, while she lays her hand on his neck, that his desire is to be the slave of a woman whom he loves. Severin offers to commit his life to Wanda, but on the condition that she embody a certain ideal. Wanda agrees, and the rest of the story is a long-winded educational process wherein Severin instructs Wanda on how she can live up to his ideal. As in the case of Socrates, Masoch's irony is that Severin seems submissive, but in fact he takes the active role of teaching Wanda to fulfil an ideal. What does this ideal look like?

Deleuze points out that the women in Masoch's literature all share some physical and psychic characteristics. They are all supercilious, violent, muscular and dominant.[48] Nevertheless, distinguishable beneath these similarities, Deleuze claims, are three different types of women. He shows that all these types can be found in *Venus im Pelz*, in a progression following the parts of the novel. The first type of woman appears at the beginning, the second kind in the middle, and the third at the end of Masoch's novel. How does Deleuze describe the first and third type?[49]

Venus im Pelz opens with a dream told by the narrator to Severin. In this dream, he finds himself in the company of the goddess of love, who complains about a Northern Christian mentality. Over there, the goddess claims, people are only interested in duties and virtue. By contrast, the goddess is excited by sensuality and cheerful love. A little later on, when Severin shares his history with Wanda, she corresponds in the first part of his story to the image of the goddess from the dream of the narrator. Neither the goddess nor Wanda (in the first part of the book) is bound to a man, and both protest against marriage. They move from one to another short-lived relationship in which they search for fiery excitement. This characterises the first type of woman, who can be called 'the pagan nymphomaniac'.

Turning to the end of the novel, we find the third type of woman, embodied by Wanda with the assistance of a Greek man. In the final scene, she binds Severin, who is thrashed by the Greek assistant. The voluptuous Wanda has now made way for the woman who sexually enjoys inflicting pain. While she clung at first to riotous love, now she is more vicious: 'Men who wish to live as the gods of Olympus did must have slaves to throw in their fish ponds and gladiators ready to do battle for them at their feast. Little do they care if they are spattered by the fighters' blood.'[50] According to Deleuze, the first and third types of woman share the fact that their lives are sensual: either through excessive love, or through sexually enjoying cruelty. This lustful love and cruelty express the sensual nature of the masochistic universe.

Neither at the beginning nor at the end of *Venus im Pelz* does Wanda incarnate the ideal that Severin has in mind. Deleuze states: 'However, it is clear that neither the hermaphrodite woman nor the sadistic woman represents the ideal of Masoch.'[51] Wanda realises the ideal in the middle part of the novel, where she moves between the first and third type. Severin's masochistic ideal therefore lies between the voluptuous love of the nymphomaniac on the one hand and sadism on the other. This ideal of the in-between is difficult for Wanda to maintain. During the many dialogues, she explores that gap and expresses the insecurity that goes with the delicate task: 'I am afraid I will not be able to do it, but I want to try it, for your sake, because I love you, Severin.'[52] What characterises that second feminine type, which must uphold the middle position, exactly?

The fact that the ideal is between two extremes implies that Wanda must conform to the image of a mother. First of all, this means that she must be tough and strict. This stringency is a mild, less extreme form of sadistic cruelty. Furthermore, Wanda must eliminate her genital desires and give up her licentious sensuality. Following the title of Deleuze's study, the ideal woman of the masochist is characterised by 'coldness' regarding the genitals. This coldness is accentuated by the frequent sneezing and is also expressed in the space in which masochism takes place. This is illustrated by the reverie of the narrator in *Der Capitulant* from 1875 after crossing a snowy plain: 'Everything is cold. The thoughts hang like ice cones on the brain, the soul is covered by an ice layer, the blood falls apart like mercury.'[53] Severin demands that Wanda turn off her genital desire. This results in the creation and maintaining of Masoch's universe, which he experiences as a lovely and playful atmosphere. Wanda does not share the bed with Severin, but she caresses his head lying on her half-naked chest, and kisses his hand while she whispers sweet words in his ears. This predatory eroticism is echoed in the following passage:

> For ten days I had not been without her for an hour, except for the nights. I was allowed to look her in the eyes, hold her hands, listen to what she said, accompany her everywhere. [. . .] We had stretched ourselves out in the meadow this afternoon, at the feet of the Venus statue, I picked flowers and threw them into her lap, and she made wreaths of them with which we decorated our goddess.[54]

The observation that Severin teaches Wanda to become a cold mother without any genital desire is expressed in the fact that he is strongly focused on a specific object. Severin is strongly fixed – not on 'shiny boots of leather' – but, as the title of Masoch's most famous novel indicates, on a fur coat.[55] This means that the fur coat is a fetish.[56] Deleuze does not understand the fetish here as Freud does in his 'Drei Abhandlungen zur Sexualtheorie'. In this text, Freud understands fetishism as an extension of sexual interest in the person to things that are connected with the person. Fetishism, according to Freud in 1905, is an effect of the overvaluation of the beloved person.[57] Deleuze's understanding of fetishism in masochism is more similar to the way in which Freud depicts fetishism in his short text 'Fetishism' from 1927.[58]

In this text, Freud presents an Oedipal understanding of fetishism.[59] This means that Freud begins from the assumption that the confrontation with the absence of the penis in the woman is an important moment in the child's development. Normally, as we have seen before, according to Freud this observation has the effect that the child takes the castration threat seriously and then represses Oedipal wishes. However, the fetishist refuses to give up faith in a mother with a penis. He denies the female genitals by attaching himself to an object that substitutes for the woman's penis. This fixation on the fetish obscures the absence of the penis and arrests the sexual desire for female genitals.[60] Severin's predatory eroticism also means that the movement towards the female genitals stops. This stoppage, which is reflected in the photographic scenes and frozen poses, is expressed in the choice of the fur coat that hides the female genitals. We must therefore understand the fur coat as a fetish in a Freudian sense, namely as a cover for the vagina, which, however, does not mean that this fetish is a substitute for the penis. Another difference from Freud is that Deleuze does not understand the fetish as a reaction to a shortcoming in reality, which requires covering. Masoch must be understood from an imaginative ideal of a non-genital mother expressing herself in the fixation on the fur coat. In other words, the fetish is not a reaction to a trauma but the expression of an erotic fantasy that is cold towards genital sexuality and suspends the movement towards the female genitalia.[61]

The central role of the cold mother in the masochistic universe is not only expressed in fetishism but also has far-reaching consequences for the father. Indeed, from a Freudian perspective, the confrontation with the female genitalia means that the child takes the father's castration threat seriously. However, the disavowal of the mother's absence of the penis leads to the father's threat losing its weight. The father is absent from Masoch and the law he represents has no meaning. The masochistic ideal evokes memories of the matriarchy. This artificial situation is not an extension of human nature. As a result, there is a constant danger that spontaneous relationships will reappear. Deleuze draws attention to the fact that Wanda and Severin therefore enter into a contract in which they swear to adhere to the masochistic fantasy.[62] In accordance with the imagination, with the submission to the maternal ideal on the one hand and the denial of the father on the other, the function of this contract is twofold.

First of all, the contract must ensure that the woman adheres to the ideal image that the masochist imposes. Wanda must be strict and sweet at the same time, without her enjoying sexual pleasure. She also adds to Severin's demands: '"You forgot something," she whispered now, "the most important thing: that I always have to wear fur."'[63] Second, the contract ensures that the men and everything reminiscent of the Oedipal father will disappear. This means not only that Wanda needs lovers in order to threaten them violently, but also that she takes the whip and scourges Severin. However, Deleuze stresses that the mother's flogging does not satisfy a need for punishment and is not an expression of guilt for a forbidden desire. The only fault for which the masochist is to blame is not moral, but stems from the fact that he, like his father, still possesses the penis. This resemblance to the father is the actual object of the mother's flogging. Thus, behind the battering mother there is no father. No, it is the father in the masochist who is beaten.[64] The enjoyment that accompanies this is not a pleasure in the humiliation itself. Masochistic pleasure is primarily an effect of what the castrating mother introduces; namely, the rebirth of a new, a-phallic man from the cold mother without the intervention of the father.[65]

Phantasm and Nature

Deleuze recalls that Masoch is familiar with *Das Mutterrecht* from 1861.[66] In this groundbreaking study, Swiss historian and anthropologist Johann Jakob Bachofen presents a grotesque Hegelian vision of history in which he distinguishes three phases. More specifically, Bachofen raises for the first time the idea, rejected today, of a matriarchy that follows hetaerism and anticipates the modern patriarchy: 'Although the matriarchy's struggle against other forms is revealed by different phenomena, the underlying principle of development is clear. The matriarchy is followed by the patriarchy and preceded by unregulated hetaerism.'[67] What do these phases involve?[68]

The first, hetairistic phase – the period of Aphrodite, the goddess of love and sexuality – is dominated by nomadic Berbers, such as the Garamantes and the Nasamones from Libya. These peoples, according to Bachofen, are characterised by the absence of the father. After all, there is a tyrant at the head of every nation who puts women at the disposal of the people. As a result, the father is unfamiliar with the children born from a promiscuous sexuality. According to Bachofen, this lifestyle is reflected in the 'wild' plant life of the marshes. Between the first and the second phase major events take place: first, the Ice Age, which drains the marshes and creates the steppe, and second, revolt against the tyrant by the Amazons, a people of female warriors. The second, gynocratic phase – the period of Demeter, the goddess of agriculture – leads to agricultural society. The wild marshes make way for planted fields. This focus on fertility, according to Bachofen, is accompanied by the rise of matriarchal power. In the second phase the man is subordinate to the woman, which means that she is no longer merely a public object of lust; now she only creates new life. Finally, the third, Apollonian phase leads to the patriarchal victory over the matriarchy. The woman is subjugated, and her fate is linked to the family and marriage.

According to Deleuze, Masoch does not read Bachofen's work out of an intellectual interest and in the capacity of the history teacher he had been at the University of Graz since 1856. The reason for Masoch's reading lies in his personal life history. Deleuze states: 'The phantasm here finds what it needs, a theoretical ideological structure that gives it the value of a general conception of human nature and of the world.'[69] According to Deleuze, what Masoch reads in Bachofen's *Das Mutterrecht* responds to a personal need: the need of fantasy.[70] What exactly does Deleuze mean by a fantasy and what does that mean in the case of Masoch? Why does this fantasy need a theoretical foundation? And in what sense does Bachofen's grotesque view of history respond to this need?

These questions can be answered by means of a short text by Masoch, namely *Souvenir d'enfance et réflexion sur le roman* from 1888.[71] In it, Masoch states that every artist is characterised by a disposition that individualises him and separates him from his environment.[72] In Masoch's youth, this predisposition manifests itself in an interest in prints of executions, legends of martyrs and the atrocities told to him by his mother. During his adolescence, this sensitivity to the joy of cruelty crystallises into a fixed idea in response to a specific event that takes place when Masoch is ten years old and plays hide and seek with the children of Countess Zénobie.[73] While playing, he hides in the Countess's bedroom behind a coat rack on which a lot of clothes are hung. Hardly has he hidden himself when Zénobie, dressed in a short Gallic fur coat, throws her lover onto the sofa in the same room. Suddenly, however, Zénobie's husband enters the room. Even before he can express his indignation, Zénobie slaps his face, causing him to fall backwards, bleeding. At the same time the coat rack falls and Zénobie notices the young Leopold. She gets very angry, throws him to the ground, presses her knee onto his shoulder and beats him. Entirely in line with Jean-Jacques Rousseau's confession that as a young man he enjoyed punishment by a governess, Masoch's pain also mixes with pleasure. Then, the Count returns and throws himself at Zénobie's feet to ask her forgiveness. Meanwhile Masoch flees, but driven by curiosity he continues to listen for a while. He hears the cracking of the whip and the moaning of the Count.

This event is not trauma in the sense that it unexpectedly surprises Masoch and counteracts his psychological economy. Rather, the opposite is the case. In Masoch's text on the novel, for example, we read: 'the impressions of life that present to the author the living figure, the prototype of which already exists in his imagination, then join this disposition'.[74] The scene with Zénobie does not disrupt Masoch's psyche but is an extension of his disposition. Submitting, witnessing and hearing Zénobie's violent actions arouses his enthusiasm and provides them with the material in which they can express themselves. This results in the psychological image, the so called 'phantasm', of being beaten by a caring but strict mother.

This image, among others, dominates Masoch's love story with Anna von Kottowitz-Wasserzieher. He talks to her about animals and is happy when she hits him in the face. Anna also notes that he makes love with great force after she has first punished him.[75] This history, just like Masoch's later sexual relations, expresses his imagination. The same image is also found in *Venus im Pelz*, which goes back to his relationship with Fanny Pistor, and in *Das Volksgericht* from 1882, in which Masoch describes the relationship between the robber Kyrilla and Feodisia, a despotic woman who leaves her husband for a large landowner.[76] Masoch's sexual life and literature are dominated by the obsessive depiction of a cold, tyrannical woman.

In the text in which he reflects on the novel, Masoch nevertheless indicates that he does not know where that image comes from or why it has appeared.[77] Precisely why that disposition is of singular interest to him and why those drives characterise his imagination is a mystery to him. In Bachofen's writings, Masoch finds the solution to this problem. In his three-part sketch of history – in Bachofen's 'mythology', Deleuze argues – Masoch discovers the contours of his own fantasy: the mother, the Demeter figure from the second phase, reflects Masoch's ideal; the two extremes, the nymphomaniac and the 'male' sadist, are a foreshadowing of Aphrodite and the Apollonian cruel patriarchy respectively. In other words, in *Das Mutterrecht*, Masoch finds what he needs. Bachofen's mythology provides him with the theoretical foundation or objective framework from which he can understand his strange disposition and fantasy. Masoch understands his mother ideal as an expression of the cold landscape and Demeter.

This means that Masoch's own way of dealing with his strange fantasy is the opposite of the traditional psychoanalytical treatment of the phantasm. Masoch does not associate his imagination with his personal history, but separates it from the individual embedding and understands it as an update of an impersonal history. This depersonalisation explains why the masochistic ideal can spread to areas of life other than sexuality. Mythologisation offers a broader, grander scope that does not hinder Masoch's sexuality, but gives it the power to unfold. Fed by reading Bachofen, he can express his ideal, for example in an exceptional Christian theology, in which the father is crucified, the son is taken from the cross by the mother, and the utopia of a communist matriarchy is installed, based on agriculture and surrounded by wide fields.[78]

IV Deleuze's Opponents

In the two previous sections we have looked at Deleuze's interpretation of the literature of Sade and Masoch. In what follows, I will show why Deleuze juxtaposes the oeuvre of the two writers. This will show that Deleuze's reading is intended as an explicit criticism of a number of leading figures who have thought about sadism and masochism. I will also show that from Deleuze's reading a second criticism can be deduced which in *Présentation de Sacher-Masoch* he does not yet explicitly mention, but which anticipates the 'anti-Oedipus project' of a few years later. In order to get a clear picture of both criticisms, we first need to briefly return to Henri Bergson.

Sadism versus Masochism

One of Bergson's best-known essays is *Le rire: Essai sur la signification du comique* dating from 1900. That essay is interspersed with countless illustrations. Bergson opens with the comical situation in which a man suddenly falls over because he trips on a stone protruding from the footpath.[79] The bystanders would not have laughed if the man had lain down on the path freely. This means that it is not the sudden fall itself that is comical, but the awkwardness of the man and the fact that he did not notice the irregularity in the footpath. According to Bergson, one laughs at the man's lack of the flexibility to adapt to an unusual situation. Another example is comic facial expressions.[80] Some of them are characterised by a tic: moving the angle of the mouth or blinking. The reason why this can make others laugh is that the face loses its normal shape and that this distortion is sometimes maintained. It is as if the face is driven by a mechanism that deprives it of the possibility of going back to its original form. Bergson points out the comicality of both the fallen man and the facial expression in the same way. According to him, a situation, action or person is comical when flexibility is affected by a rigid automatism.

We must understand this interpretation from Bergson's view of what philosophy should be. According to Bergson, according to Deleuze in *Le bergsonisme* from 1966, philosophy must focus on the ontological distinction between things that interfere with reality but differ fundamentally.[81] Of course, the philosopher's task is not to prevent substantially different things from occurring together. The philosopher searches for traces of things in reality that are mixed but between which there is a conceptual distinction. It is from this perspective that we need to understand Bergson's interest in the comic. After all, the comical shows how two virtually separate, parallel lines of force intersect during their actualisation. The laughter with the falling man originates from the intersection of suppleness and stiffness, but both go back to the lightness of the soul and the heaviness of matter, between which Bergson believes there is an essential distinction ontologically.[82]

Deleuze's *Présentation de Sacher-Masoch* must be read with that Bergsonian background. First of all, Deleuze observes that in both Sade and Masoch sadism and masochism occur together: 'More than that, the "meeting" of sadism and masochism, the appeal they make to each other, seems clearly inscribed in the oeuvre of Sade as well as in that of Masoch.'[83] In the final scene from *Venus im Pelz*, for example, Wanda becomes a sadistic woman who commissions her lover to violently whip 'the poetry out of Severin's body'. In *Les 120 journées de Sodome*, the libertines regularly organise sessions in which they allow themselves to be abused.

However, according to Deleuze, this does not mean that sadism and masochism are intrinsically linked. Firstly, sadism is not at the heart of masochism. Sadism, on the contrary, introduces the end of masochistic staging. Thus, at the end, Wanda falls out of her role as a cold, strict mother, and with the arrival of the Greek assistant, the rejected father returns as well. This accomplice does not destroy Severin's similarity to the father but does destroy his masochistic fantasy: the sadistic Greek man heals Severin of his masochism.[84] Secondly, masochism is not part of the essence of sadism. The sadist's demand that he himself needs to be mistreated is only intended to check whether his plan was successful or not. The harshness with which he threatens his victim assures him that he has gone far enough; mildness teaches him that he has saved his victim too much.[85] Masochism and sadism can intersect, but Sade's and Masoch's worlds, according to Deleuze's Bergsonian reading, are fundamentally different. While sadism is dominated by the father, reason, philosophy of nature and apathy, masochism is dominated by the mother, imagination, mythology and coldness.

The thesis that the two perversions are incompatible goes against the views of a few authoritative figures. First of all, Deleuze addresses the two pioneers of modern sexology, namely the British doctor Havelock Ellis and the German psychiatrist Richard von Krafft-Ebing.[86] In his *Psychopathia Sexualis*, the latter states: 'The counterpart of sadism is masochism. While the first wants to cause suffering and use violence, the second wants to cause pain and feel subjugated to violence.'[87] Sadism means sexual enjoyment from inflicting pain or subjugating others. The masochist enjoys the pain inflicted on him or subjugation. Masochism is thus the passive variant of active sadism.[88] This means that sadism and masochism are not incompatible. After all, the two phenomena have in common the enjoyment of pain. Krafft-Ebing's and Ellis' understanding of sadism and masochism means that both originate from the same root of pleasure-pain, of which sadism is the active and masochism the passive expression.[89]

Second, Deleuze also criticises Freud's conception of sadism and masochism.[90] In the above-mentioned text 'Drei Abhandlungen zur Sexualtheorie' Freud claims that sadism and masochism occur in one and the same person together. Every sadist, he says, is a masochist, and vice versa.[91] In 1905 Freud mentions this thesis only indirectly. However, this statement is elaborated more fully in the 1915 text 'Triebe und Triebschicksale'. In this respect, Freud distinguishes the following four phases.[92]

The first phase consists of an original sadism or a drive to overpower the other. In the second phase both the object and the purpose of the overpowering change. Now the person is no longer torturing himself, but is tortured by others. This deflection to one's own person and the associated shift from an active to a passive object of the drive also characterises the phase of sexual masochism, which is the third phase. During this third phase, the masochist does not hurt himself but is mistreated by another person. The masochist enjoys his role as victim because he can move into the active position he previously occupied himself and which is now taken by someone else. The fourth phase is that of sexual sadism, in which one enjoys the pain rather than overwhelming the other. That pleasure is only possible after the third, masochistic phase. The sadist identifies with the victim and enjoys the pain he first inflicted himself. In short, sexual masochism (third phase) presupposes an original sadistic overpowering drive (first phase), and sexual sadism (fourth phase) only becomes possible from the point of view of sexual masochism (third phase). In 1920 Freud revised the idea that the basis of masochism was an original sadism.[93] In contrast to his earlier concept, Freud now states that masochism is the starting point. Nevertheless, the underlying idea remains the same: one sexual perversion is derived from the other. What is original – sadism first, masochism later – changes, but the thesis that one perversion goes back to another is retained. Sadism and masochism are not two fundamentally different perversions, according to Freud, but can be reduced to each other.[94]

Sadism and Masochism: Non-Oedipal Perversions?

Although the tenor of his criticism is the same in both cases, Deleuze mentions Krafft-Ebing and Ellis only indirectly. The structure of his study is primarily accompanied by an explicit criticism of Freud because he states that sadism and masochism are mutually reducible. In so doing, according to Deleuze, Freud disregards the essential distinction between the two perversions. In the background of Deleuze's study, however, there is a second Bergsonian critique of Freud.[95] Deleuze does not elaborate this criticism in *Présentation de Sacher-Masoch*, but I will show that we can deduce it from his interpretation of Sade and Masoch. In order to get a good idea of what exactly Deleuze criticises, I will first investigate 'Ein Kind wird geschlagen' from 1919.[96]

With this text, as can be seen from the subtitle, Freud wants to map out the origin of the perversions.[97] For this, he bases himself on six cases, four women and two men, all characterised by the fantasy that a child is beaten.[98] According to Freud, enjoying this representation, which leads to masturbation, presupposes two preceding phases. In the first moment the performance 'my father beats the child I hate' is central. This psychological image is based on the loving bonding of the girl with her father and her jealousy towards a newly born brother or sister to whom the father pays a lot of attention. The girl imagines that her father is hitting her hated brother or sister. The message she associates with this is that the father loves her alone. At the end of the first phase, this early incestuous love translates into a genital paternal wish, which is then supressed under the pressure of the Oedipal ban. The patient cannot remember the second phase, which is a construction by Freud. During that phase, it is still the father who hits. However, he no longer beats the brother or sister, but the imaginative child herself. Freud's explanation of this masochistic fantasy is twofold. On the one hand, the fantasy satisfies an unconscious need for punishment arising from the sense of guilt about the fact that the genital desire for the father, despite the Oedipal prohibition, lives on in the unconscious. On the other hand, the masochistic fantasy meets the desire for the father. The suppression of genital sexuality, according to Freud, leads to the regression to pregenital sadistic sexuality. The genitally conceived fantasy from the first phase ('father loves only me') changes as a result into the representation 'father beats me', which causes sexual arousal. In the third phase, the idea 'a child is beaten' is forced upon the patient. In this performance, the girl observes how a teacher hits a group of boys. These boys act as substitutes for the girl. As a result, the enjoyment associated with the fantasy performance must be understood not in a sadistic sense, but in a masochistic sense.

The important point is that Freud thinks masochism in Oedipal terms in 'Ein Kind wird geschlagen.' This applies to his two interpretations of being beaten from the second phase. In one case, the desire to be beaten is an expression of a need for punishment that springs from a sense of guilt. This guilt arises because desire does not disappear, despite the ban on incest. In the other case, beating meets the desire for the parent. This emphasis on genital desire and the ban on incest is completely absent from Deleuze's reading. According to Deleuze, as we have seen, masochism is characterised by the absence of genital desires. The central feature is a predacious yet warm relationship between the masochist and the maternal figure, whose genitals are covered by a fur coat. Moreover, the consequence of the denial of the female sex is that the Oedipal patriarchal law does not become interiorised. In Masoch's world, only motherly figures reign who radically reject the father and the law he represents. It follows that, according to Deleuze, we cannot understand masochism from and as a reaction to the conflict between genital desire and the law of the father. Masochism is neither an expression of a guilt that, despite the Oedipal ban, results from the survival of the genital desire, nor a peculiar, regressive way to satisfy the desire forbidden by law. On the one hand, there is no genital desire in the masochist that unconsciously persists, causes a sense of guilt and bypasses the ban on the Oedipal father through beating; on the other hand, there is no law in Masoch's universe that forbids and supplants desire.[99]

From this we can conclude that *Présentation de Sacher-Masoch* is not only a long, spun-out, frontal attack on those views that do not recognise the essential distinction between sadism and masochism. In the background there is also a criticism that is already laying the foundations of Deleuze and Guattari's later 'anti-Oedipus project'.[100] The criticism is that Freud understands perversions such as sadism and masochism in Oedipal terms, just like neuroses.[101] In so doing, Freud denies that sadism and masochism are the expression of a reality that has nothing in common with neurosis.[102] This difference comes to light after a thorough reading of Sade's and Masoch's literature, but not after reading Sophocles. His tragedy can be instructive with regard to neurosis, but it does not help to map out the perversions.[103]

V Conclusion

Unlike the modernists and *nouveaux novanciers* of his time, Deleuze does not consider Sade's and Masoch's literature as an autonomous, self-referential object that is detached from reality. For Deleuze, the primary importance of Sade's and Masoch's literature is not that it teaches something about the lives of their writers: their desires, memories, worries, experiences – in short, *dirty little secrets*.[104] He is only interested in Sade's and Masoch's literature as far as it also has a clinical reference. The assumption on which the claim of Deleuze's study is based is that both writers are doctors or symptomatologists. Their literature is clinically pioneering: for the first time in history, Sade and Masoch have grouped together the signs and symptoms of sadism and masochism respectively.[105] According to Deleuze, von Krafft-Ebing named both perversions not after their first or best-known patients, but after those who first sharply depicted both perversions. Moreover, Sade's and Masoch's literature also teaches something about clinical reality and shows what is overlooked by psychologists, psychiatrists and psychoanalysts. (One may ask, however, how convincing Deleuze's assumption is, since Sade's and Masoch's characters clearly belong to a specific historical context, and therefore it might be expected that they differ from the perverts treated by psychologists and psychiatrists.)[106] Deleuze shares this point of view with Freud, but at the same time this also leads to a criticism of Freud's psychoanalytical theory. After all, the common thread of Deleuze's study is that a reading by Sade and Masoch shows that sadism and masochism have nothing in common. This thread also shows that for Deleuze philosophy and literature are interwoven.[107] According to Deleuze, literature itself is not harmful to the truth, nor does he understand literature as a vehicle for his thoughts. Instead, he finds in literature an ally upon which he relies in order to perform one of the main tasks of philosophy, namely criticism, in the field of the clinic.[108] According to Deleuze, who, in this respect follows Bergson's example, one of the main tasks of philosophy is to expose and thus distinguish fraudulent units. It is precisely for this reason that he is interested in Sade and Masoch. Their oeuvre meets the philosopher's task of disrupting false entities, in this case the clinical non-entity 'sadomasochism'. In other words, Deleuze is interested in Sade's literature because, when juxtaposed with Masoch's oeuvre, it illustrates the idea of two heterogeneous and parallel series operating according to different principles.

Conclusion

When Apollinaire, in the first decade of the last century, claimed that the writer and libertine Marquis de Sade might dominate the twentieth century, this probably resulted from the observation that interest in Sade was increasing after a century during which little attention was paid to his work. During the following decades, the surrealists saw Sade as an ally, various texts by Sade were found and published, and biographers dealt with the life of 'the divine Marquis'. Although the life and work of Sade still attract interest to this day, it is somewhat exaggerated to conclude that Sade dominated the past century. Nevertheless, in a sense Apollinaire has been proven right. After the Second World War, Sade enjoyed the attention of the leading figures of the intellectual Parisian scene. Among the first readers and commentators are Klossowski, Blanchot and Bataille. Later, Lacan, Barthes and Deleuze also joined in.

These commentators are aware of the Sade studies of their colleagues and also refer to them.[1] For example, Blanchot and Lacan take up the expression *Être-suprême-en-méchanceté* introduced by Klossowski; Deleuze and Bataille refer to Klossowski and Blanchot respectively; and Lacan praises Klossowski's perspicacity in *Sade mon prochain*. However, this does not mean that the various studies are very similar in terms of content. Despite the fact that these French philosophers regularly refer to each other – and often move in the same circles – it is not the case that the differences between their interpretations are minimal. When these studies are compared, it is noticeable that their scope differs, that different aspects are emphasised, that the same aspect is approached from a different perspective or that something is highlighted that no other reading pays attention to. Klossowski, for example, holds the erotic and cruel scenes against a gnostic background, while the same scenes are interpreted in a formalistic sense by Barthes and are associated with Kant's categorical imperative by Lacan. It is also striking that Deleuze states that the sadist is sexually excited by thinking, while Klossowski believes that the sadist is a dreamer and that he enjoys the pointless repetition of always doing the same thing. Bataille, on the other hand, claims that the sadist's enjoyment is an effect of unification with that which transcends ordinary, profane life. Or take, for example, the studies by Klossowski and Bataille. Both shed light on Sade from a psycho-biographical perspective, but while Klossowski believes that Sade writes in order to come to terms with a certain problem, Bataille argues that Sade starts writing in order to justify himself and that writing is also an expression of his apathy. Blanchot, for his part, claims that, while writing, language detaches itself from Sade's hands and thereby reveals its materiality and autonomy. However, despite these differences, a similarity also emerges. The authors always read Sade's literature as an illustration, reflection or expression of a theme or viewpoint that often recurs elsewhere in their oeuvre. In other words, the different Sade interpretations can, from a certain point of view, be read as a lively introduction to the thinking of some of the leading figures in French post-war philosophy.

In addition to this similarity, a second coherence emerges that is more related to the content.[2] Klossowski claims, for example, that the life of the person Marquis de Sade gravitates around the thought of sodomy and purity that keeps cropping up but nevertheless escapes him. Blanchot and Barthes agree that Sade's literature heralds the death of the author as the subject of language and text. Lacan further argues that the sadist is focused on an object that falls out of the symbolic order but that at the same time does not escape the grip of the symbolic. Finally, Bataille understands the apathetic sadist as the expression of the impersonal flux of energy and states that in the pure thinking of the sadist *natura naturans*, or first nature, expresses itself. What these interpretations have in common is that they announce a new way of thinking. In what sense?

As is well known, modern philosophy places man at the heart of our concerns. This is one of the distinctions between modern and classical philosophy. After all, in pre-modern times, it was not man but God who was the centre of reality: He created the world and He functioned as the centre of man's thinking and acting. This means that in pre-modernity man was only the passive recipient of the knowledge and the law that God revealed to him. In modern philosophy, on the other hand, man occupied the sovereign position that used to be reserved for God. The basis of knowledge and action was no longer with Him, but with man. A typical example is the Copernican revolution Kant caused in epistemological thinking. After all, according to Kant, knowledge is created by the human cognitive capacities that bring order to the sensory world. In his moral philosophy, too, Kant extends this turn to man. Moral action, according to Kant, does not obey a heteronomous, divine law but, on the basis of the autonomy of reason, springs from 'the moral law within me'. In the six interpretations that this book has investigated, the idea always recurs that man – in this case the sadist and Sade as a person or writer – as the sovereign subject of reality 'dies' and disappears from the centre of reality. Marquis de Sade and his characters are 'neither God nor master' over reality, but are subjected to and determined by language, thought or the flux that precedes their will, freedom or Ego. In short, the studies discussed above can also be read as a fresh introduction to postmodernism through sadism. That may not be the most common way to get to know that thinking, but at least it has the advantage of appealing to the imagination.

Notes

Introduction

1. This book is based upon my Dutch book *Markies de Sade: Essays over ethiek en kliniek, literatuur en natuur.*
2. 'The divine Marquis' is a frequently used expression among Sade interpreters. It was first used by Apollinaire.
3. Apollinaire, *L'œuvre du marquis de Sade*, p. 17; my translation.
4. By 'Sade' I mean the literature of the Marquis. In cases where I refer to the life of Sade as a person, I mention this explicitly.
5. Apart from the philosophers mentioned, de Beauvoir also wrote an essay on Sade, 'Faut-il brûler Sade?' I will not devote a separate chapter to that essay because de Beauvoir's text is highly biographical in nature, and also because she describes rather than interprets. For more information, see Butler, 'Beauvoir on Sade', and Lauwaert, 'Not Just Free but Flesh'. Foucault also regularly returns to Sade, without, however, writing a separate comprehensive study. For a discussion of Foucault's literature, see Marty, *Pourquoi le XXe siècle*, pp. 131–70. Camus, for his part, writes about Sade in the well-known *L'homme révolté*, but too little to be relevant here. Finally, one could ask: why do I not mention Sartre? The reason is that Sartre, in *L'être et le néant*, does not depart from, and never speaks of, Sade. He only discusses sadism in a (non-)clinical sense.
6. These names, which are well known, are often brought together under the somewhat tired term 'postmodern'. Later in the Introduction, I come back to this briefly.

7. For a historical overview of the reception of the work of Sade, see Marty, *Pourquoi le XXe siècle*.
8. In what follows, 'libertine' is synonymous with 'sadist'.
9. Needless to say, I will not highlight every aspect of those interpretations. It would undoubtedly be particularly interesting, for example, to explore Bataille's suggestion that Sade is a Christian thinker, or to take a closer look at the humour Deleuze discovers in Sade. However, there is no space here to go into all these matters in greater depth.

Chapter 1

1. A first rough version of this chapter has been published earlier as 'Pierre Klossowski Reads Sade Theologically: Modernity and Salvation'.
2. Klossowski, 'Protase et apodose', p. 9; my translation.
3. What Klossowski means by 'pathological' will be made clear in the fourth section.
4. Klossowski, *Sade mon prochain*. 'Éléments d'une étude' is included as an abridged version as the second appendix, entitled 'Le père et la mère dans l'œuvre de Sade' (ibid., pp. 189–201). 'Le mal et le négation d'autrui' appears in a slightly different form as 'Esquisse du système de Sade' (ibid., pp. 47–95). The central idea of 'Le monstre' is included in the last part of 'Delectatio morosa' (ibid., pp. 118–32, 129–32). 'L'hommage à la vierge' (ibid., pp. 105–17) and 'Destruction et pureté' (ibid., pp. 99–104) appear in 1947 for the first time, and this under the heading 'Sous le masque de l'athéisme'. 'Le marquis de Sade et la révolution' is included as 'Sade et la révolution' (ibid., pp. 13–43). 'Le corps du néant' has the same title in *Sade mon prochain* as before (ibid., pp. 155–83). In *Sade mon prochain* one can also read 'Don Juan selon Kierkegaard' (ibid., pp. 135–52) and 'Qui est mon prochain?' This last text is divided into the first (ibid., pp. 185–7) and third appendices (ibid., pp. 203–4).
5. Apart from a few footnotes, the first version of 'Sade et la révolution' is identical to the second version (Klossowski, *Sade mon prochain, précédé de: Le philosophe scélérat*, pp. 59–87; this text is also included in Marquis de Sade, *Œuvres complètes. Tome III*). This is also the case for the three parts of 'Sous le masque de

l'athéisme' (this text also appears in Marquis de Sade, *Œuvres complètes. Tome X*): 'Destruction et pureté' (Klossowski, *Sade mon prochain, précédé de: Le philosophe scélérat*, pp. 139–43), 'L'hommage à la vierge' (ibid., pp. 145–58) and 'Delectatio morosa' (ibid., pp. 159–70). This is not so for 'Esquisse du système de Sade' (ibid., pp. 91–136; this text is also included in Marquis de Sade, *Œuvres complètes. Tome XIII*). In 1967 Klossowski rewrote the beginning and end of the essay. The second appendix, 'Le père et la mère dans l'œuvre de Sade' (Klossowski, *Sade mon prochain, précédé de: Le philosophe scélérat*, pp. 177–86), has also been changed heavily: the last six lines in the text have been deleted. The other appendix, 'Qui est mon prochain?', has not been changed (ibid., pp. 175–6, 187–8).

6. In the same year this text was also published in Marquis de Sade, *Œuvres complètes. Tome XVI*, and as 'Sade ou le philosophe scélérat.' 'L'androgynie dans la représentation sadienne', one of the last paragraphs from 'Le philosophe scélérat', was published later in *Obliques* 1977. Klossowski's other texts on Sade are 'De l'opportunité à étudier l'œuvre du marquis de Sade'; 'À propos d'une anthologie du marquis de Sade'; 'Préface'; 'Justine et Juliette' (this text is included in a shorter version as 'Note additionnelle sur Justine' in *Sade mon prochain, précédé de: Le philosophe scélérat*, pp. 156–8); and 'Sade et Fourier.'
7. This is, however, what Klossowski himself holds in his 'Avertissement', which is the foreword to the republication in 1967 (*Sade mon prochain, précédé de: Le philosophe scélérat*, p. 11).
8. Faulkner, 'The Vision, the Riddle, and the Vicious Circle'; Gallop, *Intersections*, pp. 67–112; Van Pelt, *Pierre Klossowski*, pp. 154–6.
9. Klossowski derives the title 'Sade mon prochain' from St Benedict Joseph Labre, who lived in the eighteenth century. When the saint was asked what he thought of his contemporary, as is written on the page preceding the first chapter of the 1947 edition, he replied that Sade was his neighbour.
10. De Sade, *De 120 dagen van Sodom*, p. 82.
11. Klossowski, *Sade mon prochain, précédé de: Le philosophe scélérat*, pp. 29–31.
12. Ibid., pp. 44–9.
13. De Sade, *De 120 dagen van Sodom*, pp. 32–3; my translation.

14. Ibid., p. 124; my translation.
15. Klossowski, *Sade mon prochain, précédé de: Le philosophe scélérat*, p. 45; my translation.
16. Ibid., pp. 31–7.
17. De Sade, *De 120 dagen van Sodom*, pp. 22–3; my translation.
18. De Sade, *De slaapkamerfilosofen*, p. 76; my translation.
19. De Sade, *De 120 dagen van Sodom*, p. 113; my translation.
20. Ibid., p. 59; my translation.
21. De Sade, *Juliette*, p. 35; my translation.
22. Klossowski, *Sade mon prochain, précédé de: Le philosophe scélérat*, pp. 20–2. Klossowski's interpretation is here based upon the section 'Sade et le révolution' (ibid., pp. 59–87).
23. Ibid., p. 91.
24. Ibid., pp. 96–7.
25. De Sade, 'Gesprek tussen een priester en een stervende', p. 75; my translation.
26. Klossowski, *Sade mon prochain, précédé de: Le philosophe scélérat*, pp. 103–9.
27. Sade himself does not use the expression *L'Être Suprême en méchanceté* but has *L'Être Suprême* (*Juliette*, p. 372).
28. Ibid., pp. 112–15.
29. Ibid., pp. 97, 107, 113.
30. Ibid., pp. 117–22. For the Pope's discussion to which Klossowski refers, see de Sade, *Juliette*, pp. 730–48.
31. Klossowski (*Sade mon prochain, précédé de: Le philosophe scélérat*, pp. 123–5) states that nature's desire is an illustration of what Freud calls 'the death drive'. This similarity can be seen, among other things, in a passage from *Das Unbehagen der Kultur* from 1930 in which Freud describes the death drive as the destruction of the capacity to revive (Freud, 'Het onbehagen in de cultuur', p. 510).
32. Klossowski, *Sade mon prochain, précédé de: Le philosophe scélérat*, p. 140; my translation.
33. This explanation is based upon Leisegang, *La gnose*, pp. 9–47; Loth and Michel, *Dictionnaire de théologie catholique: Sixième partie*, pp. 1434–67; Pelikan, *Christian Tradition*, pp. 68–120; Runciman, *Le manichéisme médiéval*, pp. 7–29; *Sacramentum mundi*, pp. 1–12.

34. Klossowski, *Sade mon prochain, précédé de: Le philosophe scélérat*, pp. 140–3.
35. Ibid., p. 127.
36. Ibid., p. 143.
37. Ibid., p. 121.
38. De Sade, *De slaapkamerfilosofen*, p. 97; my translation.
39. Pelikan, *Een geschiedenis van Maria*, pp. 201–12.
40. Ibid., pp. 125–35.
41. De Sade, *De 120 dagen van Sodom*, p. 36; my translation.
42. Ibid., p. 29; my translation.
43. Klossowski, *Sade mon prochain, précédé de: Le philosophe scélérat*, p. 146.
44. Ibid., pp. 141–2, 159–60, 163.
45. Here I rely on Praz, *Lust, dood en duivel*, pp. 21–33.
46. De Sade, *Juliette*, p. 59; my translation.
47. Klossowski, *Sade mon prochain, précédé de: Le philosophe scélérat*, pp. 146–7, 163.
48. Ibid., pp. 146, 166.
49. Although in this context she is not talking about the sadist, but about the person Marquis de Sade, this thesis is diametrically opposed to what de Beauvoir claims. According to de Beauvoir, the Marquis has no feeling in his body. It is to remedy this that he hurts the other. By letting the body of the other come to the surface in pain, Sade hopes to be able to regain a feeling in his own body ('Moeten wij Sade verbranden?', pp. 30–1).
50. Ibid., p. 148.
51. Klossowski, *Sade mon prochain, précédé de: Le philosophe scélérat*, p. 159.
52. Ibid., p. 166.
53. Ibid., p. 171.
54. Ibid., p. 149.
55. When he discusses Sade in his seventh seminar, Lacan also mentions the expression *delectatio morosa*, without going back over it any further (*L'éthique de la psychanalyse*, p. 232). Klossowski uses the expression *delectatio morosa* not only in his Sade studies, but also in other places in his oeuvre. See Van Pelt, *Pierre Klossowski*, pp. 108–14.

56. Klossowski, *Sade mon prochain, précédé de: Le philosophe scélérat*, p. 160.
57. Ibid., pp. 161–2. For a more comprehensive explanation of the meaning of *delectatio morosa* in scholasticism, see Baladier, *Érôs au Moyen Âge*, pp. 171–98; Loth and Michel, *Dictionnaire de théologie catholique: Deuxième partie*, pp. 245–50.
58. Klossowski, *Sade mon prochain, précédé de: Le philosophe scélérat*, pp. 162–3.
59. Ibid., p. 164.
60. See, for example, Castanet, *Pierre Klossowski*, p. 35.
61. Klossowski, *Sade mon prochain, précédé de: Le philosophe scélérat*, p. 168.
62. Ibid., p. 169.
63. 'Je ne suis ni un romancier, ni un philosophe, ni même un artiste avant d'être d'abord un maniaque – un pur et simple manique.' (Huser, 'Eros, Belzébuth et Cie', p. 6; my translation.)
64. Klossowski, *Les lois de l'hospitalité*, pp. 43–4.
65. Klossowski, 'Protase et apodose', p. 10. For Augustine's interpretation of the simulacrum, I rely on Lugan-Dardigna, *Klossowsk*, and Van Pelt, *Pierre Klossowski*, pp. 62–4.
66. For Klossowski's interpretation of the Roman plays at the theatre, see Klossowski, *Origines culturelles et mythiques*, and Van Pelt, *Pierre Klossowski*, pp. 62–4.
67. For Klossowski's interpretation of the simulacrum, see Foucault, 'Het proza van Actaeon'; Klossowski, *Nietzsche et le cercle vicieux*, pp. 359–63; Lugan-Dardigna, *Klossowski*; Smith, 'Impulses'; Van Pelt, *Pierre Klossowski*, pp. 62–4.
68. Klossowski, *La ressemblance*, p. 104.
69. 'Il y a une telle abondance qui lui est offerte, qu'elle l'écrase s'il ne trouve pas une réplique à cette richesse qui l'accable.' (Ibid., p. 111; my translation.)
70. Klossowski, *Sade mon prochain, précédé de: Le philosophe scélérat*, pp. 31–4.
71. Quoted in Pauvert, *Markies de Sade*, p. 14; my translation.
72. Quoted in Guilbert and Leroy, *50 lettres*, p. 169; my translation.
73. Klossowski, *Sade mon prochain, précédé de: Le philosophe scélérat*, p. 50.
74. De Sade, *De slaapkamerfilosofen*, p. 107; my translation.

75. Klossowski, *Sade mon prochain, précédé de: Le philosophe scélérat*, pp. 22–3.
76. Ibid., p. 139.
77. Ibid., p. 185.
78. Ibid., p. 184.
79. Ibid., p. 185. Klossowski states this in the second appendix, 'Le père et la mère dans l'oeuvre de Sade', which, as already mentioned, relies on 'Eléments d'étude'. In this text, it turns out, Klossowski does not interpret Sade in classical Oedipal terms. Sade's aggression is not against the father, but against the mother. The result of this contrary interpretation is that Klossowski was dismissed by the psychoanalyst René Laforgue, for whom he was currently working as secretary.
80. Klossowski, *Sade mon prochain, précédé de: Le philosophe scélérat*, p. 24.

Chapter 2

1. This chapter is partly based on my publications 'De Terreur van het schrijven' and 'A Poststructuralist Interpretation of Art'.
2. Quoted in Nordholt, '*Het schuwe denken*', p. 11; my translation.
3. Several texts were published later in Blanchot, *Faux pas*.
4. The text was later included in Blanchot, *La condition critique*.
5. Blanchot, 'La raison de Sade', in: Blanchot, *Lautréamont et Sade*, 1949 and 1963, and in: Blanchot, *Sade et Restif de la Bretonne*. Here I discuss this study only tangentially, citing *Sade et Restif de la Bretonne*. For a more comprehensive study, see Loughead, 'More than Adequate Logic'.
6. The 1986 publication is in Blanchot, *Sade et Restif de la Bretonne*. It is this last volume that will be used in the remainder of this chapter.
7. Originally, this text was published in two parts: Blanchot, 'Le règne animal de l'esprit' and 'La littérature et le droit à la mort'. Later both texts were published in Blanchot, *La Part du feu* and *De Kafka à Kafka*.
8. Blanchot, 'Literatuur en het recht op de dood', p. 145; my translation.

9. In what follows, I do not explain Blanchot's thesis that Sade is the author par excellence. After all, this would mean that I compared Blanchot's reading of Sade with his reading of Mallarmé, for example. I shall confine myself to explaining what is inherent in this thesis, namely that Sade meets a particular ideal that Blanchot has in mind.
10. For these facts I rely on Nordholt, '*Het schuwe denken*', pp. 13–20.
11. Blanchot, 'De la révolution à la littérature'.
12. Blanchot, 'L'insurrection, la folie d'écrire', p. 94.
13. Blanchot, 'Literatuur en het recht op de dood', p. 144.
14. Blanchot, 'L'insurrection, la folie d'écrire', p. 81.
15. Ibid., pp. 84–5. This passage can be found in de Sade, *De slaapkamerfilosofen*, p. 211.
16. Blanchot, 'L'insurrection, la folie d'écrire', p. 82.
17. Blanchot, 'La raison de Sade', pp. 13–14.
18. Ibid., p. 39.
19. Ibid., p. 46. On the page where he deals with *Être-suprême-en-méchanceté*, Blanchot indicates that he derives the expression from Klossowski, who introduced it in 1934–5 ('Le mal et la négation d'autrui', p. 18). Another commentator who pays attention to this is the French avant-garde writer and essayist Philippe Sollers. In 1989, in the name of Sade, he wrote a letter in which he associated *Être-suprême-en-méchanceté* with the Reign of Terror and Robespierre's speech from 1794 about 'the cult of the Highest Being' (Sollers, *Sade*). For a discussion of this, see Stockwell, 'Sade and Sollers'. In addition to this letter, Sollers wrote several short contributions about Sade. For more information see Marty, *Pourquoi le XXe siècle*, pp. 345–61.
20. Blanchot, 'La raison de Sade', pp. 46–7. The passage to which Blanchot refers can be found in de Sade, *Juliette*, pp. 375–76.
21. Blanchot, 'La raison de Sade', p. 50.
22. De Sade, 'Gesprek tussen een priester en een stervende', p. 55; my translation.
23. Blanchot, 'La raison de Sade', pp. 49–53.
24. Ibid., p. 54.
25. Blanchot in this context refers to Klossowski, who holds that the sadist needs the other to get rid of his wounded ideal of purity (Blanchot, 'La raison de Sade', p. 43). According to Blanchot,

Klossowski therefore ignores the radicalism of the negation. The sadist does not destroy the other in order to achieve something else; he only needs the other to be able to execute the movement of radical negation.

26. This is a good example of what Bataille calls 'useless negation'.
27. Blanchot, 'L'insurrection, la folie d'écrire', p. 86; my translation.
28. Hegel, *Werke 3*, pp. 431–41.
29. For a more comprehensive discussion of Hegel's conception of the French Revolution and the Reign of Terror, see Arthur, 'Hegel and the French Revolution', and also Stolzenberg, 'Hegel's Critique of the Enlightenment'. For a comment on Blanchot's Hegelian interpretation of the French Revolution, see De Kesel, 'Recht op de dood'.
30. Blanchot, 'L'insurrection, la folie d'écrire', p. 91.
31. Blanchot understands the Sadean universe as anarchy (ibid., pp. 89–91). He does not mean that there are no laws in Sade's world; he rather understands anarchy as the lack of any solid ground that keeps the whole together.
32. Ibid., p. 72.
33. Ibid., pp. 70–1.
34. De Sade, *De slaapkamerfilosofen*, p. 195.
35. Blanchot, 'L'insurrection, la folie d'écrire', p. 77. That Sade as a writer wants to say everything is also reflected in the words he puts in various places in the mouths of his characters. For example, Dolmancé states in the final paragraph of *La philosophie dans le boudoir*: 'Wel, alles is gezegd' ('Well, everything is said'). (De Sade, *De slaapkamerfilosofen*, p. 287; my translation.)
36. Blanchot, 'L'insurrection, la folie d'écrire', p. 77.
37. According to Blanchot, the desire to say everything characterises not only the work of Sade but also that of Jean-Jacques Rousseau (*Le livre à venir*, pp. 63–4).
38. Blanchot, L'insurrection, la folie d'écrire', p. 76.
39. Ibid., p. 72.
40. Ibid., p. 79.
41. Ibid., pp. 77–8.
42. The word 'aesthetic' comes from the Greek *aisthesis*, which means 'empirical' or 'feeling'.
43. Blanchot, 'L'insurrection, la folie d'écrire', p. 78.

44. Ibid., pp. 91–2.
45. Ibid., pp. 147, 149–50.
46. By the term 'neutral,' I allude to the term 'Neutrum,' which was at the heart of Blanchot's thinking from the 1960s. He understands the Neutrum in the original sense of the Latin expression *ne utrum*, which means 'neither one nor the other.' For Blanchot's discussion of the Neutrum see his 'La voix narrative.' For a comment on this text, see Manoury, 'Le Neutre blanchotien'; Hill, '"Not in Our Name"'; Zarader, *L'être et le neutre*.
47. For the relation between Blanchot's and Hegel's understanding of literature, see Dubost, 'La littérature comme épreuve.'
48. See, among others, Blanchot, *L'espace littéraire*.
49. Not only in his phenomenology of the corpse, but also in his reflections on the image and night, Blanchot distinguishes a first and a second version (ibid., pp. 345–59, 215–26). For a discussion of Blanchot's views of the image and the corpse see Vande Veire, 'De imaginaire bevreemding'; Ropars-Wuilleumier, 'On Unworking'; Toumayan, *Encountering the Other*, pp. 115–68.
50. In this way the corpse and language can be seen as an incarnation of Lévinas' *il y a*. For the link between Blanchot and Emmanuel Lévinas, see, among others, Cools, *Langage et subjectivité*; Lafond, 'Des Forêts, Blanchot et Lévinas'; Hansel, 'Maurice Blanchot.'
51. Hegel, *Werke 3*, pp. 294–311. In that paragraph Hegel discusses work in general. Both Kojève (*Introduction à la lecture de Hegel*, p. 90) and Hyppolite (*Genèse et structure de la Phénoménologie de l'Esprit de Hegel*, p. 287) in their interpretation of Hegel give a central place to the workings of the intellectual. It is clear that Blanchot is indebted to this interpretation. Blanchot understands Hegel's paragraph as an analysis of the writer's work.
52. Hegel, *Werke 3*, p. 310.
53. Sartre, *Situations II*, p. 72.
54. Ibid., p. 74.
55. Blanchot, 'Literatuur en het recht op de dood,' p. 153.
56. Ibid., p. 153; my translation.
57. The term 'outside' has a central place in Blanchot's thinking. According to Foucault, Blanchot is focused not on nothing but, as in the title of Foucault's essay on Blanchot, on 'the thinking of the outside.' See Foucault, 'Het denken van het Buiten.'

58. Blanchot, 'L'insurrection, la folie d'écrire', p. 9.
59. Blanchot, 'L'absence de livre'. For a comprehensive interpretation of this text, see van Rooden, 'De list van de beschaving'.
60. Blanchot, 'L'absence de livre', p. 621.
61. Ibid., p. 620.
62. Exodus 35: 1.
63. 'comme s'il fallait le langage (le discours) pour que l'écriture donne lieu à la lisibilité commune'. (Blanchot, 'L'absence de livre', p. 631; my translation.)
64. Ibid., p. 624.
65. Blanchot, 'L'athéisme et l'écriture: L'humanisme et le cri', in: Blanchot, *L'entretien infini*. I cite this edition below unless otherwise stated. For a more comprehensive reading of this text, see ten Kate, 'De schreeuw van het humanisme'.
66. The first part was published into two parts: Blanchot 'L'athéisme et l'écriture: L'humanisme et le cri (1)' and 'L'athéisme et l'écriture: L'humanisme et le cri (fin)'.
67. Blanchot, 'L'athéisme et l'écriture', p. 370.
68. Deuteronomy 4: 11–12.
69. Blanchot, 'L'athéisme et l'écriture', pp. 380–3.
70. Foucault, *De woorden en de dingen*, p. 453; my translation.
71. For a discussion of Blanchot's idea of humanism, see Dalton, 'Man is the Indestructible'.

Chapter 3

1. This chapter is based upon my Dutch text 'Batailles lezing van Sade: Genot en literatuur als expressies van kracht'.
2. One year later, this text was published as 'Sade et la morale'. See also Bataille, 'Le mal dans le platonisme et dans le sadisme', and 'Sade et la morale' in: Bataille, *Œuvres complètes. Tome VII*. I cite this latter version of 'Sade et la morale' below.
3. Bataille, 'Le secret de Sade' and 'Le secret de Sade (II).
4. Bataille, 'Sade', in: Bataille, *La littérature et le mal* and in *Œuvres complètes. Tome IX*.
5. Bataille, 'Le bonheur, l'érotisme et la littérature (II)'.
6. 'Le bonheur, l'érotisme et la littérature (II)' is also the basis for the study 'L'érotisme sans limite'. See also Bataille, 'L'homme souverain de Sade', in: Bataille, *Œuvres complètes. Tome X*.

7. Bataille, 'Sade et l'homme normal,' in: Bataille, *L'érotisme* and in: Bataille, *Œuvres complètes. Tome X.*
8. It is surprising that in recent secondary literature no attention is paid to the fact that Bataille mentions the formal aspects of Sade's literature. See, for example, Roche, 'Black Sun,' and Stoekl, *Bataille's Peak*, pp. 3–31.
9. Bataille, 'L'homme souverain de Sade,' pp. 167–8.
10. De Sade, *De 120 dagen van Sodom*, p. 158; my translation.
11. De Sade, *De slaapkamerfilosofen*, p. 163; my translation.
12. De Sade, *Juliette*, p. 160; my translation.
13. Bataille, 'Le secret de Sade (II),' p. 311.
14. Bataille, 'L'homme souverain de Sade,' p. 174.
15. Ibid., pp. 168–72.
16. These lines are based on 'Théorie de la religion.' For Bataille's framework, see Groot, *Vier ongemakkelijke filosofen*, pp. 275–309.
17. Bataille, 'L'érotisme,' pp. 48–9.
18. This is based on Bataille, 'L'économie à la mesure de l'univers,' 'La part maudite' and 'La limite de l'utile.' For a comprehensive discussion, see Hochroth, 'Scientific Imperative.'
19. Bataille, 'L'homme souverain de Sade,' p. 171. In this context, Bataille quotes from Blanchot's Sade study (ibid., pp. 171–2). For the passage that Bataille quotes, see Blanchot, 'La raison de Sade,' pp. 58–60.
20. Bataille, 'L'homme souverain de Sade,' pp. 169–70. See also Bataille, 'Le secret de Sade (II),' pp. 308–9.
21. See also Bataille, 'L'érotisme,' pp. 90–109.
22. Bataille, 'Le secret de Sade (II),' p. 308.
23. Bataille, 'Le bonheur, l'érotisme et la littérature (II),' p. 407. See also Bataille, 'L'érotisme,' p. 18.
24. Bataille, 'L'homme souverain de Sade,' p. 170.
25. Bataille, 'Le secret de Sade,' p. 159.
26. Bataille, 'Le secret de Sade (II),' p. 307.
27. Bataille, 'L'homme souverain de Sade,' p. 172.
28. De Sade, *Juliette*, p. 18; my translation.
29. What follows is based on Graver, *Stoicism and Emotion*; Holowchak, *The Stoics*, pp. 47–53; van Reijen, 'Ik denk dus ik voel.'
30. Sade and eroticism are only two examples of phenomena that, according to Bataille, should be thought of in terms of *l'économie*

générale. Other phenomena are war, sport and art, among others. See, for example, Bataille, 'La part maudite', pp. 51–79, and 'Théorie de la religion', pp. 281–345. For a comprehensive and critical discussion of these phenomena, see Corbey, 'Gift en transgressie', and ten Kate, *De lege plaats*, pp. 167–264.

31. As we have seen before, not only Bataille but also Klossowski writes about the sadist's apathy. The latter interprets this in two ways. The first interpretation, stemming from the first version of *Sade mon prochain*, holds that the sadist longs for apathy because he aims at the maximum development of energy. In this way, Klossowski holds, the sadist reflects nature (Klossowski, *Sade mon prochain, précédé de: Le philosophe scélérat*, pp. 127–36). In *Le philosophe scélérat* from 1967 he writes that the sadist is obsessed by the law and its transgression, and his aim finally is to behave in such a way that he is insensitive to both law and transgression (ibid., pp. 37–42).
32. As stated before, Bataille understands both eroticism and sadism as expressions of impersonal and aimless energy. In eroticism, however, the emphasis is on goallessness, while in Sade the emphasis is on apathy. Nevertheless, according to Bataille, eroticism always has something apathetic in the sense that the ties with oneself and with the other become looser. Sadistic acts are not themselves aimed at a purpose.
33. Bataille, 'L'homme souverain de Sade', p. 173.
34. De Sade, *Juliette*, p. 15; my translation.
35. Thus, according to Bataille, Sade, as we have seen, is in line with usual eroticism. In addition to this anthropological lecture, Bataille reads Sade, although to a limited extent, from a historical perspective. Indeed, he refers to the sovereign rulers and princes of the *Ancien Régime* (Bataille, 'L'homme souverain de Sade', pp. 164–5). Those decadent sovereigns do not work but only consume the products that others produce for them. In that regard, Bataille says, they lead a life beyond the profane order. According to him, it is exactly this fact that lies at the base of the French Revolution. At the end of the eighteenth century, the revolutionaries do not revolt against the aristocratic class because they want to destroy the country. No, the insurgency

is based on the desire that every human being has, but that until then only the sovereign could satisfy, namely the desire to transcend ordinary life. Sovereign life meets this desire, and it is for this reason that the people attack the Bastille. The people want to take part in the life of luxury and thus satisfy the desire for transcendence. From a certain point of view, we must understand Sade against this background. *L'homme souverain de Sade*, according to Bataille, takes the position once occupied by the sovereign. Through the apathetic act he has the 'inner experience' of a life beyond the profane order that at that time belonged only to the sovereign and that the people could only look at from a certain distance. For Bataille's analysis of sovereign life, see 'La souveraineté'. See also De Kesel, 'Anatomie van een soeverein'.

36. Bataille, 'L'homme souverain de Sade', p. 173.
37. Ibid.; Bataille, 'Le secret de Sade (II)', p. 307.
38. Bataille, 'Sade et la morale', pp. 449–51, and 'L'érotisme sans limite', p. 148.
39. What follows is based on Moyaert, *De mateloosheid van het christendom*, pp. 173–303.
40. The sadist must also be understood in negative terms. Just like the mystic, the sadist is characterised by the fact that he loosens the relation with himself and the other. The difference is, however, that the negation in the case of the mystic is deliberately pursued while in the case of the sadist the release of the self and the other is an effect. In addition, the mystic destroys not only every bond but also his involvement in the world in general.
41. Here, I refer to the title of Bataille's text, published for the first time in 1943, *L'expérience intérieure*.
42. Bataille, 'L'érotisme', p. 13.
43. See also Direk, 'Erotic Experience', p. 110; Durançon, *Georges Bataille*, p. 130; Guerlac, '"Recognition"', pp. 90–2; Hollier, 'Dualist Materialism', pp. 129–30.
44. Bataille, 'L'homme souverain de Sade', p. 174, and 'Sade et l'homme normal', in: Bataille, *L'érotisme*, pp. 194–5.
45. From what we have seen above, it appears that Bataille emphasises the fact that the sadist exceeds a certain kind of boundary. In his Sade studies, he does not focus on, for example, the

question of how the transgression and the boundary relate to each other. The latter is discussed elsewhere (see, for example, 'L'érotisme', pp. 66–72) and is rethought by Foucault later on ('Inleiding tot de transgressie', pp. 59–60). In this context, see also ten Kate, '"Vlug niets zonder weg terug"'.

46. It is in the controversy between Bataille and Breton about Sade that the break between Bataille and the surrealist movement can be felt most strongly.
47. See Bataille's posthumously published letter: 'La valeur d'usage de D. A. F. de Sade (I)', pp. 54–8.
48. Bataille, 'Préface', pp. ix–xi.
49. For a more comprehensive discussion of the relation between the surrealists and Bataille, see Surya, *Georges Bataille*, pp. 142–78.
50. Bataille, 'Sade et l'homme normal', in: Bataille, *Œuvres complètes. Tome X*, pp. 176–7.
51. Ibid., pp. 187–8.
52. When Bataille deals with the activity of writing, he only discusses the involvement with the other and not with the self.
53. De Sade, *De slaapkamerfilosofen*, p. 277; my translation.
54. Bataille, 'Sade et l'homme normal', in: Bataille, *Œuvres complètes. Tome X*, p. 189.
55. De Beauvoir too claims that Sade writes to justify his deeds ('Moeten wij Sade verbranden?', pp. 61–3). Also, note the difference between Bataille's and Klossowski's psycho-biographical reading. Klossowski, as we have seen, suggests that Sade is interested in philosophy not to justify his cruelties, but to put what obsesses him at a distance.
56. Bataille, 'Sade et l'homme normal', in: Bataille, *Œuvres complètes. Tome X*, pp. 186, 190.
57. De Sade, *De slaapkamerfilosofen*, p. 76; my translation.
58. De Sade, *Juliette*, p. 748; my translation.
59. Bataille, 'Sade et l'homme normal', in: Bataille, *Œuvres complètes. Tome X*, p. 187.
60. This interpretation is later stressed by Deleuze (*Présentation*, p. 19).
61. Bataille, 'Sade et l'homme normal', in: Bataille, *Œuvres complètes. Tome X*, p. 190.
62. Bataille, 'Le secret de Sade (II)', pp. 304–5.

63. Ibid., p. 304; Bataille, 'Le secret de Sade', p. 160.
64. De Sade, *De slaapkamerfilosofen*, p. 7; my translation.
65. Bataille, 'Sade et l'homme normal', in: Bataille, *Œuvres complètes. Tome X*, p. 187.

Chapter 4

1. This chapter is partly based upon my text 'Kant met Sade: Sade met Kant'.
2. 'Personne n'a d'ailleurs fait la moindre attention à cet article. Il y a un tout petit bonhomme qui l'a commenté quelque part; je ne sais même pas si c'est paru. Mais jamais personne ne m'a répondu sur cet article. C'est vrai que je suis incompréhensible.' (Lacan, 'Conférence de presse', p. 24; my translation.)
3. 'Kant avec Sade' is mainly based upon the lectures from 23 December 1959 (Lacan, *L'éthique de la psychanalyse*, pp. 87–97), 20 January 1960 (ibid., pp. 129–31), 23 March 1960 (ibid., pp. 221–3), 30 March 1960 (ibid., 232–9) and 4 May 1960 (ibid., pp. 248–56). In what follows, I concentrate on 'Kant avec Sade'. I only refer to Lacan's seminary to better understand 'Kant avec Sade'.
4. Allouch, 'Ça de Kant, cas de Sade', p. 27.
5. Also in 1966, another slightly modified version of Lacan's essay was published in *Écrits*. A last version was published in 1971, namely in the pocket version of *Écrits*, titled *Écrits II*. In what follows, I use the 1966 version from *Écrits* unless otherwise stated.
6. De Beauvoir, 'Moeten wij Sade verbranden?', p. 76.
7. Bataille, 'Sade et la morale', p. 452.
8. Horkheimer and Adorno, *Dialectiek van de Verlichting*, pp. 95–133. This study was first published in New York and three years later in German at Querido in Amsterdam.
9. Later, in 1967, Deleuze also talks about both Kant and Sade.
10. During his seminar, Lacan stated that the pornographic pages in Sade's oeuvre are of little interest to him (Lacan, *L'éthique de la psychanalyse*, p. 221). He also goes against these authors who read Sade's literature as a detailed phenomenology of sadism in the clinical sense (Lacan, 'Kant avec Sade', p. 765). He refers to

Paulhan, among others, who puts Sade on the same level as, for example, von Krafft-Ebing, and who states that Sade's literature should be read as a case study (Paulhan, 'Le marquis de Sade', p. 50). Bataille also opposes those who consider Sade's literature clinically relevant ('Sade et l'homme normal', in: Bataille, *Œuvres complètes. Tome X*, pp. 181–2). In the final chapter we will see that they are diametrically opposed to Deleuze in that respect.

11. 'qu'elle donne la vérité de la *Critique*.' (Lacan, 'Kant avec Sade', p. 766; my translation.) Lacan introduces this thesis by drawing attention to the fact that Kant's *Kritik der Praktischen Vernunft* and Sade's *La philosophie dans le boudoir* succeed one another in time. He writes that Sade's novel is published eight years later (Lacan, 'Kant avec Sade', p. 765). During his seminar on ethics, Lacan states that Sade's text is published six years after Kant's text (*L'éthique de la psychanalyse*, p. 95). Lacan's information is incorrect here both times. *La philosophie dans le boudoir* was published in 1795, seven years after *Kritik der praktischen Vernunft*'s publication in 1788.
12. Zupančič, *Ethics of the Real*.
13. Baas, *Le désir pur*, pp. 22–82, and Žižek, *For They Know Not What They Do*, pp. 229–77.
14. Lacan, *L'éthique de la psychanalyse*, p. 93.
15. Kant, *Kritiek van de praktische rede*, pp. 81–2.
16. Ibid., p. 104.
17. According to Kant, what is pathological is what moves man: passions, desires, lust and displeasure.
18. Lacan, *L'éthique de la psychanalyse*, p. 93.
19. Lacan, 'Kant avec Sade', p. 767.
20. Kant, *Kritiek van de praktische rede*, p. 72.
21. Kant distinguishes 'maxim' from 'law'. A maxim is a rule that is only valid for one's own will. A maxim becomes a law when the rule applies to any reasonable being (ibid., p. 57).
22. Lacan, 'Kant avec Sade', p. 767. For Kant's example, see *Kritiek van de praktische rede*, pp. 67–8.
23. Lacan, 'Kant avec Sade', p. 767.
24. 'Vive la Pologne, car s'il n'y a avait pas de Pologne, il n'y aurait pas de Polonais.' (Ibid.; my translation.)

25. Ibid., p. 768.
26. This criticism of Kant's ethics is Hegelian in nature. For more information, see Heyde, *De verwerkelijking van de vrijheid*, pp. 123–48. The fact that Lacan's criticism is highly Hegelian in inspiration once again illustrates the interest of French post-war philosophy in Hegel. It is not unlikely that Lacan derives his interpretation of the example from Hyppolite. For this, see Hyppolite, *Introduction à la philosophie*, pp. 82–7.
27. 'cette réjection radicale du pathologique, de tout égard pris à un bien, à une passion, voire à une compassion.' (Lacan, 'Kant avec Sade,' p. 770; my translation.)
28. Lacan therefore does not claim that Sade's libertines reject the law. However, this interpretation of Lacan's reading can be found in Sample, 'Lacan, Kant, and Sade,' pp. 11–12.
29. Lacan, 'Kant avec Sade,' p. 770.
30. On this point, Žižek links Lacan's study with Hannah Arendt's account of Eichmann's 1961 trial (Žižek, *Het subject en zijn onbehagen*, pp. 68–75). There, Arendt emphasises that Eichmann refers to Kant during the police interrogation (Arendt, *Eichmann in Jeruzalem*, pp. 238–41). Like the sadist, Eichmann must not be understood from a pathological motivation in a Kantian sense; we must understand him from the motivation of the performance of duty for duty's sake. Žižek stresses, however, that the similarity between sadism and Nazism stops at the apathetic obedience of the sadist and the executioner to the empty law. As a regime, Nazism was by no means formalistic. It was explicitly aimed at creating a strong German community. More generally, it is striking that in the French studies on Sade – written shortly after the Second World War – the oeuvre of Sade and fascism are not linked. It is therefore remarkable that the Italian director Pier Paolo Pasolini, in the 1975 *Bibliografia essenziale of Salò, or the 120 days of Sodom* – a film of Sade's book that is transferred to an explicitly fascist context – refers to the Sade studies of Klossowski, Blanchot and Barthes.
31. '"J'ai le droit de jouir de ton corps, dirai-je à qui me plaît, et ce droit, je l'exercerai, sans qu'aucune limite m'arrête dans le caprice des exactions que j'aie le goût d'y assouvir."' (Lacan, 'Kant avec Sade,' *Critique* 191/1963, p. 294; my translation.)

32. Lacan, 'Kant avec Sade', p. 771. The same idea can also be found in Blanchot's study ('La raison de Sade', pp. 14–15). During his seminar on ethics, Lacan urged his audience to read Blanchot's interpretation (Lacan, *L'éthique de la psychanalyse*, p. 236).
33. De Sade, *De slaapkamerfilosofen*, p. 216. Although Lacan's formulation of the Sadean law is nowhere to be found in Sade's literature in exactly the same words, what Lacan says is very similar to the previous passage from Sade's thesis. It is therefore not unlikely that Lacan found this idea therein for his formulation of the Sadean categorical imperative. This presumption is reinforced by Lacan's assertion that the hard core of Sade's morality can be found in his politico-philosophical pamphlet from *La philosophie dans le boudoir* ('Kant avec Sade', p. 768).
34. '"J'ai le droit de jouir de ton corps, peut me dire quiconque, et ce droit, je l'exercerai, sans qu'aucune limite m'arrête dans le caprice des exactions que j'aie le gout d'y assouvir."' (Ibid., pp. 768–9; my translation)
35. During his seminar on moral philosophy, he formulated Sade's law as follows: 'Prêtez-moi la partie de votre corps qui peut me satisfaire un instant, et jouissez, si cela vous plaît, de celle du mien qui peut vous être agréable.' (Lacan, *L'éthique de la psychanalyse*, p. 237.)
36. See Blanchot, 'La raison de Sade', p. 15.
37. De Sade, *De slaapkamerfilosofen*, pp. 219–20.
38. Lacan, *L'éthique de la psychanalyse*, pp. 96–7.
39. Rüdiger Safranski, without mentioning Lacan's study, also comes to this conclusion (*Het kwaad*, pp. 166–8).
40. I have already pointed out in the introduction to this chapter that Horkheimer and Adorno also connect Kant's and Sade's work. The scope of their study, however, is different from Lacan's. The point of their study is that Sade, in an enlarged form, shows that the Enlightenment has not left the mythical-religious stage but has mimicked it. For a more detailed explanation, see Comay, 'Adorno avec Sade', and Thérien, 'Les Lumières et la dialectique'.
41. That's what Deleuze calls 'Sade's irony'. It lies in the fact that Sade, while Kant has loosened the law from the substantial determination of the good, fills Kant's void with a new substance, namely evil (Deleuze, *Présentation de Sacher-Masoch*, pp. 71–9).

42. Lacan, *L'éthique de la psychanalyse*, p. 96.
43. For a reading of Kant's ethics in the light of 'the logic of appearances' from his first criticism see De Kesel, *Eros en ethiek*, pp. 135–42, and Rogozinski, *Le don de la loi*, pp. 46–9.
44. According to Lacan, Sade shows that Kant's ethics do not guarantee the good and that his ethics require substantive determination. However, it should be noted that Lacan's criticism only applies to the extent that he only looks at Kant's first formulation of the categorical imperative. After all, Kant's ethics is less empty than Lacan makes it appear. Kant's second formulation gives more substance to his ethics. It states that every human being must always be treated as an end in itself and must never be used as a means to an end. With this, Kant immunises himself against a criticism such as that of Lacan. From this perspective, Lacan's thesis should be watered down. This thesis then no longer holds that Sade exposes the shortcoming of Kant, but implies instead that Sade shows the reason why Kant supplements his first formulation of the categorical imperative with a second one.
45. 'Ici Sade est le pas inaugural d'une subversion, dont [. . .] Kant est le point tournant.' (Lacan, 'Kant avec Sade', p. 765; my translation.) According to Marty (*Pourquoi le XXe siècle*, pp. 40–1) this passage is only present in the version from *Critique*. It is clear from the above that this is not the case.
46. For Kant's four forms of evil see Kant, *De religie binnen de grenzen van de rede*, pp. 70–9.
47. Lacan, 'Kant avec Sade', p. 773.
48. De Sade, *Juliette*, p. 372.
49. Ibid., p. 375.
50. Note that not only Lacan but also Klossowski and Blanchot refer to the passage in which the Supreme Being is discussed.
51. Lacan, 'Kant avec Sade', p. 772.
52. Kant, *Kritiek van de praktische rede*, p. 171.
53. Ibid., pp. 160–2.
54. Ibid., pp. 173–81.
55. De Sade, *Justine*, p. 9.
56. Recall that the subtitles of *Justine* and *Juliette* are *les malheurs de la vertu* and *les prospérités du vice* respectively.

57. 'l'axe ancien de l'éthique: qui n'est rien d'autre que l'égoïsme du bonheur. Dont on ne peut dire que toute référence en soit éteinte chez Kant.' (Lacan, 'Kant avec Sade,' p. 786; my translation.)
58. Ibid., p. 790.
59. Ibid.
60. Ibid., p. 786.
61. Ibid., p. 790. As early as the opening lesson in which he announces the programme of his seventh seminar, Lacan clearly states that the 'naturalist liberation from desire' by the libertines has turned out to be a failure (*L'éthique de la psychanalyse*, p. 12).
62. Lacan summarises that in the formulation *Noli tangere matrem* (Lacan, 'Kant avec Sade,' p. 790). He alludes here to the Bible verses in which Jesus, after his resurrection, says to Mary Magdalene: 'Touch me not' (John 20: 17). In Latin, Jesus' commandment is *Noli me tangere.*
63. Revelation 21: 8.
64. Lacan, 'Kant avec Sade,' pp. 775–6. The expression 'the second death' appears for the first time in Lacan's seventh seminar (Lacan, *L'éthique de la psychanalyse*, p. 291).
65. In 'Kant avec Sade,' Lacan does not refer to the passage from *Juliette* on the basis of which he introduces the term 'the second death.' During his seminary on ethics, on the other hand, he reads the passage in its entirety (ibid., pp. 249–50).
66. De Sade, *Juliette*, p. 738.
67. Lacan, *L'éthique de la psychanalyse*, p. 291.
68. Like Klossowski, Lacan relates Sade's philosophy of nature to Freud's death drive (Lacan, 'Kant avec Sade,' pp. 776–7). Lacan is very laudatory about Klossowski's study. At the end of 'Kant avec Sade' he states that *Sade mon prochain* originates from 'the perspicacity of Klossowski' (p. 789).
69. 'il y a quelque part, mis assurément hors du monde de la nature, l'au-delà de cette chaine.' (Lacan, *L'éthique de la psychanalyse*, pp. 251–2; my translation.)
70. In the second chapter we saw that Blanchot also makes a distinction between a first and second death. According to Lacan, however, this second death does not create any meaning but, on the contrary, leads to the destruction of meaning.
71. Kant, *Kritiek van het oordeelsvermogen*, pp. 91–9.

72. I would like to remind you that, according to Klossowski, the victims of Sade are not bound to any body either.
73. Lacan, 'Kant avec Sade', pp. 775–6.
74. Ibid., p. 776. In his seminar on ethics, Lacan states that he borrows the expression *l'entre-deux-morts* from one of his listeners (*L'éthique de la psychanalyse*, p. 369).
75. Beauty is symbolic in the sense that the symbolic order creates meaning by marking a distinction not only between man and woman, man and animal, but also between the ugly and the beautiful.
76. Lacan, *L'éthique de la psychanalyse*, p. 256.
77. Lacan also refers to the Saint-Fond fantasy from *Juliette* (Lacan, 'Kant avec Sade', p. 776). This fantasy reflects both the longing for second death and the law to which this longing is bound. For example, Saint-Fond dreams of a hell in which the victims are tortured forever after their first death. Such torture is intended to prevent the dead from being reintegrated into the natural cycle. At the same time, the fact that the crimes continue forever shows the failure of the sadist's project. For Saint-Fond's vision of eternal suffering, see de Sade, *Juliette*, pp. 343–5. Blanchot also refers to the fantasy of Saint-Fond ('La raison de Sade', p. 36).
78. Lacan, 'Kant avec Sade', p. 779.
79. Bataille also refers to and quotes from Sade's will (Bataille, 'Le secret de Sade', pp. 152–3).
80. This is only true in so far as no account is taken of the sequel of the frequently quoted passage from Sade's will. Sade does want to disappear from people's minds, but, he continues, 'except for the small number of those who wanted to love me to the end and whose lovely memory I take with me in my grave'. (Pauvert, *Markies de Sade*, p. 376; my translation).
81. In his third seminar, Lacan states that a skeleton is human when lying in a grave (*Les psychoses*, p. 111).
82. Lacan, 'Kant avec Sade', p. 779.
83. Ibid., p. 765.
84. The third gymnasium, not mentioned by Lacan, is the Kynosarges where Antisthenes develops his cynical theory.
85. The title *La philosophie dans le boudoir* has been translated as *Philosophy in the Bedroom*. This is a somewhat unfortunate

translation. The *boudoir*, popular in the eighteenth century, is not a bedroom, but a room next to the bedroom to which the woman of the house can withdraw to wash and dress.

86. Lacan, 'Kant avec Sade', p. 765.
87. Ibid., p. 771.
88. Kant, *Kritiek van de praktische rede*, p. 118.
89. See also Žižek, 'Kant and Sade', p. 22.
90. Lacan, 'Kant avec Sade', p. 778.
91. Ibid., p. 781. For Kant's parable see Kant, *Kritiek van de praktische rede*, p. 71.
92. Lacan, 'Kant avec Sade', pp. 781–2.
93. In this I am paraphrasing *Et non propter vitam vivendi perdere causas*, which literally means 'and not for the sake of life lose the reasons to live'. This is Lacan's variant of a line from Juvenal's eighth *Satire* (Lacan, 'Kant avec Sade', p. 782). Lacan probably read this in Kant's second criticism (Kant, *Kritiek van de praktische rede*, p. 209).
94. Lacan, 'Kant avec Sade', p. 773.
95. For a discussion of the relationship between Lacan's and Kant's thinking in general see Mooij, 'Kant en Lacan', and Bernet, 'Wet en natuur bij Kant en Lacan'.
96. Lacan, 'Kant avec Sade', p. 772.
97. Lacan calls the voice and the gaze, among other things, 'amboceptive objects' (ibid., p. 772; see also Lacan, *Les quatre concepts fondamentaux*, p. 89). He refers to the fact that these objects appear to be on a border and are therefore connected to two different areas. The term 'amboceptor' comes from the nineteenth-century haematologist and immunologist Paul Ehrlich, who used it to refer to an antibody in the blood that can combine with both an antigen and immunity molecules because it has two receptors.

Chapter 5

1. This chapter is partly based upon my texts 'Erotiek en moderniteit', 'Roland Barthes, lezer van markies de Sade: Van klassieke naar moderne literatuur', and 'Sadisme als formalisme: Roland Barthes' semiologische lezing van Sade'.
2. Barthes, 'Pour la libération d'une pensée pluraliste', p. 1705; my translation.

3. See Barthes, 'Michelet', p. 306; 'Le silence de don Juan', p. 379; '"Dom Juan"', p. 386.
4. Barthes, 'La métaphore de l'œil'.
5. As already indicated in the Introduction, Barthes also presented this text in a workshop organised by Tel Quel. In the same year, Barthes' text was also included unchanged in Marquis de Sade, *Œuvres complètes. Tome XVI*.
6. From now on, I refer to the Dutch translation: *Sade, Fourier, Loyola*, 1984.
7. For a more detailed overview of the passages in which Barthes refers casually to Sade, see Roger, 'Traitement de faveur'.
8. Ibid., p. 40.
9. Barthes, *Sade, Fourier, Loyola*, p. 39.
10. Ibid., p. 7.
11. Barthes, 'Flaubert en de zin', p. 91. See Barthes, *De nulgraad van het schrijven*, p. 51.
12. Barthes, *Sade, Fourier, Loyola*, p. 8.
13. For Barthes' view on classical literature, see *De nulgraad van het schrijven*, pp. 9–74.
14. When I write about Sade's literature in this part, I do not refer to his oeuvre in general. I aim at these parts of his work that are still classically inspired.
15. For a more extensive Barthes-inspired argumentation of the statement that Justine belongs to classical literature, see Delers, '"Mais où est le cul?"', and McMorran, 'Intertextuality'.
16. For the whole episode, see de Sade, *Justine*, pp. 65–95.
17. Here, I rely on Bal, *De theorie van vertellen en verhalen*. Bals relies on Barthes, 'Introduction à l'analyse structurale des récits'.
18. Barthes, *Sade, Fourier, Loyola*, p. 145.
19. In this chapter I understand the notion of meaning in three ways. This first interpretation holds that something gets a meaning by being taken into a larger whole.
20. De Sade, 'De schrijver'.
21. De Sade, 'Faxelange'.
22. De Sade, 'De schrijver', p. 576. The book *Les crimes de l'amour*, unlike most of Sade's novels, was well received. The reason is, as it appears here, that Sade praises the good in this collection.

23. What Barthes sees as modern literature is explained in, among others, Perloff, 'Barthes and the Zero Degree', and Monier-Bérenguier, 'Roland Barthes et le roman'.
24. Barthes, *Sade, Fourier, Loyola*, pp. 145, 155–6.
25. As in the previous section, I do not refer here to Sade's oeuvre in general here either. When I write about Sade in this section, I mean these parts that show that Sade is already in the track of modern literature.
26. Barthes, *Sade, Fourier, Loyola*, p. 18.
27. For a comprehensive summary of Justine's life history, see Carter, *De sadeaanse vrouw*, pp. 50–95.
28. A more detailed description of Juliette's road trips can be found in Von Der Thüsen, 'Juliette at the Volcano'.
29. *Pícaro* is Spanish for 'rogue'.
30. Barthes, *Sade, Fourier, Loyola*, p. 18.
31. Here, I rely on Airaksinen, *Philosophy*, pp. 141–6.
32. We have seen earlier that Bataille and Klossowski also point to repetition. Bataille refers to repetition when he discusses the influence of Sade's text on the reader. Klossowski discusses repetition from his psycho-biographical perspective on Sade.
33. Barthes, *Sade, Fourier, Loyola*, pp. 128–9.
34. De Sade, *De 120 dagen van Sodom*, p. 74.
35. De Sade, *Justine*, p. 217.
36. For a more detailed Barthesian-inspired discussion of the details in Sade see Thomas, *Sade*.
37. Barthes, 'Het werkelijkheidseffect', pp. 101–4.
38. This interpretation, according to which the absence of meaning is central to Sade's oeuvre, goes against several recent Sade interpretations. See, for example, Edmiston, 'Nature', p. 129.
39. I am referring here to the title of a previously mentioned book by Barthes, *Le degré zéro de l'écriture*.
40. Ibid., p. 10.
41. De Sade, *Justine*, pp. 75–6; my translation.
42. Ibid., p. 76; my translation.
43. Ibid., p. 77; my translation.
44. De Sade, *De slaapkamerfilosofen*, pp. 15–16; my translation.
45. Barthes, *Sade, Fourier, Loyola*, p. 11.

46. Ibid., p. 12.
47. Barthes, 'De dood van de auteur', p. 115.
48. Ibid., p. 118.
49. This is evident not only from Barthes' reading, but also from the fact that, according to him, in Sade's literature, the writer Sade returns as a friend (Barthes, *Sade, Fourier, Loyola*, p.12). The choice of the term 'return' shows that Sade, according to Barthes, has already died, namely as an author or as the person who gives substance to the text.
50. This reading goes against the fact that Sade strongly emphasises the role of the author himself. See de Sade, 'Gedachte over de romans', p. 15.
51. In Blanchot's reading, too, as I have shown in the second chapter, the central idea is that the reference to Sade disappears as an author due to the absence of a content.
52. Barthes, *Sade, Fourier, Loyola*, p. 173.
53. In the *Decameron*, probably written between 1349 and 1353, three young men and seven young ladies fill their days with stories, at a rate of ten a day. It is not unlikely that Sade had read it. Indeed, during his imprisonment in Vincennes he asks his wife, in a letter, to send him this book (de Sade, *Brieven*, p. 141).
54. Barthes, *Sade, Fourier, Loyola*, pp. 36, 143.
55. De Sade, *De 120 dagen van Sodom*, p. 346; my translation.
56. My comment is partly based on Harari and Pellegrin, 'Exogamy'.
57. De Sade, *De slaapkamerfilosofen*, pp. 267–8; my translation.
58. Barthes, *Sade, Fourier, Loyola*, p. 33.
59. Ibid., pp. 30, 175. Contemporary Sade interpretations also draw attention to the fact that eroticism in Sade is bound by rules. See, for example, Piret, *De geschiedenis als slachtbank*, pp. 46–7.
60. De Sade, *De slaapkamerfilosofen*, p. 93; my translation.
61. Barthes, *Sade, Fourier, Loyola*, pp. 32–4.
62. De Sade, *De slaapkamerfilosofen*, pp. 97–8; my translation.
63. De Sade, *De 120 dagen van Sodom*, p. 58; my translation.
64. Ibid., pp. 195–6; my translation.
65. Ibid., p. 358; my translation.
66. Ibid., p. 349; my translation.
67. Barthes, *Sade, Fourier, Loyola*, pp. 39–41, 134, 141.

68. Ibid., p. 173. By 'eroteme', Barthes alludes to 'grapheme' and 'morpheme', respectively the letters of a language system and the word parts that cannot be split up further into meaningful parts.
69. For a detailed analysis of Sade's language, please see Riffaterre, 'Sade, or Text as Fantasy', and Pyrhönen, 'Imagining the Impossible'.
70. Barthes, *Sade, Fourier, Loyola*, p. 138.
71. De Sade, *De 120 dagen van Sodom*, p. 49.
72. Bataille too, as we saw in the third chapter, does not understand sadism as a transgression of the law. The difference is that with Bataille this idea arises from a more metaphysical perspective on Sade, while with Barthes this thought follows from his interpretation of the erotic scenes.
73. Barthes, *Sade, Fourier, Loyola*, pp. 9, 143–4.
74. Ibid., p. 143.
75. In the first section I stated that the meaning of things must be understood from their participation in a harmonious whole. Here I understand 'meaning' in a structuralist sense: things get meaning from their reference to and difference from other things.
76. What I call 'classic' corresponds to what Foucault calls 'the pre-classic era'. In addition, I use the term 'classic' in a broad sense. Unlike Foucault, who refers to the sixteenth century as being pre-classical, I refer to the Middle Ages and antiquity as 'classical'.
77. Foucault, *De woorden en de dingen*, pp. 39–71.
78. Ibid., pp. 43–51.
79. Ibid., p. 51.
80. Ibid.
81. Ibid., p. 43.
82. This involves a third interpretation of the notion of meaning: something gets meaning because it is a symbol of something else.
83. Barthes, *Sade, Fourier, Loyola*, p. 24.
84. Ibid., pp. 21–2.
85. De Sade, *Justine*, p. 87; my translation.
86. De Sade, *De 120 dagen van Sodom*, p. 108; my translation.
87. Ibid., p. 192; my translation.
88. Barthes, *Sade, Fourier, Loyola*, p. 22.

89. Ibid., p. 23.
90. Ibid., p. 56.
91. De Sade, *Justine*, pp. 148–9.
92. Barthes, *Sade, Fourier, Loyola*, p. 24.
93. Ibid., p. 27.
94. For a more detailed description, see Cryle, 'Taking Sade Serially.'
95. De Sade, *De 120 dagen van Sodom*, pp. 53–60; my translation.
96. Ibid., p. 61.
97. Barthes, *Sade, Fourier, Loyola*, p. 35; my translation.

Chapter 6

1. This chapter is partly based upon my texts 'The Enjoyment of Pure Reasoning' (with Erica Harris), 'Gilles Deleuze on Sacher-Masoch and Sade: A Bergsonian Criticism of Freudian Psychoanalysis' (with Will Britt) and 'Gilles Deleuze leest Sade en Sacher-Masoch: Literatuur en kliniek.'
2. In the remainder of this chapter I will use not 'von Sacher-Masoch' but 'Masoch.' In doing so, I follow the secondary literature.
3. That text is very similar to the introduction in *Présentation de Sacher-Masoch*, but the two texts are not identical, as some interpreters have claimed (Sauvagnargues, *Deleuze et l'art*, p. 41).
4. For an overview of the other texts in which Deleuze refers to Masoch, see Gelas and Micolet, *Deleuze et les écrivains*, p. 576.
5. For the texts in which Deleuze briefly refers to Sade, see ibid.
6. Le Brun also defends this thesis in *Soudain un bloc d'abîme*, pp. 254–6. It is striking, however, that Le Brun, who in her study nevertheless refers to the French post-war Sade interpreters, does not refer to Deleuze in this context.
7. This means that by 'sadism' Deleuze is referring not only to a literary reality but also to a clinical reality. He differs in this respect from the Sade interpreters discussed in the previous chapters.
8. De Sade, *De 120 dagen van Sodom*, p. 143; my translation.
9. De Sade, *Juliette*, p. 204; my translation.
10. Deleuze, *Présentation de Sacher-Masoch*, p. 23.
11. Ibid., p. 26.
12. This description corresponds to the way I explained apathy in the first chapter.

13. Deleuze, *Présentation de Sacher-Masoch*, p. 27.
14. Deleuze relies for this distinction on Klossowski, 'Éléments d'une étude.'
15. Deleuze, *Présentation de Sacher-Masoch*, pp. 24–5.
16. De Sade, *De slaapkamerfilosofen*, p. 46; my translation.
17. Ibid., p. 89; my translation.
18. Deleuze, *Présentation de Sacher-Masoch*, p. 25.
19. De Sade, *Juliette*, p. 734; my translation.
20. Ibid., p. 498; my translation. For Deleuze's reference to this passage, see *Présentation de Sacher-Masoch*, p. 26.
21. Freud, 'Het Ik en het Es,' p. 415; my translation.
22. Deleuze, *Présentation de Sacher-Masoch*, p. 106.
23. Ibid., p. 106; my translation.
24. Ibid., p. 106.
25. Freud, 'Het masochisme als economisch probleem,' pp. 28–9. See also Freud, 'Het onbehagen in de cultuur,' p. 515.
26. Deleuze, *Présentation de Sacher-Masoch*, p. 53.
27. This interpretation is in line with Deleuze and Guattari's study on Kafka. See Deleuze and Guattari, *Kafka*, pp. 21–2.
28. Deleuze and Guattari, *Anti-Oedipus*, pp. 374–5.
29. Deleuze, *Présentation de Sacher-Masoch*, p. 108.
30. Freud, 'Het Ik en het Es,' p. 394.
31. Ibid., p. 42.
32. Deleuze, *Présentation de Sacher-Masoch*, p. 100.
33. De Sade, *Justine*, pp. 284–5.
34. De Sade, *De slaapkamerfilosofen*, pp. 45–6; my translation.
35. Ibid., p. 46; my translation.
36. Deleuze, *Présentation de Sacher-Masoch*, pp. 18–19.
37. Ibid., p. 108.
38. Dee Sade, *De slaapkamerfilosofen*, p. 79; my translation.
39. Freud, 'Drie verhandelingen,' pp. 59–62.
40. Ibid., p. 61.
41. This means that sadism, according to Deleuze, is not a sublimation in a Freudian sense. While, according to Freud, sublimation goes along with the destruction of sexual goals, in Sade, Deleuze holds, sexualisation increases when desexualisation continues. The more energy is freed, the more the sadist is sexually excited because the activity of thinking can continue itself unhindered.

42. Deleuze, *Présentation de Sacher-Masoch*, pp. 100–1.
43. Ibid., p. 104.
44. Freud also states that thinking can be sexually exciting and that this lust functions not as a motive but as an effect of thinking (Freud, 'Drie verhandelingen', p. 81).
45. In Deleuze's interpretation, Masoch's life and work are interwoven.
46. Deleuze, *Présentation de Sacher-Masoch*, pp. 21–2.
47. *Venus im Pelz* is part of *Die Liebe*, the first part of *Des Vermächtnis Kains*, the title of Masoch's large but unfinished novel project.
48. Ibid., p. 42.
49. Deleuze, *Présentation de Sacher-Masoch*, pp. 42–4.
50. Ibid., p. 143.
51. Ibid., p. 44; my translation.
52. Von Sacher-Masoch, *Venus in bont*, p. 32; my translation
53. Von Sacher-Masoch, 'De capitulant', pp. 100–1; my translation.
54. Von Sacher-Masoch, *Venus in bont*, p. 34; my translation.
55. 'Shiny boots of leather' is the opening sentence of 'Venus in furs', the fourth song from the 1967 album *The Velvet Underground and Nico* by the Velvet Underground. That Lou Reed sings about leather here is because in the S&M scene after the Second World War the leather took over the role of fetish from fur. See Hekma, *ABC van perversies*, pp. 135–6.
56. Deleuze, *Présentation de Sacher-Masoch*, pp. 28–9.
57. Freud, 'Drie verhandelingen', pp. 35–6.
58. Freud, 'Het fetisjisme'.
59. See also Freud, 'De splitsing van het Ik'.
60. Freud, 'Het fetisjisme', pp. 421–2.
61. In this context, Deleuze (*Présentation de Sacher-Masoch*, pp. 74–5) refers to Theodor Reik, who also states that fantasy – in addition to provocation, proof and suspense – characterises masochism. See Reik, *Masochism*, pp. 44–58.
62. Deleuze, *Présentation de Sacher-Masoch*, pp. 79–89.
63. Von Sacher-Masoch, *Venus in bont*, p. 66; my translation.
64. Deleuze, *Présentation de Sacher-Masoch*, pp. 53–4. The fact that, according to Deleuze, in masochism the father does not strike but is beaten himself goes against Freud's understanding of masochism in 'Ein Kind wird beaten'.

65. In this context, Deleuze also points to the humour of masochism. While beating normally punishes the forbidden pleasure, being beaten for the masochist is a prerequisite of the pleasure. See *Présentation de Sacher-Masoch*, pp. 71–9.
66. Ibid., p. 47.
67. Bachofen, *Myth, Religion, and Mother Right*, p. 93; my translation.
68. Ibid., pp. 92–120.
69. Deleuze, *Présentation de Sacher-Masoch*, p. 47; my translation.
70. Ibid.
71. This text was included as a second appendix in Deleuze's study.
72. Ibid., p. 251.
73. Ibid., p. 252.
74. Ibid., p. 251; my translation.
75. Kossmann, 'Over leven en werk', pp. 45–6.
76. Von Sacher-Masoch, 'Het volksgericht'.
77. Von Sacher-Masoch, 'Souvenir d'enfance', p. 254.
78. Deleuze, *Présentation de Sacher-Masoch*, p. 87.
79. Bergson, *Lachen*, p. 16.
80. Ibid., pp. 24–6.
81. Deleuze, *Le bergsonisme*, pp. 11–22.
82. In addition to the distinction between soul and matter, there are many other Bergsonian dualisms: *durée*/space, perception/memory, instinct/intelligence, etc.
83. Deleuze, *Présentation de Sacher-Masoch*, p. 34; my translation.
84. Ibid., pp. 57–60.
85. Ibid., p. 35.
86. Ibid., p. 34.
87. Von Krafft-Ebing, *Psychopathia Sexualis*, p. 99; my translation.
88. This view is also reflected in the US Diagnostic and Statistical Manual today. See American Psychiatric Association, *Diagnostic and Statistical Manual of Mental Disorders*, pp. 572–4.
89. Deleuze, *Présentation de Sacher-Masoch*, p. 41.
90. Ibid., pp. 33–42, 89–96.
91. Freud, 'Drie verhandelingen', pp. 40–1.
92. Freud, 'Driften en hun lotgevallen', pp. 32–4.
93. Freud, 'Aan gene zijde', p. 25.

94. Ibid., p. 210. See also Freud, 'Het masochisme als economisch probleem', p. 25.
95. See Geyskens, 'Gilles Deleuze over Sacher-Masoch', pp. 779–82; Kazarian, 'Revolutionary Unconscious', pp. 91–4; Sigler, '"Read Mr. Sacher-Masoch"'.
96. Freud, 'Een kind wordt geslagen'.
97. The subtitle is 'Bijdrage tot de kennis over het ontstaan van seksuele perversies'.
98. The differences that Freud sees between women's and men's fantasies are unimportant in this context. I limit myself to the female fantasy. It is also this to which Freud pays the most attention.
99. Deleuze (*Présentation de Sacher-Masoch*, p. 90) refers to a lecture by Béla Grunberger, who also proposes a non-Oedipal interpretation of masochism, but who nevertheless neglects the central role of the mother. See Grunberger, 'Esquisse d'une théorie psychodynamique'.
100. It is therefore not surprising that 'Ein Kind wird geschlagen', among other things, is also discussed in *L'anti-Œdipe*. See Deleuze and Guattari, *Anti-Oedipus*, pp. 80–4. In *Présentation de Sacher-Masoch* Deleuze also devotes attention to this text. In it, however, he emphasises not Freud's Oedipal interpretation of masochism, but rather the fact that sadism and masochism can be deduced from each other. See Deleuze, *Présentation de Sacher-Masoch*, pp. 51–2.
101. Thus far, I have only focused on masochism. In the first section of this chapter I have already shown that Deleuze does not understand Sade in Oedipal terms.
102. In the year Deleuze's study was published, Lacan states: 'you must radically distinguish the perverse act from the neurotic act'. (Lacan, *Logic of Phantasy*, p. 12.) Psychoanalysts have also recently picked up Deleuze's criticism. See Jonckheere, *Het seksuele fantasma voorbij*, pp. 121–38, and David-Ménard, *Deleuze et la psychanalyse*, pp. 31–42.
103. In line with Deleuze, Lacan also states that we must read Masoch in order to map out masochism. During the seventh seminar, for example, he says the following: 'Read M. de Sacher-Masoch, a highly informative author.' (Lacan, *L'éthique de la psychanalyse*, p. 281; my translation.)

104. Deleuze, 'La littérature et la vie,' p. 12.
105. Deleuze, *Présentation de Sacher-Masoch*, p. 16, and *Pourparlers*, p. 195.
106. In this respect, there is a certain similarity between Blanchot's, Lacan's and Deleuze's Sade studies. Blanchot and Lacan also use Sade's literature to bring to light something that normally does not get attention. According to Blanchot, Sade's work, for example, allows the reader to get a feel for the materiality and autonomy of language. According to Lacan, Sade's literature reminds us of some forgotten aspects of moral experience.
107. Deleuze, 'Mystique et masochisme,' p. 183.
108. I am referring here to the title of Deleuze's 1993 collection of essays, *Critique et clinique*.

Conclusion

1. An exception to this is Barthes, who does not refer to any other Sade study in his 1967 study.
2. Here I rely on Foucault ('Les problèmes de la culture,' p. 1244).

Bibliography

Airaksinen, T., *The Philosophy of the Marquis de Sade,* London and New York: Routledge, 1995.

Allouch, J., 'Ça de Kant, cas de Sade: Érotologie analytique III. Sur "Kant avec Sade" de Jacques Lacan', *Cahiers de L'Unebévue,* Paris, 2001.

American Psychiatric Association, *Diagnostic and Statistical Manual of Mental Disorders: Fourth Edition, Text Revision,* Washington, DC: American Psychiatric Association, 2000.

Apollinaire, G., *L'œuvre du marquis de Sade,* Paris: Bibliothèque des Curieux, 1909.

Arendt, H., *Eichmann in Jeruzalem: De banaliteit van het kwaad,* trans. W. J. P. Scholtz, Amsterdam/Antwerpen: Uitgeverij Atlas, 2005.

Arthur, C., 'Hegel and the French Revolution', *Radical Philosophy* 52 (1989), pp. 18–21.

Baas, B., *Le désir pur: Parcours philosophiques dans les parages de J. Lacan,* Leuven: Peeters, 1992.

Bachofen, J. J., *Myth, Religion, and Mother Right,* trans. R. Manheim, Princeton: Princeton University Press, 1967.

Bal, M., *De theorie van vertellen en verhalen: Inleiding in de narratologie,* Utrecht: Dick Coutinho, 1978.

Baladier, C., *Érôs au Moyen Âge: Amour, désir et 'delectatio morosa',* Paris: Les Éditions du Cerf, 1999.

Barthes, R. 'L'arbre du crime', *Tel Quel* 28 (1967), pp. 22–37.

Barthes, R., 'L'arbre du crime', in: Marquis de Sade, *Œuvres complètes. Tome XVI,* Paris: Éditions du Cercle du Livre Précieux, 1967, pp. 509–32.

Barthes, R., *De nulgraad van het schrijven: Inleiding tot de semiologie,* trans. E. A. van Caspel, Amsterdam: Meulenhoff, 1970.

Barthes, R., *Sade, Fourier, Loyola,* Paris: Éditions du Seuil, 1971.

Barthes, R., *Sade, Fourier, Loyola,* trans. M. Luccioni, Amsterdam: Uitgeverij De Arbeiderspers, 1984.

Barthes, R., 'Michelet,' in: Barthes, *Œuvres complètes. Tome I (1942–1965),* Paris: Éditions du Seuil, 1994, pp. 243–373.

Barthes, R., 'Le silence de don Juan,' in: Barthes, *Œuvres complètes. Tome I (1942–1965),* Paris: Éditions du Seuil, 1994, pp. 377–9.

Barthes, R., 'Dom Juan', in: Barthes, *Œuvres complètes. Tome I (1942–1965),* Paris: Éditions du Seuil, 1994, pp. 384–6.

Barthes, R., 'La métaphore de l'œil,' in: Barthes, *Œuvres complètes. Tome I (1942–1965),* Paris: Éditions du Seuil, 1994, pp. 1346–51.

Barthes, R., 'Introduction à l'analyse structurale des récits,' in: Barthes, *Œuvres complètes. Tome II (1966–1973),* Paris: Éditions du Seuil, 1994, pp. 74–103.

Barthes, R., 'Pour la libération d'une pensée pluraliste,' in: Barthes, *Œuvres complètes. Tome II (1966–1973),* Paris: Éditions du Seuil, 1994, pp. 1699–709.

Barthes, R., 'Flaubert en de zin,' in: Barthes, *Het werkelijkheidseffect,* trans. R. Hofstede, Brussels: Historische Uitgeverij, 2004, pp. 89–100.

Barthes, R., 'Het werkelijkheidseffect,' in: Barthes, *Het werkelijkheidseffect,* trans. R. Hofstede, Brussels: Historische Uitgeverij, 2004, pp. 101–12.

Barthes, R., 'De dood van de auteur,' in: Barthes, *Het werkelijkheidseffect,* trans. R. Hofstede, Brussels: Historische Uitgeverij, 2004, pp. 113–22.

Bataille, G., 'Le secret de Sade,' *Critique* 15–16 (1947), pp. 147–60.

Bataille, G., 'Le secret de Sade (II),' *Critique* 17 (1947), pp. 304–12.

Bataille, G., 'Sade et la morale,' in: *La profondeur et le rythme,* Troisième volume des Cahiers du Collège Philosophique, Grenoble: Arthaud, 1948, pp. 333–44.

Bataille, G., 'Le bonheur, l'érotisme et la littérature (II),' *Critique* 36 (1949), pp. 401–11.

Bataille, G., 'Préface,' in: D. A. F. de Sade, *Justine ou les malheurs de la vertu,* Paris: Jean-Jacques Pauvert, 1954, pp. vii–xxxvi.

Bataille, G., 'Sade,' in: Bataille, *La littérature et le mal,* Paris: Éditions Gallimard, 1957, pp. 120–48.

Bataille, G., 'L'homme souverain de Sade,' in: Bataille, *L'érotisme,* Paris: Les Éditions de Minuit, 1957, pp. 183–96.

Bataille, G., 'Sade et l'homme normal', in: Bataille, *L'érotisme*, Paris: Les Éditions de Minuit, 1957, pp. 197–218.

Bataille, G., 'La valeur d'usage de D. A. F. de Sade (I) (lettre ouverte à mes camarades actuels)', in: Bataille, *Œuvres complètes. Tome II*, Paris: Éditions Gallimard, 1970, pp. 54–69.

Bataille, G., 'L'économie à la mesure de l'univers', in: Bataille, *Œuvres complètes. Tome VII*, Paris: Éditions Gallimard, 1976, pp. 9–16.

Bataille, G., 'La part maudite', in: Bataille, *Œuvres complètes. Tome VII*, Paris: Éditions Gallimard, 1976, pp. 19–179.

Bataille, G., 'La limite de l'utile', in: Bataille, *Œuvres complètes. Tome VII*, Paris: Éditions Gallimard, 1976, pp. 185–280.

Bataille, G., 'Théorie de la religion', in: Bataille, *Œuvres complètes. Tome VII*, Paris: Éditions Gallimard, 1976, pp. 281–345.

Bataille, G., 'Le mal dans le platonisme et dans le sadisme', in: Bataille, *Œuvres complètes. Tome VII*, Paris: Éditions Gallimard, 1976, pp. 365–80.

Bataille, G., 'Sade et la morale', in: Bataille, *Œuvres complètes. Tome VII*, Paris: Éditions Gallimard, 1976, pp. 445–52.

Bataille, G., 'L'érotisme sans limite', in: Bataille, *Œuvres complètes. Tome VIII*, Paris: Éditions Gallimard, 1976, pp. 148–57.

Bataille, G., 'La souveraineté', in: Bataille, *Œuvres complètes. Tome VIII*, Paris: Éditions Gallimard, 1976, pp. 243–456.

Bataille, G., 'Sade', in: Bataille, *Œuvres complètes. Tome IX*, Paris: Éditions Gallimard, 1979, pp. 239–58.

Bataille, G., 'L'homme souverain de Sade', in: Bataille, *Œuvres complètes. Tome X*, Paris: Éditions Gallimard, 1987, pp. 164–75.

Bataille, G., 'Sade et l'homme normal', in: Bataille, *Œuvres complètes. Tome X*, Paris: Éditions Gallimard, 1987, pp. 176–95.

Bergson, H., *Lachen: Essay over de betekenis van het komische*, trans. E. de Marez Oyens, Amsterdam: Boom, 2010.

Bernet, R., 'Wet en natuur bij Kant en Lacan', in: P. Van Haute and S. IJsseling (eds), *Ethiek en deconstructie*, Leuven/Assen: Universitaire Pers/Van Gorcum, 1992, pp. 29–49.

Blanchot, M., 'De la révolution à la littérature', *L'insurgé* 1 (1937), p. 3.

Blanchot, M., *Faux pas*, Paris: Éditions Gallimard, 1943.

Blanchot, M., 'Quelques remarques sur Sade', *Critique* 3–4 (1946), pp. 239–49.

Blanchot, M., 'Le règne animal de l'esprit', *Critique* 18 (1947), pp. 387–405.

Blanchot, M. 'À la rencontre de Sade', *Les Temps Modernes* 25 (1947), pp. 577–612.

Blanchot, M., 'La littérature et le droit à la mort', in: Blanchot, *La Part du feu*, Paris: Éditions Gallimard, 1948, pp. 291–331.

Blanchot, M., 'La littérature et le droit à la mort', *Critique* 20 (1948), pp. 30–47.

Blanchot, M., 'La raison de Sade', in: Blanchot, *Lautréamont et Sade*, Paris: Les Éditions de Minuit, 1949, pp. 17–49.

Blanchot, M., *L'espace littéraire*, Paris: Éditions Gallimard, 1955.

Blanchot, M., *Le livre à venir*, Paris: Éditions Gallimard, 1959.

Blanchot, M., 'La raison de Sade', in: Blanchot, *Lautréamont et Sade*, Paris: Les Éditions de Minuit, 1963, pp. 17–49.

Blanchot, M., 'L'inconvenance majeure', in: D. A. F. Sade, *Français, encore un effort . . .*, Paris: Éditions J.-J. Pauvert, 1965, pp. 9–51.

Blanchot, M., 'L'inconvenance majeure', *Nouvelle Revue Française* 154 (1965), pp. 600–18.

Blanchot, M., 'L'athéisme et l'écriture: L'humanisme et le cri (1)', *La Nouvelle Revue Française* 178 (1967), pp. 586–604.

Blanchot, M., 'L'athéisme et l'écriture: L'humanisme et le cri (fin)', *La Nouvelle Revue Française* 179 (1967), pp. 812–21.

Blanchot, M., 'La voix narrative (le "il", le neutre)', in: Blanchot, *L'entretien infini*, Paris: Éditions Gallimard, 1969, pp. 556–67.

Blanchot, M., 'L'insurrection, la folie d'écrire', in: Blanchot, *L'entretien infini*, Paris: Éditions Gallimard, 1969, pp. 323–42.

Blanchot, M., 'L'athéisme et l'écriture: L'humanisme et le cri', in: Blanchot, *L'entretien infini*, Paris: Éditions Gallimard, 1969, pp. 367–93.

Blanchot, M., 'L'absence de livre', in: Blanchot, *L'entretien infini*, Paris: Éditions Gallimard, 1969, pp. 620–36.

Blanchot, M., 'La littérature et le droit à la mort', in: Blanchot, *De Kafka à Kafka*, Paris: Éditions Gallimard, 1981, pp. 11–61.

Blanchot, M., 'La raison de Sade', in: Blanchot, *Sade et Restif de la Bretonne*, Brussels: Éditions Complexe, 1986, pp. 9–66.

Blanchot, M., 'L'insurrection, la folie d'écrire', in: Blanchot, *Sade et Restif de la Bretonne*, Brussels: Éditions Complexe, 1986, pp. 67–101.

Blanchot, M., 'Literatuur en het recht op de dood', in: Blanchot, *Literatuur en het recht op de dood*, trans. J. Beerten and P. Bosse, Kampen: Kok Agora, 2000, pp. 119–74.

Blanchot, M., 'Quelques remarques sur Sade', in: Blanchot, *La condition critique: Articles 1945–1998*, Paris: Éditions Gallimard, 2010, pp. 83–94.

Butler, J., 'Beauvoir on Sade: Making Sexuality into an Ethic', in: C. Card (ed.), *The Cambridge Companion to Simone de Beauvoir*, Cambridge: Cambridge University Press, 2003, pp. 168–88.

Carter, A., *De sadeaanse vrouw: Een cultuurhistorisch essay*, trans. L. Broeder, Amsterdam: Uitgeverij Contact, 1986.

Castanet, H., *Regard et perversion à partir des Lois de l'hospitalité de Pierre Klossowski*, Nice: Z'Editions, 1993.

Castanet, H., *Pierre Klossowski: La pantomime des esprits. Suivi d'un entretien de Pierre Klossowski avec Judith Miller*, Nantes: Éditions Cécile Defaut, 2007.

Comay, R., 'Adorno avec Sade', *difference:. A Journal of Feminist Cultural Studies* 17 (2006), pp. 6–19.

Cools, A., 'Inleiding', in: M. Blanchot, *Literatuur en het recht op de dood*, trans. J. Beerten and P. Bosse, Kampen: Kok Agora, 2000, pp. 7–73.

Cools, A., *Langage et subjectivité: Vers une approche du différend entre Maurice Blanchot et Emmanuel Lévinas*, Louvain-la-Neuve: Éditions de l'Institut supérieur de philosophie, 2007.

Corbey, R., 'Gift en transgressie: Kanttekeningen bij Bataille', *Tijdschrift voor filosofie* 56 (1994), pp. 272–312.

Cryle, P., 'Taking Sade Serially: "Les cent vingt journées de Sodome"', *Substance* 20 (1991), pp. 91–113.

Dalton, J., 'Man is the Indestructible: Blanchot's Obscure Humanism', *COLLOQUY text theory critique* 10 (2005), pp. 150–70.

David-Ménard, M., *Deleuze et la psychanalyse*, Paris: Presses universitaires de France, 2005.

De Beauvoir, S., 'Moeten wij Sade verbranden?', in: de Beauvoir, *Markies de Sade*, trans. C. Veerman, 's-Gravenhage: BZZTôH, 1985.

De Graaf, B., *Op weg naar Armageddon: De evolutie van fanatisme*, Amsterdam: Boom, 2012.

De Kesel, M., 'Anatomie van een soeverein: Het "antieke" in Batailles moderniteit en de impact ervan op zijn politieke denken', in: G. Coppens (ed.), *Rondom Georges Bataille: Tien lezingen over filosofie, kunst en politiek*, Leuven: Acco, 1997, pp. 57–94.

De Kesel, M., 'Recht op de dood: Blanchot over de verhouding tussen literatuur en revolutie', in: A. S. Nordholt, L. ten Kate and

F. Vande Veire (eds), *Het wakende woord: Literatuur, ethiek en politiek bij Maurice Blanchot,* Nijmegen: Uitgeverij SUN, 1997, pp. 101–20.

De Kesel, M., *Eros en ethiek: Een lectuur van Jacques Lacans Séminaire VII,* Leuven: Acco, 2002.

De Rougemont, D., *Liefde en avondland,* trans. P. Hijmans, Amsterdam: Uitgeversmaatschappij Holland, 1949.

De Sade, D. A. F., 'Gesprek tussen een priester en een stervende', in: de Sade, *Gesprek tussen een priester en een stervende en andere teksten,* trans. H. Leus, Bruges: Uitgeverij De Galge, 1965, pp. 49–77.

De Sade, D. A. F., *De slaapkamerfilosofen: Dialogen, bestemd voor de opvoeding van jongedames,* The Hague: Bert Bakker/Daamen nv, 1968.

De Sade, D. A. F., 'Gedachte over de romans', in: de Sade, *Liefde's misdaden: Heroïsche en tragische verhalen,* trans. H. Warren, The Hague: Bert Bakker/Daamen nv, 1970, pp. 5–28.

De Sade, D. A. F., 'Faxelange of de misdaden van de eerzucht', in: de Sade, *Liefde's misdaden: Heroïsche en tragische verhalen,* trans. H. Warren, The Hague: Bert Bakker/Daamen nv, 1970, pp. 210–43.

De Sade, D. A. F., 'De schrijver van "Liefde's misdaden" aan Villeterque de krantenluis', in: de Sade, *Liefde's misdaden: Heroïsche en tragische verhalen,* trans. H. Warren, The Hague: Bert Bakker/Daamen nv, 1970, pp. 570–9.

De Sade, D. A. F., *Justine, of de tegenspoed der deugdzaamheid,* trans. G. Pappot, The Hague: Bert Bakker nv, 1971.

De Sade, D. A. F., *Juliette, of de voorspoed van de ondeugd,* trans. H. Warren, Amsterdam: Ooievaar Pockethouse, 1995.

De Sade, D. A. F., *Brieven uit de gevangenis,* trans. T. Buckinx, Amsterdam: Uitgeverij Bert Bakker, 1996.

De Sade, D. A. F., *De 120 dagen van Sodom,* trans. H. Warren, n.p.: Uitgave van De Morgen, 2005.

Delers, O., '"Mais où est le cul?" Life and form in Sade's *Les infortunes de la vertu* and *La nouvelle Justine*', *Eighteenth-Century Fiction* 22 (2010), pp. 657–72.

Deleuze, G., 'De Sacher Masoch au masochisme', *Arguments* 21 (1961), pp. 40–6.

Deleuze, G., *Le bergsonisme,* Paris: Presses universitaires de France, 1966.

Deleuze, G., *Présentation de Sacher-Masoch: Le froid et le cruel*, Paris: Les Éditions de Minuit, 1967.
Deleuze, G., *Capitalisme et schizophrénie 2: Mille plateaux*, Paris: Les Éditions de Minuit, 1980.
Deleuze, G., *Francis Bacon: Logique de la sensation*, Paris: Éditions du Seuil, 1984.
Deleuze, G., *Pourparlers 1972–1990*, Paris: Les Éditions de Minuit, 1990.
Deleuze, G., 'La littérature et la vie', in: Deleuze, *Critique et clinique*, Paris: Les Éditions de Minuit, 1993, pp. 11–17.
Deleuze, G., 'Représentation de Masoch', in: Deleuze, *Critique et clinique*, Paris: Les Éditions de Minuit, 1993, pp. 71–4.
Deleuze, G., 'Mystique et masochisme', in: Deleuze, *L'île déserte et autres textes: Textes et entretiens 1953–1974*, Paris: Les Éditions de Minuit, 2002, pp. 182–6.
Deleuze, G. and Guattari, F., *Kafka: Pour une littérature mineure*, Paris: Les Éditions de Minuit, 1975.
Deleuze, G. and Guattari, F., *Anti-Oedipus: Kapitalisme en schizofrenie*, trans. J. Beerten, Kampen: Uitgeverij Klement, 2010.
Delon, M., 'Dix ans d'études sadiennes (1968–1978)', *Dix-huitième siècle* 11 (1979), pp. 394–426.
Delon, M., *Sade en son temps, Sade après Sade*, Paris: Éditions Textuel, 2007.
Deprun, J., 'Sade et le rationalisme des Lumières', *Raison présente* 3 (1967), pp. 75–90.
Deprun, J., 'Sade philosophe', in: Marquis de Sade, *Œuvres I*, Paris: Éditions Gallimard, Bibliothèque de la Pléiade, 1990, pp. lix–lxix.
Descombes, V., *Modern French Philosophy*, trans. L. Scott-Fox and J. M. Harding, Cambridge: Cambridge University Press, 1980.
Direk, Z., 'Erotic Experience and Sexual Difference in Bataille', in: S. Winnubst (ed.), *Reading Bataille Now*, Bloomington: Indiana University Press, 2007, pp. 94–116.
Dubost, M., 'La littérature comme épreuve: Blanchot, lecteur de Hegel', in: É. Hoppenot and A. Milon (eds), *Maurice Blanchot et la philosophie*, Nanterre: Presses universitaires de Paris ouest, 2010, pp. 87–101.
Durançon, J., *Georges Bataille*, Paris: Éditions Gallimard, 1976.

Edmiston, W. F., 'Nature, Sodomy and Semantics in Sade's *La philosophie dans le boudoir*', *Studies in Eighteenth Century Culture* 24 (1995), pp. 121–36.

Faulkner, J., 'The Vision, the Riddle, and the Vicious Circle: Pierre Klossowski Reading Nietzsche's Sick Body through Sade's Perversion', *Textual Practice* 21 (2007), pp. 43–69.

Foucault, M., 'Spreken tot in het oneindige', in: Foucault, *De verbeelding van de bibliotheek: Essays over literatuur*, trans. J. F. Vogelaar and Y. van Kempen, Nijmegen: SUN, 1986, pp. 8–21.

Foucault, M., 'Inleiding tot de transgressie: Over Georges Bataille', in: Foucault, *De verbeelding van de bibliotheek: Essays over literatuur*, trans. J. F. Vogelaar and Y. van Kempen, Nijmegen: SUN, 1986, pp. 55–77.

Foucault, M., 'Het denken van het Buiten', in: Foucault, *De verbeelding van de bibliotheek: Essays over literatuur*, trans. J. F. Vogelaar and Y. van Kempen, Nijmegen: SUN, 1986, pp. 95–122.

Foucault, M., 'Het proza van Actaeon', in: Foucault, *De verbeelding van de bibliotheek: Essays over literatuur*, trans. J. F. Vogelaar and Y. van Kempen, Nijmegen: SUN, 1986, pp. 79–94.

Foucault, M., 'Les problèmes de la culture: Un débat Foucault–Preti', in: Foucault, *Dits et écrits. Tome I (1954–1975)*, Paris: Éditions Gallimard, 2001, pp. 1237–48.

Foucault, M., *De woorden en de dingen: Een archeologie van de menswetenschappen*, trans. W. van der Star, Amsterdam: Boom, 2006.

Freud, S., 'Driften en hun lotgevallen', in: Freud, *Werken 4 (1915–1919)*, trans. W. Oranje, Amsterdam: Boom, 2006, pp. 17–44.

Freud, S., 'Een kind wordt geslagen', in: Freud, *Werken 8 (1917–1923)*, trans. W. Oranje, Amsterdam: Boom, 2006, pp. 65–89.

Freud, S., 'Aan gene zijde van het lustprincipe', in: Freud, *Werken 8 (1917–1923)*, trans. W. Oranje, Amsterdam: Boom, 2006, pp. 162–218.

Freud, S., 'Het Ik en het Es', in: Freud, *Werken 8 (1917–1923)*, trans. W. Oranje, Amsterdam: Boom, 2006, pp. 371–427.

Freud, S., 'Het masochisme als economisch probleem', in: Freud, *Werken 9 (1924–1929)*, trans. W. Oranje, Amsterdam: Boom, 2006, pp. 18–31.

Freud, S., 'De ondergang van het oedipuscomplex', in: Freud, *Werken 9 (1924–1929)*, trans. W. Oranje, Amsterdam: Boom, 2006, pp. 32–40.

Freud, S., 'Het fetisjisme', in: Freud, *Werken 9 (1924–1929)*, trans. W. Oranje, Amsterdam: Boom, 2006, pp. 416–24.

Freud, S., 'Het onbehagen in de cultuur', in: Freud, *Werken 9 (1924–1929)*, trans. W. Oranje, Amsterdam: Boom, 2006, pp. 456–532.

Freud, S., 'De splitsing van het Ik in het afweerproces', in: Freud, *Werken 10 (1930–1938)*, trans. W. Oranje, Amsterdam: Boom, 2006, pp. 512–17.

Freud, S., 'Drie verhandelingen over de theorie van de seksualiteit', in: Freud, *Werken 4 (1905–1909)*, trans. W. Oranje, Amsterdam: Boom, 2006.

Gallop, J., *Intersections: A Reading of Sade with Bataille, Blanchot and Klossowski*, Lincoln/London: University of Nebraska Press, 1981.

Gelas, B. and Micolet, H., *Deleuze et les écrivains*, Nantes: Éditions Cécile Defaut, 2007.

Geyskens, T., 'Gilles Deleuze over Sacher-Masoch: Literatuur als symptomatologie', *Tijdschrift voor Filosofie* 68 (2006), pp. 779–801.

Graver, M. R., *Stoicism and Emotion*, Chicago/London: University of Chicago Press, 2007.

Groot, G., *Vier ongemakkelijke filosofen: Nietzsche, Cioran, Bataille, Derrida*, Amsterdam: Uitgeverij SUN, 2003.

Grunberger, B., 'Esquisse d'une théorie psychodynamique du masochisme', *Revue française de psychanalyse* 18 (1954), pp. 193–241.

Guerlac, S., '"Recognition" by a Woman! A Reading of Bataille's *L'érotisme*', *Yale French Studies* 78 (1990), pp. 90–105.

Guilbert, C. and Leroy, P., *50 lettres du marquis de Sade à sa femme*, Paris: Flammarion, 2009.

Hansel, G., 'Maurice Blanchot, lecteur de Lévinas', in: É. Hoppenot and A. Milon (eds), *Blanchot et la philosophie*, Nanterre: Presses universitaires de Paris ouest, 2010, pp. 315–73.

Harari, J. and Pellegrin, H., 'Exogamy and Incest: De Sade's Structures of Kinship', *Comparative Literature* 6 (1973), pp. 1212–37.

Hegel, G. W. F., *Werke 3: Phänomenologie des Geistes*, Frankfurt am Main: Suhrkamp, 1970.

Hekma, G., *ABC van perversies*, Amsterdam: Meulenhoff, 2009.

Hermans, W. F., *Het sadistische universum*, Amsterdam: De Bezige Bij, 1965.

Heyde, L., *De verwerkelijking van de vrijheid: Een inleiding in Hegels rechtsfilosofie*, Leuven: Universitaire Pers Leuven, 1987.

Hill, L., '"Not in Our Name": Blanchot, Politics, the Neuter', *Paragraph* 30 (2007), pp. 141–59.

Hochroth, L., 'The Scientific Imperative: Improductive Expenditure and Energeticism', *Configurations* 3 (1995), pp. 47–77.

Hollier, D., 'The Dualist Materialism of Georges Bataille', *Yale French Studies* 78 (1990), pp. 124–39.

Holowchak, M. A., *The Stoics: A Guide for the Perplexed*, London/New York: Continuum, 2008.

Horkheimer, M. and Adorno, T., *Dialectiek van de Verlichting: Filosofische fragmenten*, trans. M. van Nieuwstadt, Amsterdam: Boom, 2007.

Huser, F., 'Eros, Belzébuth et Cie', *Le Nouvel Observateur* 20 (1982), pp. 74–7.

Hyppolite, J., *Genèse et structure de la Phénoménologie de l'Esprit de Hegel*, Paris: Aubier, 1946.

Hyppolite, J., *Introduction à la philosophie de l'histoire de Hegel*, Paris: Éditions du Seuil, 1983.

Janin, J., 'Le marquis de Sade', *Revue de Paris* 11 (1834), pp. 321–60.

Jonckheere, L., *Het seksuele fantasma voorbij: Zeven psychoanalytische gevalsstudies*, Leuven/Leusden: Acco, 2003.

Kant, I., *De religie binnen de grenzen van de rede*, trans. G. Van Eekert, W. Van Herck and W. Lemmens, Amsterdam: Boom, 2004.

Kant, I., *Kritiek van de praktische rede*, trans. J. Veenbaas and W. Visser, Amsterdam: Boom, 2009.

Kant, I., *Kritiek van het oordeelsvermogen*, trans. J. Veenbaas and W. Visser, Amsterdam: Boom, 2009.

Kavanagh, T. M., 'The Libertine Moment', *Yale French Studies* 94 (1998), pp. 79–100.

Kazarian, E. P., 'The Revolutionary Unconscious: Deleuze and Masoch', *SubStance* 2/39 (2010), pp. 91–106.

Klossowski, P., 'Éléments d'une étude psychanalytique sur le marquis de Sade', *Revue française de psychanalyse* 6 (1933), pp. 458–75.

Klossowski, P., 'Le mal et la négation d'autrui dans la philosophie de D. A. F. de Sade', *Recherches philosophiques* 4 (1934–5), pp. 268–93.

Klossowski, P., 'Le monstre', *Acéphale* 1 (1936), pp. 6–7.

Klossowski, P., 'De l'opportunité à étudier l'œuvre du marquis de Sade', *Les Cahiers du Sud* 285 (1947), pp. 717–20.

Klossowski, P., *Sade mon prochain*, Paris: Éditions du Seuil, 1947.

Klossowski, P., 'À propos d'une anthologie du marquis de Sade', *Paru* 43 (1948), pp. 60–3.

Klossowski, P., 'Préface', in: D. A. F. de Sade, *Œuvres complètes. Vol. IX*, Paris: Jean-Jacques Pauvert, 1963, pp. i–xvii.

Klossowski, P., *Les lois de l'hospitalité*, Paris: Éditions Gallimard, 1965.

Klossowski, P., 'Esquisse du système de Sade', in: Marquis de Sade, *Œuvres complètes. Tome XIII*, Paris: Éditions du Cercle du Livre Précieux, 1966, pp. xliii–lxxi.

Klossowski, P., 'Sade et la révolution', in: Marquis de Sade, *Œuvres complètes. Tome III*, Paris: Éditions du Cercle du Livre Précieux, 1966, pp. 349–65.

Klossowski, P., 'Justine et Juliette', in: Marquis de Sade, *Œuvres complètes. Tome VI*, Paris: Éditions du Cercle du Livre Précieux, 1966, pp. 67–79.

Klossowski, P., 'Sous le masque de l'athéisme', in: Marquis de Sade, *Œuvres complètes. Tome X*, Paris: Éditions du Cercle du Livre Précieux, 1966, pp. xxxvii–lvii.

Klossowski, P., 'Le philosophe scélérat', in: Marquis de Sade, *Œuvres complètes. Tome XVI*, Paris: Éditions du Cercle du Livre Précieux, 1967, pp. 477–505.

Klossowski, P., *Sade mon prochain, précédé de: Le philosophe scélérat*, Paris: Éditions du Seuil, 1967.

Klossowski, P., 'Sade ou le philosophe scélérat', *Tel Quel* 28 (1967), pp. 3–22.

Klossowski, P., *Origines culturelles et mythiques d'un certain comportement des dames romaines*, Montpellier: Fata Morgana, 1968.

Klossowski, P., *Nietzsche et le cercle vicieux*, Paris: Mercure de France, 1969.

Klossowski, P., 'Protase et apodose', *L'Arc* 43 (1970), pp. 8–20.

Klossowski, P., 'Sade et Fourier', *Topique* 4 (1970), pp. 79–98.

Klossowski, P., 'L'androgynie dans la représentation sadienne', *Obliques* 12–13 (1977), pp. 245–7.

Klossowski, P., *La ressemblance,* Marseille: André Dimanche, 1984.

Kojève, A., *Introduction à la lecture de Hegel,* Paris: Éditions Gallimard, 1947.

Kossmann, A., 'Over leven en werk van Leopold von Sacher-Masoch', in: Kossmann, *Leopold von Sacher-Masoch: Martelaar voor een dagdroom,* Uitgever: BZZTôH, 1985, pp. 8–93.

Lacan, J., 'Kant avec Sade', in: D. A. F. de Sade, *Œuvres complètes. Tome III,* Paris: Éditions du Cercle du Livre Précieux, 1963, pp. 551–77.

Lacan, J., 'Kant avec Sade', *Critique* 191 (1963), pp. 291–313.

Lacan, J., 'Kant avec Sade', in: Lacan, *Écrits,* Paris: Éditions du Seuil, 1966, pp. 765–90.

Lacan, J., 'Kant avec Sade', in: Lacan, *Écrits II,* Paris: Éditions du Seuil, Coll. Points Essais, 1971, pp. 119–48.

Lacan, J., *Les quatre concepts fondamentaux de la psychanalyse: Le séminaire (Livre XI),* Paris: Éditions du Seuil, 1973.

Lacan, J., 'Conférence de presse du docteur Jacques Lacan au Centre culturel français de Rome le 29 octobre 1974', *Lettres de l'École freudienne* 16 (1975), pp. 6–26.

Lacan, J., *Les psychoses: Le séminaire (Livre III),* Paris: Éditions du Seuil, 1981.

Lacan, J., *L'éthique de la psychanalyse: Le séminaire (Livre VII),* Paris: Éditions du Seuil, 1986.

Lacan, J., *The Logic of Phantasy: The Seminar, Book XIV,* trans. C. Gallagher (from unedited French manuscripts), Eastbourne: Antony Rowe, 2002.

Lafond, N., 'Des Forêts, Blanchot et Lévinas: Pour un "autrement dire"', in: É. Hoppenot and A. Milon (eds), *Maurice Blanchot et la philosophie,* Nanterre: Presses universitaires de Paris ouest, 2010, pp. 49–60.

Lauwaert, L., 'Batailles lezing van Sade: Genot en literatuur als expressies van kracht', *Tijdschrift voor Filosofie* 73 (2011), pp. 231–60.

Lauwaert, L., 'Erotiek en moderniteit', *Frame: Tijdschrift voor literatuurwetenschap* 25 (2011), pp. 69–78.

Lauwaert, L., 'Roland Barthes, lezer van markies de Sade: Van klassieke naar moderne literatuur', *Streven: Cultureel-maatschappelijk Maandblad* 79 (2012), pp. 42–51.

Lauwaert, L., 'Sadisme als formalisme: Roland Barthes' semiologische lezing van Sade', *Tijdschrift voor Filosofie* 74 (2012), pp. 425–59.

Lauwaert, L., 'Gilles Deleuze leest Sade en Sacher-Masoch: Literatuur en kliniek', *Psychoanalytische Perspectieven* 30 (2012), pp. 249–75.

Lauwaert, L., 'Kant met Sade: Sade met Kant', *Psychoanalytische Perspectieven* 31 (2013), pp. 36–64.

Lauwaert, L., 'Pierre Klossowski Reads Sade Theologically: Modernity and Salvation', *International Journal of Philosophy and Theology* 74 (2013), pp. 174–82.

Lauwaert, L., *Markies de Sade: Essays over ethiek en kliniek, literatuur en natuur*, Kalmthout: Pelckmans, 2014.

Lauwaert, L., 'Not Just Free but Flesh: Simone de Beauvoir's Existentialist Approach to Sade's Life and Work', *The Journal of the British Society for Phenomenology* 45 (2014), pp. 162–74.

Lauwaert, L., 'De Terreur van het schrijven', *Psychoanalytische Perspectieven* 33 (2015), pp. 75–95.

Lauwaert, L., 'A Poststructuralist Interpretation of Art', *Philosophy Today* (forthcoming).

Lauwaert, L. and Britt, W., 'Gilles Deleuze on Sacher-Masoch and Sade: A Bergsonian Criticism of Freudian Psychoanalysis', *Deleuze Studies* 9 (2015), pp. 153–84.

Lauwaert, L. and Harris, E., 'The Enjoyment of Pure Reasoning', *Philosophy Today* 59 (2015), pp. 191–206.

Le Brun, A., *Soudain un bloc d'abîme, Sade*, Paris: Jean-Jacques Pauvert, 1986.

Leisegang, H., *La gnose*, trans. J. Gouillard, Paris: Payot, 1971.

Loth, B. and Michel, A., *Dictionnaire de théologie catholique: L'exposé des doctrines de la théologie catholiques. Leurs preuves et leur histoire: Deuxième partie*, Paris: Librairie Letouzey et Ané, 1911.

Loth, B. and Michel, A., *Dictionnaire de théologie catholique: L'exposé des doctrines de la théologie catholiques. Leurs preuves et leur histoire: Sixième partie*, Paris: Librairie Letouzey et Ané, 1911.

Loughead, T., 'More than Adequate Logic: Blanchot avec Sade', *Journal of the British Society for Phenomenology* 41 (2010), pp. 33–47.

Lugan-Dardigna, A.-M., *Klossowski: L'homme aux simulacres*, Paris: Navarin, 1986.

McMorran, W., 'Intertextuality and Urtextuality: Sade's Justine Palimpsest', *Eighteenth Century Fiction* 19 (2007), pp. 637–90.

Manoury, D., 'Le Neutre blanchotien, reflets et réflexions à partir de *L'Amitié*', in: É. Hoppenot and A. Milon (eds), *Maurice Blanchot et la philosophie*, Nanterre: Presses universitaires de Paris ouest, 2010, pp. 243–57.

Marty, É., 'Maurice Blanchot, Roland Barthes, "une ancienne conversation"', in: É. Hoppenot and A. Milon (eds), *Maurice Blanchot et la philosophie*, Nanterre: Presses universitaires de Paris ouest, 2010, pp. 299–313.

Marty, É., *Pourquoi le XXe siècle a-t-il pris Sade au sérieux?*, Paris: Éditions du Seuil, 2011.

Mengue, P., *L'ordre sadien: Loi et narration dans la philosophie de Sade*, Paris: Éditions Kimé, 1996.

Monier-Bérenguier, N., 'Roland Barthes et le roman', *French Review* 59 (1986), pp. 730–42.

Mooij, A., 'Kant en Lacan', in: N. Kok and K. Nuijten (eds), *In dialoog met Lacan*, Amsterdam: Boom, 1996, pp. 110–20.

Moyaert, P., *De mateloosheid van het christendom: Over naastenliefde, betekenisincarnatie en mystieke liefde*, Nijmegen: Uitgeverij SUN, 1998.

Nordholt, A. N., '*Het schuwe denken*: Inleiding', in: A. S. Nordholt, L. ten Kate and F. Vande Veire (eds), *Het wakende woord: Literatuur, ethiek en politiek bij Maurice Blanchot*, Nijmegen: Uitgeverij SUN, 1997, pp. 11–43.

Ost, F., *Sade et la loi*, Paris: Odile Jacob, 2005.

Pappot, G., *De markies de Sade: Een portret uit brieven en documenten*, Amsterdam: N. V. De Arbeiderspers, 1967.

Paulhan, J., 'Le marquis de Sade et sa complice ou les revanches de la pudeur', in: Paulhan, *Le marquis de Sade et sa complice*, Brussels: Editions Complexe, 1987, pp. 23–76.

Pauvert, J.-J., *Markies de Sade in levenden lijve: Pornograaf en stilist 1783–1814*, trans. T. Buckinx, Baarn: Uitgeverij de Prom, 1993.

Pelikan, J., *The Christian Tradition. A History of the Development of Doctrine, Part 1: The Emergence of the Catholic Tradition (100–600)*, Chicago/London: University of Chicago Press, 1971.

Pelikan, P., *Een geschiedenis van Maria*, trans. A. Haacke and R. van der Helm, Baarn: Uitgeverij Ten Have b.v., 1997.

Perloff, P., 'Barthes and the Zero Degree of Genre', *World Literature Today* 59 (1985), pp. 510–16.

Piret, J.-M., *De geschiedenis als slachtbank: Reflexieve modernisering en de wet bij Joseph de Maistre, Marquis de Sade en G. W. F. Hegel*, Brussels: Uitgeverij VUBPRESS, 2009.

Praz, M., *Lust, dood en duivel in de literatuur van de romantiek*, trans. A. Haakman, Amsterdam: Uitgeversmaatschappij Agon BV, 1990.

Puchner, M., 'Sade's Theatrical Passions', *Yale Journal of Criticism* 18 (2005), pp. 111–25.

Pyrhönen, H., 'Imagining the Impossible: The Erotic Poetics of Angela Carter's "Bluebeard" Stories', *Textual Practice* 21 (2007), pp. 93–111.

Queneau, R., 'Premières confrontations avec Hegel', *Critique* 195–6 (1963), pp. 694–700.

Reichler, C., *L'âge libertin*, Paris: Les Éditions de Minuit, 1987.

Reik, T., *Masochism in Sex and Society*, trans. M. H. Beigel, New York: Grove Press, 1941.

Riffaterre, M., 'Sade, or Text as Fantasy', *Diacritics* 2 (1971), pp. 2–9.

Roche, G., 'Black Sun: Bataille on Sade', *Janus Head* 9 (2006), pp. 157–80.

Roger, P., 'Traitement de faveur (Barthes lecteur de Sade)', *Nottingham French Studies* 36 (1997), pp. 34–44.

Rogozinski, J., *Le don de la loi: Kant et l'énigme de l'éthique*, Paris: Presses universitaires de France, 1999.

Ropars-Wuilleumier, M.-C., 'On Unworking: The Image in Writing According to Blanchot', in: C. B. Gill (ed.), *Maurice Blanchot: The Demand of Writing*, London/New York: Routledge, 1996, pp. 138–52.

Roudinesco, É., *Jacques Lacan: Esquisse d'une vie, histoire d'un système de pensée*, Paris: Fayard, 1993.

Runciman, S., *Le manichéisme médiéval: L'hérésie dualiste dans le christianisme*, Paris: Payot, 1949.

Ryland, H., 'Recent Developments in Research on the Marquis de Sade', , *French Review* 25 (1951), pp. 10–15.

Sacramentum mundi: Theologisch lexicon voor de praktijk. Handboek bij het gebruik van de nieuwe katechismus. Deel V, Bussum: Uitgeverij Paul Brand, 1969.

Safranski, R., *Het kwaad*, trans. M. Wildschut, Amsterdam: Olympus, 1998.

Sample, R., 'Lacan, Kant, and Sade', *Journal of the British Society for Phenomenology* 26 (1995), pp. 5–16.

Sartre, J.-P., *Situations II: Qu'est-ce que la littérature?*, Paris: Éditions Gallimard, 1948.

Sauvagnargues, A., *Deleuze et l'art,* Paris: Presses universitaires de France, 2006.

Sigler, D., '"Read Mr. Sacher-Masoch": The Literariness of Masochism in the Philosophy of Jacques Lacan and Gilles Deleuze', *Criticism* 53 (2011), pp. 189–90.

Smith, D. W., 'Impulses, Phantasms, Simulacra, Stereotypes', *Diacritics* 35 (2005), pp. 8–21.

Sollers, P., *Sade: Contre l' Être Suprême,* Paris: Quai Volaire, 1992.

Stockwell, C., 'Sade and Sollers: Hoax or Ventriloquism?', *Substance* 40 (2011), pp. 22–36.

Stoekl, A., *Bataille's Peak: Energy, Religion, and Postsustainability,* Minneapolis/London: University of Minnesota Press, 2007.

Stolzenberg, J., 'Hegel's Critique of the Enlightenment in "The Struggle of the Enlightenment with Superstition"', in: K. R. Westphal (ed.), *The Blackwell Guide to Hegel's Phenomenology of Spirit,* Oxford: Wiley-Blackwell, 2009, pp. 190–206.

Surya, M., *Georges Bataille, la mort à l'œuvre,* Paris: Éditions Gallimard, 1992.

Ten Kate, L., *De lege plaats: Revoltes tegen het instrumentele leven in Bataille's atheologie,* Kampen: Kok Agora, 1994.

Ten Kate, L., '"Vlug niets zonder weg terug": De grens in Batailles denken, uitgelegd aan de hand van zijn theorie van de erotiek', in: R. te Velde (ed.), *In het spoor van Plato: Eros in de westerse cultuur,* Nijmegen: Vlakhof Pers/Thijngenootschap, 2010, pp. 178–201.

Ten Kate, L., 'De schreeuw van het humanisme: Om-schrijvingen van mens en God bij Blanchot onder verwijzing naar Foucault', in: M. Blanchot, *De stem en het schrift: Drie opstellen over de esthetische distantie in de vertelling, het humanisme en de toekomst van de boekcultuur,* Kalmthout/Zoetermeer: Pelckmans/Klement, 2012, pp. 105–32.

Thérien, C., 'Les Lumières et la dialectique: De Hegel à Adorno et Horkheimer', *Revue Philosophique de Louvain* 101 (2003), pp. 568–92.

Thomas, C., *Sade, la dissertation et l'orgie,* Paris: Éditions Payot & Rivages, 2002.

Toumayan, A. P., *Encountering the Other: The Artwork and the Problem of Difference in Blanchot and Levinas,* Pittsburgh: Duquesne University Press, 2004.

Tulard, J., 'Sade et la censure sous le premier empire', in: Centre aixois d'études et de recherches sur le dix-huitième siècle (ed.), *Le marquis de Sade,* Paris: Librairie Armand Colin, 1968, pp. 209–15.

Van Pelt, C., *Pierre Klossowski: Filosoof van de Eros,* Amsterdam/ Warder: Elders Special Productions, 2006.

Van Reijen, M., 'Ik denk dus ik voel: Een stoïcijnse filosofie van emoties', in: Van Reijen (ed.), *Emoties: Van stoïcijnse apatheia tot heftige liefde,* Kampen: Uitgeverij Klement, 2005, pp. 40–64.

Van Rooden, A., 'De list van de beschaving: Over het boek als cultuurdrager', in: M. Blanchot, *De stem en het schrift: Drie opstellen over de esthetische distantie in de vertelling, het humanisme en de toekomst van de boekcultuur,* Kalmthout/Zoetermeer: Pelckmans/Klement, 2012, pp. 133–54.

Van Sevenant, A., *Kleine filosofie van het vrijen,* Antwerpen/Apeldoorn: Garant, 2009.

Vande Veire, F., 'De imaginaire bevreemding', in: A. S. Nordholt, L. ten Kate and F. Vande Veire (eds), *Het wakende woord; Literatuur, ethiek en politiek bij Maurice Blanchot,* Nijmegen: Uitgeverij SUN, 1997, pp. 69–88.

Verdonk, W. E., *Peut être: De betekenis van Sade's antropologie voor de ethiek. Een hoofdstuk uit de problematiek van de verlichting,* Amsterdam: Editions Rodopi N.V.

Villeterque, A.-L. de 'De kritiek van Villeterque in de "Journal des Arts, des Sciences et de Littérature", van 30 vendémiaire An IX (22 october 1800)', in: D. A. F. de Sade, *Liefde's misdaden: Heroïsche en tragische vertellingen,* The Hague: Bert Bakker/Daamen nv, 1970, pp. 580–2.

Von Der Thüsen, J., 'Juliette at the Volcano: Reflections on the Sadean Journey', *Studies in Eighteenth Century Culture* 22 (1993), pp. 87–103.

Von Krafft-Ebing, R., *Psychopathia sexualis: Eine klinisch-forensische Studie,* Stuttgart: Verlag von Ferdinand Enke, 1907.

Von Sacher-Masoch, L., 'Souvenir d'enfance et réflexion sur le roman', in: G. Deleuze, *Présentation de Sacher-Masoch: Le froid et le cruel*, Paris: Les Éditions de Minuit, 1967, pp. 251–4.

Von Sacher-Masoch, L., *Venus in bont*, trans. A. Kossmann, Amsterdam: De Arbeiderspers, 1969.

Von Sacher-Masoch, L., 'De capitulant', in: A. Kossmann, *Leopold von Sacher-Masoch: Martelaar voor een dagdroom*, 's-Gravenhage: BZZTôH, 1985, pp. 95–156.

Von Sacher-Masoch, L., 'Het volksgericht', in: A. Kossmann, *Leopold von Sacher-Masoch: Martelaar voor een dagdroom*, 's-Gravenhage: BZZTôH, 1985, pp. 159–250.

Zarader, M., *L'être et le neutre: À partir de Maurice Blanchot*, Paris: Éditions Verdier, 2001.

Žižek, S., *For They Know Not What They Do: Enjoyment as a Political Factor*, London/New York: Verso, 1991.

Žižek, S., *Het subject en zijn onbehagen: Vijf essays over psychoanalyse en het cartesiaanse cogito*, trans. J. Schokker, Amsterdam/Meppel: Boom, 1997.

Žižek, S., 'Kant and Sade: The Ideal Couple', *lacanian ink* 13 (1998), pp. 12–25.

Zupančič, A., *Ethics of the Real: Kant, Lacan*, London/New York: Verso, 2000.

Index

aeon, 19–20
Ancien Régime, 46
androgyny, 8–9, 13, 15, 33
Augustine, 31–2, 38
auto-eroticism, 146, 152
autonomy, 51–2, 55, 169–70

Badiou, A., 6
Barthes, R., 1–2, 4, 117–41, 168–9
Bataille, G., 1–2, 4, 7, 62–88, 90, 117, 168–9
Blanchot, M., 1–2, 4, 39–62, 66, 168–9

Camus, A., 55, 163
Christianity, 15–16, 18, 22, 38, 59, 60, 125
coldness, 155, 163
continuity, 70, 72–6

de Beauvoir, S., 90, 117
decentralisation, 5, 61
delectatio morosa, 8, 15, 27–9, 38
Deleuze, G., vi, 1–2, 4–6, 142–69
depersonalisation, 35, 149, 160
destruction, 2, 14, 17–18, 26, 44–5, 67, 74, 76, 79, 81, 84, 102, 104, 107, 130, 145–6, 148–9, 151
discontinuity, 69, 72–4, 76, 81

energy, 62–88, 150–1, 169
enjoyment, 27–8, 38, 63–4, 78, 80–2, 105, 112, 118–19, 128, 133, 135–6, 152, 157, 163, 165, 169
erotemes, 132
ethics, 89–116, 150
Être-Suprême-en-méchanceté, 16–17, 35, 95, 99, 100–1, 123
evil, 16–17, 35, 59–60, 81, 136–7, 171

first nature, 143
formalism, 141

Foucault, M., 1, 59–60, 81, 136–7, 171
freedom, 10, 46–7, 82, 96, 99, 100, 105

general economy, 68, 82
gesture, 8, 10–11, 15
Gnosticism, 8, 15, 18–20
Gute, 93

Hegel, G. W. F., 2, 46, 50, 54, 79, 157, 179–80, 188
humanism, 41, 55, 59, 60–1

immanence, 14
impersonal, 36, 67, 71, 77–8, 87, 129, 148, 160, 169
inconvenance, 47–9, 50

Janin, J., 82
Jarry, A., 94

Klossowski, P., 1–2, 4, 39–62, 66, 168–9

Lacan, J., vi, 1–2, 4–5, 89–116, 129, 168–9
love, 12, 20, 25, 32, 36, 44, 79, 97, 100, 111–19, 150, 154, 155, 158, 160, 165

madness, 48–9, 52
maniac, 30, 33
masochism, 142–3, 153, 155–6, 161–7
materiality, 20, 50–5, 58, 169
Meillassoux, Q., 6
modernity, 8–9, 14–15, 21, 24, 38, 59–60, 104, 111, 136, 170
monotheism, 57
mysticism, 79

natura naturans, 45, 151, 169
nature, 5, 7, 9, 12, 15–18, 20–2, 24–6, 28, 34–6, 38, 44–5, 60, 73, 84–5, 92–3, 96, 98–9, 101, 103, 106–8, 111–12, 123, 126, 134, 136, 144–6, 148–9, 151, 154, 157–8, 163, 169
negation, 44–7, 50–1, 61, 139
Neutre, 55
Nietzsche, F., 37–8, 55

pathology, 7
postmodern, 5, 34, 77, 115, 150
psychoanalysis, 89, 107

repetition, 2, 27, 29, 37, 63–4, 86–7, 118, 121, 123, 125, 130, 152, 169
restricted economy, 68

sadism, 26, 63, 76, 98, 111, 118, 143, 146, 148–9, 150, 152, 155, 161–4, 166–7, 170

sadomasochism, 142, 167
Sartre, J.-P., 54
second death, 51, 105–10
second nature, 143–6
simulacrum, 4, 30–2
sodomy, 8–9, 12–13, 33–5, 37, 169
Stoicism, 74–6, 111
Summum Bonum, 101, 104
Super-Ego, 147–9, 150–2
theology, 8, 28, 38, 100
transcendence, 14, 79, 184
transgression, 4, 13, 42, 63–4, 80–2, 102, 128–9, 132, 133

violence, 48, 73, 76, 83, 102, 118, 142, 163
von Sacher-Masoch, L., 142

Wohl, 92–3, 96, 111

EU Authorised Representative:
Easy Access System Europe Mustamäe tee 50, 10621 Tallinn, Estonia
gpsr.requests@easproject.com

Printed and bound by CPI Group (UK) Ltd, Croydon, CR0 4YY
18/06/2026
02142305-0001